Society and the Policeman's Role

The role of the policeman in the community and attitudes towards the police are now matters of active public concern. In this important and enlightening study, first published in 1973, Maureen Cain gives an account of how the police operate in the United Kingdom. Her book will be of great value to sociologists, criminologists and policemen alike.

Society and the Policeman's Role

Maureen E. Cain

Routledge
Taylor & Francis Group

First published in 1973
by Routledge & Kegan Paul

This edition first published in 2015 by Routledge
2 Park Square, Milton Park, Abingdon, Oxon, OX14 4RN
and by Routledge
711 Third Avenue, New York, NY 10017

Routledge is an imprint of the Taylor & Francis Group, an informa business

© 1973 Maureen E. Cain

Publisher's Note
The publisher has gone to great lengths to ensure the quality of this reprint but
points out that some imperfections in the original copies may be apparent.

Disclaimer
The publisher has made every effort to trace copyright holders and welcomes
correspondence from those they have been unable to contact.

A Library of Congress record exists under LC control number: 73157212

ISBN 13: 978-1-138-91826-9 (hbk)
ISBN 13: 978-1-315-68854-1 (ebk)
ISBN 13: 978-1-138-91836-8 (pbk)

Society and the policeman's role

Maureen E. Cain

Routledge & Kegan Paul

London and Boston

First published 1973
by Routledge & Kegan Paul Ltd
Broadway House, 68-74 Carter Lane,
London EC4V 5EL and
9 Park Street,
Boston, Mass. 02108, U.S.A.

Printed in Great Britain by
Unwin Brothers Limited
The Gresham Press, Old Woking, Surrey, England
A member of the Staples Printing Group
© Maureen E. Cain 1973

ISBN 0 7100 7490 5

Contents

		page
Acknowledgments		vii
1	**The background of the study**	1
	Introduction	1
	The original theoretical framework	2
	The method of study	7
	Recent contributions to the sociology of the police	13
	The present research in context	25
	Summary	26
2	**Rural police work**	28
	The research division	28
	Rural beats	33
	Work away from the beat	37
	Town police work	40
	Mobile patrols	42
	Administration	44
	CID	44
	Summary	45
3	**City police work**	46
	Introduction	46
	The research division	46
	CID work	49
	Uniform men	53
	Specialist work	75
	Summary	79

4 **Interdependence with the community**   81

Introduction   81
Influences of police organization on relationships with the general public   82
Relationship with the community—social   84
Interdependence of wives and families with the community   90
Biographical indicators of a shared reality   98
Work relationships with the community   104
Effects of differential interdependence   120
Summary   124

5 **Interdependence with family—marital integration and domestic life**   125

Introduction   125
Marital integration scores   125
Practical difficulties in domestic life   132
Marital integration and conflict solution   138
Summary   139

6 **Interdependence with senior officers**   141

Introduction   141
Duties of superiors   141
Communication patterns   144
Perceived interdependence   146
Dependence of men on senior officers   148
Dependence on immediate and intermediate superiors   160
Dependence of superiors on the constables   166
Processes of bureaucratization   168
Attitudes of sergeants to men   172
Qualities admired in senior officers   174
Interview evidence   176
Effectiveness of senior officers as role-definers   179
Summary   180

7 **Interdependence with colleagues**   183

The index of interdependence with police   183
Interdependence at work—city force   189
Interdependence at work—county force   201
Relationships between departments   208
Social relationships between the men   214
Relationships between wives   217
Effectiveness of colleagues as role-definers   218
Summary   220

8 Summary, conclusions and a forward look 223

Introduction 223
Who defines the policeman's role? A recapitulation 223
Quantitative evidence 233
Conclusions 238

Appendices 247

I The policemen's interview schedule 247
II The wives' interview schedule 269
III Supplementary information about research techniques 280
IV Additional tables referred to in the text 286
V The Police (Discipline) Regulations, 1952 294

Notes 298

References 305

Index 313

Acknowledgments

I am indebted to many people for the publication of this book. They include the police men and women of all ranks from chief constable to cadet in the two forces in which this research was carried out; Mr J. E. Hall Williams and Dr A. Little, my supervisors, and Professor Howard Jones, who discussed the manuscript with me; the many people who have worked at successive typescripts of thesis and book, in particular Miss D. Mann, Miss H. Tolliday, Mrs M. Parish, Mrs C. Durrant, Mrs F. Fraser, and Mrs C. Conway; the friends who helped me when I needed it, especially Mrs N. Simpson and my good neighbours Mrs J. Malone and Mrs M. McNeal; my parents and family; and finally Mr Tony Connor, Mr P. Hollowell, and, importantly, Professor T. P. Morris, who all in different ways helped me to maintain my identity as a professional sociologist while I divided my time between boiling nappies on the gas stove and holding punch cards up to the light. To all these, and to my friends from Manchester where the arduous write-up was begun, I can only say thank you.

I am grateful for permission to reproduce material from *Police (Discipline) Regulations, S.I. 1952 No. 1705* (HMSO, Crown copyright) in Appendix V. Professor N. Gross gave permission for adaptations of his job and career satisfaction scales to be used. Three of the 'conflict situations' presented are free adaptations of those devised by Professor M. Banton.

1 The background of the study

The whole conceptual field is suffering from 'a mass of
verbalization, logical circularity, terms used in many and
confusing ways, terms used for concepts diametrically opposed
to the usage of others, refusal to recognize the difference
between another's concerns and one's own, utilization of various
levels of abstraction with no recognition of problems thus
introduced, and tedious, continual redefinition of terms'

(Biddle, 1961)

Introduction

The introduction to William Westley's recently published *Violence
and the Police* (1970) expresses so many of my own thoughts on
preparing this study for publication that I can do little better than
refer the reader to it. I too return to a work which was designed ten
years ago (in Westley's case the time lag was doubled) and find that
I barely recognize either the incipient academic who dreamed up the
theoretical framework or the young woman who stepped out with
self-confident ignorance to tackle field research. The delighted
surprise and nostalgia which visit me when re-reading my field
diaries are constantly checked by dismay at what I now regard as
crucial gaps in my evidence. Moreover, while Westley's work was an
attempt at what we should now call grounded theory, my own was
couched initially in the form of hypotheses for testing. Thus, because
theories by their nature supersede each other, the central problem
which this research set out to tackle can no longer claim to be the
most useful approach to the sociology of police work. The formal
organization of policing in this country has also changed markedly
in the last decade, since the widespread introduction of Unit Beat

1

Policing; and since the Police Act of 1964 even the legal and constitutional position of police officers has been altered (Marshall, 1965).

None the less, I offer this book to the reader as what I hope will be a useful supplement to the only two similar works which have as yet been published in this country, those of Banton (1964a) and Lambert (1970). If it were legitimate to re-formulate the central concern of the work, one could argue that the source of the policeman's world view is still a relevant question. At times in this study I have re-formulated problems in this way, but by and large the text is still in the form in which it was presented as a doctoral dissertation in 1969, for which the original theoretical propositions were unmodified. I have done this because I believe that conceptual gymnastics of this kind are often dangerous, if only because they tend to obscure major differences of standpoint. Where such translation has seemed useful and has been attempted, I have tried to make the exercise explicit.

The statement at the beginning of the chapter is about theoretical developments making use of the concept of role. This work was conceived with the twin purposes of (a) throwing some light on police organization and behaviour, and (b) clarifying the conceptual morass described by Biddle and moving towards an explanation of behaviour in terms of role pressures and definition on the lines of Gross et al. (1958). The specific problems to be investigated were set by developments in role theory.

The initial planning for the study took place in 1961 and 1962. At the time there was little published research in the area of police work.[1] In the intervening years new problems in this substantive area have emerged. As theory and research about deviance and crime has focused increasingly on sociological as distinct from social problems, analysis of the practices of enforcement agencies has become an integral part of the deviancy field. The research reported here throws incidental light on some of these problems, though its main focus is on police organization itself, rather than on the effects of police activity on those outside the police force. I have, therefore, considerably abridged the original theoretical discussion, leaving what seemed to be minimally necessary for the reader both to understand the starting point and to be able to guide himself through the material presented. I have also added, in this chapter, some discussion of more recent theoretical and empirical work about the police.

The original theoretical framework

In the design of the study a Levinsonian approach was adopted.

Levinson's suggestion (1959) that the fruitless attempt to define the essence of a reified role be abandoned remains perhaps the most significant advance in this field since the term 'role' was first coined by James in the 1890s (Banton, 1964b). Expectations about how people will behave, actual behaviour in response to these, and the various intervening cognitive processes, are analytically distinct, and it helps little in either explanation or theory building to attach the label 'role' to any particular one. Variations in each can be separately observed, for example in range or degree of institutionalization of expectations, regularity in response in different circumstances, or, as here, in the effectiveness of expectations in producing a particular response. Problems can be discretely identified and the confusion indicated by Biddle (1961) can be avoided.

In the early 1960s two main tendencies could be noted in role and role-conflict theory. The first was a convergence of historically opposed schools of thought and the second was an increased attention to the sources of role definitions. Traditionally one school of thought regarded role as a property of a person (Cooley, 1902; Meade, 1934; Davis, 1949; Newcombe and Charters, 1950; Sargent, 1951; Goffman, 1956) and the other regarded role as a property of a social system (e.g., Linton, 1936; Parsons, 1951). By the 1950s theorists in both schools were taking account of, or seeking to incorporate, the opposing position. Explicit attempts to isolate the essential elements of the theory (Nadel, 1957; Gross et al., 1958; Levinson, 1959; Banton, 1964b, 1965) and to provide an all-embracing framework of theory further facilitated the task of internal classification and highlighted the links between the various approaches. It was shown that antagonisms between opposing schools resulted from lack of clarity of definition as well as from fundamental differences of standpoint.

The second development, the *attention to the source of role definitions*, was in part a necessary consequence of the growth of the theory itself. Once a theory built to suggest explanations for particular orderings of empirical data reached the stage where the formulation of more specific hypotheses for testing seemed necessary, attention had to shift to areas where testing was possible, and conceptual tools had to be further refined before they could be used for this purpose. The major work of Gross et al. (1958) still leads the field here, though more recently other writers such as Ehrlich (1962), Preiss and Ehrlich (1966), and Musgrove (1967) have also shown that role theory can be a useful basis for prediction and analysis.

Empirical studies have focused upon role conflict, first, because theory can only be tested when there is variation in response, and, second, because of the endemic benevolence of social scientists

3

who see their function as ameliorating stresses and strains. The main result of the development of this micro-theory of conflict has been an increasing emphasis on the source of role definitions or expectations.

Just as the concept of role came to supersede that of status as a more flexible analytical tool (Goode, 1960) so analyses in terms of role conflict became more popular than the earlier analyses in terms of status conflict. This latter type of analysis persisted mainly in studies of 'marginality' in the original sense of the term (e.g., Dickie-Clark, 1966) involving duality of race or culture.

Because of the emphasis on status conflict, stemming from the works of Park and Stonequist, studies in the area until the middle 1950s tended to concentrate on multiple group membership and discrepancies in role definition resulting from this, although the term 'role conflict' was coined along the way by Hughes (e.g., Whyte *et al.*, 1945; Hughes, 1944, 1949; Roethlisberger, 1945; Linton, 1945; Hartley, 1951; Killian, 1952; Stern and Keller, 1953; Getzels and Guba, 1954). Later, the problem of different sets of expectations for the same role was recognized (e.g., Stouffer, 1948b; Gullahorn, 1956; Merton, 1957b; Ben-David, 1958; Gross *et al.*, 1958). Attempts to develop typologies of role conflict were severely restricted by the emphasis on multiple group membership. They took the form of efforts to identify the *area of behaviour* in conflict (e.g., Parsons, 1951; Seeman, 1953; Sarbin, 1954; Gross *et al.*, 1958.) Gross and his colleagues, however, noted the importance of the *source* of the expectation and, also, together with Banton (1963, 1964a, 1965), recognized the importance of the degree of consensus both between and within counterpositions. Biddle (1961) and Kahn *et al.* (1964) also paid attention to this variable. Since the publication of Gross's work it has been generally recognized that not all of those who attempt to define a role for another are equally capable of doing so. The argument thus came to centre round an explanation of these differences in power.

The recognition that the clue to role behaviour lay with the role-definers rather than the area of behaviour defined as a role was but a short step away from the realization that role theory and reference-group theory were tackling essentially the same problem, namely, that of the reasons for conformity to or deviance from the norms and standards of others. Role theory has traditionally dealt with more heavily institutionalized sets of expectations (how a man should behave *qua* policeman or *qua* father, for example) though the recognition of lack of consensus among role definitions broke down this simplistic view of a unitary role. Reference-group theory, though it too tended to emphasize group solidarity, focused attention on the *nature of the relationship* between the focal

4

person and his reference groups, for example in the typologies of reference groups developed by Turner (1956) and Merton (1957b).

Bott (1957) has well summarized the wide-ranging discrepancies in definitions of reference groups. The specific term 'reference group' was first used by the psychologist Hyman in 1942, in a study concerned with the perception of status. Since Hyman regarded role and status as inseparable, the concept has been from the very first linked indirectly with that of role. During the next decade the concept of reference group underwent considerable attempts at refinement, notably by Sherif and Cantril (1947), Sherif and Sherif (1948), Lindesmith and Strauss (1949), Newcombe (1950, and—following the publication of *The American Soldier* (Stouffer, 1949a)—by Merton and Kitt in 1951. In 1951 and 1953 Sherif added yet further contributions. By this time distinctions had been drawn between in-groups and out-groups, positive and negative reference groups, membership groups and non-membership groups, and discussion had been centred around these problems.

Merton and Turner moved forward from this base and a combination of their typologies enabled the overlap with role theory to be mapped (Cain, 1968b). It is perhaps worth emphasizing that the concept of reference group is built upon the notion of the orientation of the actor to others.

The theory on which this research was based explicitly focused attention on the *source* of role definitions (derived from role theory) and on the importance of these to the focal person (derived largely from reference-group theory). In a previous paper (ibid.) it was pointed out that the identification of role-definers (those projecting expectations) is only a preliminary step. There are differences in the importance of the definition to the role definers themselves, and in the meaning of the received definitions to the actor. More important, even given equivalent definitions and interpretations, there are structural differences in the power of different role-defining individuals or groups. Some will be more effective in influencing the behaviour of the focal person than others. Ehrlich tested the hypothesis developed by Gross *et al.*, that this variability resulted from differences in sanctions and differences in perceived legitimacy, and found that much of the variance remained unaccounted for. This, then, was the theoretical problem with which this research was primarily concerned. What are the reasons for the differences in power between role-defining groups in affecting the direction (rather than the mode) of response to discrepant role definitions?

The literature in this area, even as late as Musgrove's work (1967), has presumed that stress results from the perception of discrepant role definitions, despite the finding of Kahn *et al.* (1964) that stress is unrelated to objective conflict. This has given rise to the notion

5

that the actor or focal person seeks at all costs to avoid such 'conflict situations'. Rommetveit (1957), for example, pointed out that all conflict solutions must either be total or partial, the implication being that partial solutions leave a residue of stress for the actor and possibly also for others involved in the system. The idea of the compromise or conflict solution runs right through the literature (the trend was set by Stouffer, 1949b) and results directly from a failure to disentangle conceptually the focal person's experience of stress from his perception of himself as being the object of discrepant role definitions. There has been some confusion too as to whether these solutions should be viewed from the focal person's or the counterposition's point of view (e.g., Parsons, 1951), and also in distinguishing solutions which involve permanent structural change (e.g., Hughes, 1949; Hermann and Schild, 1960) from others of a more temporary nature. Attempts by the individual to reorganize his cognitive structure are different from impact on structure as a result of actions in a conflicted situation. The former are mechanisms which may follow the choice of solution and which enable the individual to live without stress experience.

The issue about response to conflict which is considered here is *whether the role-definer*—a term which includes counter positions and certain types of reference group—*gets his own way*. Does the focal person act in the way the role-definer wishes, or at least expects, or does he not? And in either case, why? Alternatively expressed, the dependent variable is the policeman's (focal person's) action; the independent variables are his relationships with the role-definers.

The argument which provided the basis for this study (Cain, 1968b) was that variations in the potency or effectiveness of role-definers may be linked with the degree to which the actor perceives himself to be interdependent with them. It is not just the actor's dependence, whether structural or affective, on the role-definer which determines the latter's power; it is also the actor's perception that the role-definer is reciprocally dependent on him (Berkowitz and Levy, 1956; Berkowitz, 1957; Dittes and Kelly, 1956). In deciding how to act he takes into account his estimate of the effects of his action on relevant others. Thus the theory was closely linked with the very earliest discussions surrounding the concepts of role and role-taking.

The differential power of role-definers, noted for example by Killian (1952), Sarbin (1954), Getzels and Guba (1954) and Gullahorn (1956), as well as Gross, Ehrlich, Kahn, and the other more recent role theorists previously discussed, was therefore considered in this study to be related to the extent to which the actor considers his relationship to the role-definer to be one of reciprocal dependence.

It was argued that this holds true whether or not the actor's perception of the situation is veridical in fact.

From this general theoretical position specific propositions were derived (Cain, 1968b). The two propositions which shaped this research were:

(1) that an individual with higher (measured) interdependence with a particular role-definer would act in the direction of the perceived role definitions of this group more frequently than an individual with a lower (measured) interdependence with that role-definer;

(2) that the individual with the higher (measured) interdependence with a particular role-definer would act in accordance with his perception of the role definition of that role-definer in a wider range of situations than the individual with lower (measured) interdependence.

It was also hoped in a more general way to offer explanations for the variations in power and interdependence by means of data gathered during the period of observation.

The method of study

A preliminary analysis of such evidence as was then available indicated that policemen were indeed subject to conflicting expectations, and therefore that role theory as here discussed would provide a useful approach to the understanding of police organization and behaviour. A number of these indications of conflict emerged from the evidence submitted to the Royal Commission on the Police, whose final report (1962a) was then awaited. One of the main practical problems for the police at the time of study, as now, was unnecessary wastage of long-serving officers, for which there seemed no adequate explanation (Royal Commission on the Police, 1960a). In their evidence to the 1960 Royal Commission on the Police (ibid), the Association of Chief Police Officers remarked: 'A police constable does not merely take a job, he embarks on a new way of life . . . the first claim on him must be made by his duty, and the convenience of his wife and family must be a secondary consideration'. (Royal Commission on the Police, 1960b). The Police Federation supported this view of the impingements of a policeman's work on his private life, emphasizing the importance of a reduction in or a re-organization of the policeman's hours of work in order to reduce wastage. They argued that the men had insufficient time for normal family life. Later they substantiated their opinion on this matter by carrying out a survey among their members

(Police Federation, 1963). Five hundred and twenty-five of 1,750 men leaving said they did so for 'domestic reasons'; 147 said more specifically that dissatisfaction with the hours was a cause; a further 768 expressed a general preference for other employment. The remainder of the sample said that pay was their reason for leaving, despite the 1961 pay award.

Potential conflicts engendered by the relationship of the police with the community at large were also indicated by the Association of Chief Police Officers (1960): a policeman 'must be part of the community and yet at the same time it is always dangerous to become on too intimate terms with people to whom at any time he may have to apply due process of law'.

Taken together these statements suggested the possibility of three counterpositions all projecting discrepant role definitions for the policeman, namely, his family, the community at large, and the force itself. It seemed reasonable to assume that for some policemen all three might be identification groups and therefore effective role-definers (Cain, 1968b). The short pilot study, discussed in detail in appendix III, confirmed these assumptions. It therefore seemed that it would be both useful and possible to test the proposition that the policeman's perception of his interdependence with each of these groups affected their relative success in projecting their role definitions.

Permission was initially obtained from a county force to carry out the project, and at this stage it was not clear whether or not permission could also be obtained from a city force. A pilot study in the county force was first carried out, after which the specific hypotheses were formulated and a questionnaire for interviews with both the policemen and their wives was designed (see appendix III). Given that a sample of forces of varying sizes was impossible within the constraints of time and funds, it was decided that two polar forces in terms of structural differences should be examined if possible. Accordingly, the most rural division—that with the lowest population to acreage ratio—was selected for study in the county area. Subsequently permission was obtained to continue the research in a large city force where a single division was also selected for intensive study.

The focus of the research, as has been indicated, was on the police as an organization, and role theory was used to elucidate this. Because of these two interests the relationship of the policeman with his client was not considered to be of *paramount* importance; indeed, the role approach dictated that equal consideration be given to a wide range of role-definers and to behaviour in a wide range of situations. The theoretical problem also dictated hypothesis-testing in directly comparable situations, which in turn necessitated a questionnaire/interview approach as the nearest approximation to comparability. Thus the men were asked about their behaviour in directly comparable but hypothetical (and perhaps unrealistic) situations. Discrepancies of interpretation of these situations between respondents were often apparent, since free answers to the questions were possible. Yet in order to 'test' the hypothesis as formulated, these different meanings had to be treated as the same. For the purposes of the analysis the responses had to be treated as answers to the same question.

The main hypotheses of the research were tested by means of a structured interview, details of which, together with a discussion of the scales and questions used, are given in appendices I—III. In brief, the questionnaire included items designed to measure or indicate the policeman's perceived interdependence with the community, with his family, and with the police force itself; six hypothetical situations (owing much to Banton (1964a) in their form) coupled with questions designed to indicate the policeman's likely response and also the normative expectations of relevant others; and questions designed to elicit factual information which might not readily be available from administrative records. The wives' questionnaires included items designed to assess marital integration (interdependence), a large number of opinion questions, and further questions eliciting factual information not available from other sources, for example about the children's schooling.

In addition it was decided to spend a period of 'participant' observation with the police. This part of the research was first intended simply to enliven the rather bald discussion of tabulated responses; very rapidly it became apparent that it also served the purpose of establishing *rapport*, so that in many cases it would be fair to say that it was the observation work which made the interviews possible. I would guess, though there can be no evidence for this, that it also improved their validity. As time went by, and I became more of a participant and less of an observer, a third, very important value of the observation work became apparent. It was this to which I gave most emphasis in my first report of these data (1969), and which is still the primary value of the observations for this particular piece of research. The observational records make it possible to 'go behind' the interview data so that the responses given are themselves explained in terms of the structure of the policeman's life space and the sense which he makes of it.

By the end of the research a fourth position had been reached. As my knowledge of on-going police work became more complete the inappropriateness of many of the questionnaire items became increasingly evident, on two levels. First, some of the situations and sentiments about which questions were asked were more meaningful in the researcher's world than in the policeman's. Second, even when the situation or feeling under discussion was one which was recognized by the policeman it was not always presented or expressed in his concepts or language, so that he was constantly having to make conceptual leaps, assumptions that what the researcher was *really* on about was a situation or feeling about which he *did* have knowledge and experience. The extent to which the men were prepared to make this effort was no doubt a function of their varying relationships with the researcher, which affected such things as their assumption that she really knew what was relevant but expressed it differently—in which case they would answer what they thought she meant—or the more negative assumption that an outsider, and this outsider in particular, could never understand police work and that these ridiculous questions proved it, in which case the man might give a meaningless answer to a (for him) meaningless question. For these reasons when the questionnaire data and observational data conflict—as in the discussion of differential interdependence with the community in rural and urban areas, which is not fully reflected in the scaled scores or in the responses to the hypothetical situations—in these cases I have chosen to regard the data gathered by observation and informal conversation as more valid than those gathered in answer to the structured interview questions.

The sample

One division of each force was studied intensively. In the county division all the men of all ranks were interviewed, including those on the point of transfer and their replacements. This gave a total sample of sixty-four in the county, although the establishment of the division was only sixty-two and its actual strength fifty-six. The breakdown by rank of those in the county census was: superintendents, 1; inspectors, 2; sergeants, 7; constables, 54. This included one detective sergeant and two detective constables.

In the city, officers above the rank of sergeant were excluded from the sample, since it was felt that so small a number of men did not constitute a statistically meaningful group, even without further internal divisions by rank. The strength of the research division in the city was 193 uniform constables and 35 sergeants. A 1 : 3 sample was taken of these, and a reponse rate of 72.4 per cent achieved. The sample was based on an alphabetical list within each of the three sub-divisions, and copies of this list with each third name underlined were posted in each sub-divisional station so that the men should have no anxieties as to the basis of selection. The sample numbered seventy-six; the number of respondents was fifty-five, of whom forty-seven were married. The sample included eleven sergeants, ten of whom agreed to be interviewed. CID men were not part of divisional strength, and were not included.

Fifty-seven of the sixty wives were interviewed in the county area and thirty of the forty-seven wives of the men in the sample agreed to be interviewed in the city.

Administration of the questionnaire

Interviewing began on the third day of the research in the county and on the twenty-sixth day in the city. In both areas the pattern was for the researcher to interview men posted to the area on which she was simultaneously conducting participant observation, and to start the interviewing with the men based at the DHQ with whom there was likely to be most frequent contact. This was an attempt to obviate the bias which might have arisen if some men were considerably better known than others at the time of interview.

Observational fieldwork

County Motor patrols conducted by the researcher in the county area (excluding the pilot study period) involved approximately fifty-three working hours. These patrols covered all the shifts worked by the men, and each driver was accompanied at least once. In addition, sixty-five hours were spent patrolling with the 'crime van'. These were four-hour tours of duty from 11 p.m.—3 a.m., of which the main purpose was the checking of valuable property on the division.

Foot patrols did not play a very important part in the work of the rural beat man. They were operated only in two small and one slightly larger towns on the division. Men were accompanied on foot patrols on five occasions, three eight-hour shifts and two half-shifts, totalling thirty-six hours.

Men were also accompanied when they received calls out from the station to accidents, crimes, road blocks and emergencies of various kinds. The researcher had the use of an office in the sub-division stations, and was therefore available at all times.

For the rural beat man his bicycle patrol round his 'patch' was the most important aspect of his work. Distances to be covered prevented the researcher from accompanying all the beat men on such patrols, but thirty-three hours were spent patrolling in this way on nine different occasions. One man was accompanied twice.

The total number of hours spent on formal routine patrols was, therefore, 187. Also CID or uniform men were accompanied on crime enquiries on fifteen occasions, the duration of these ranging from an hour to a whole day.

11

Special occasions, such as, for example, two town carnivals, the county show and a motor-cycle scramble, were also attended.

City In the city 180 hours (approximately) were spent patrolling on foot and 231 hours (approximately) on mobile patrols. These hours were divided as shown in Table 1. Patrols where records were incomplete have not been included.

TABLE 1 *Foot patrols*

First watch (6 a.m.–2 p.m.)	Second watch (2 p.m.–10 p.m.)	First night watch (6 p.m.–2 a.m.)	Night watch (10 p.m.–6 a.m.)
60	44	8	68

The hours for men on motor patrols were staggered, to avoid having the entire staff of the police force changing shifts at any one time. However, they followed broadly the same system of watches, displaced by either one or two hours. Recorded research hours were allocated as in Table 2.

TABLE 2 *Mobile patrols*

	First watch	Second watch	Nights	Total
Area cars	24 (3)*	64 (16)	56 (7)	144 (26)
Landrover		36 (9)		36 (9)
Traffic car			8 (1)	8 (1)
Dog van		8 (1)	8 (1)	16 (2)
Night CID			27 (3)	27 (3)
	24 (3)	108 (26)	99 (12)	231 (41)

*Brackets indicate number of occasions on which men were accompanied.

In addition an inspector and a sergeant were accompanied on semi-mobile patrols on six occasions, two evenings were spent with the plain clothes section, and a number of special events, both social and connected with the work, were attended. As in the county, the researcher made use of office facilities in the stations where she was working and was thus able to respond to the many unpredictable situations from a murder to an office party which arose in the course of the field work.

The field work was organized similarly in the two forces; an initial period of observational work was carried out at DHQ, followed by a period of observational work on the other sub-division(s), with a third and final phase at DHQ collecting statistical data and tying up the loose ends of interviewing. Patrols continued to be carried out during the final phase.

It is difficult to estimate the degree of acceptance of a field worker, but the subjective impression was that acceptance was in both cases at its height in phase two, with some renewed suspicion creeping in during the third phase when it became known that hard statistical facts about the men were being collected, and also because during this winding-up period there was rather more interaction than hitherto with senior officers.

Recent contributions to the sociology of the police

In this section I shall very briefly outline some of the trends which have been apparent in discussions of policing over the last decade, and thus put the present work in its academic context. This should also indicate lines along which the sociology of the police could most usefully be developed.

Three main sets of questions seem to have been posed. The first questions stem from a concern with citizen rights and are about police modes of operation and the exercise of police discretion. The second body of work is devoted to the question of *why* policemen operate in the way that they do. Here answers have been sought—and found—in the areas of community structure, police organization, the policeman's interpretation of his task, and the policeman's view of particular sub-groups within the population. The third set of questions arises from a concern with the *effects* of the policeman's actions, leading to a demand for more detailed descriptive work on what choices the policeman actually makes, and why. Although current interest in police work stems largely from this third set of questions, most research on the 'why' questions has had the policeman rather than the client as the underlying focus of concern, that is, most research to date falls under the second rather than the third heading.

The categories are not discrete: some works make contributions in more than one area, while others do not fit comfortably under any of the headings. None the less, these have been the most important areas of discussion. There is also a fourth, as yet barely touched upon, which concerns the place of police forces in society at a much higher level. Here the questions posed are dependent on the general model of society with which the sociologist is operating. Questions about who controls the way policemen work must be linked with these larger theoretical models if they are to have any real value.

Citizen rights

There has for some time, indeed, since the beginning of police forces as we now know them, been concern about what the police could legally do. Naturally, this has been most evident among lawyers. The concern has been with their rights to stop and search, to enter property, to question suspects, and with their means of getting evidence (e.g., Hall, 1953; Donnelly, 1962; and papers in Sowle, (ed), 1962, especially that by Remington). They looked to legal changes, to ombudsmen and independent enquiries, and to new procedural rules as solutions to what they perceived as problems.

Social scientists shared this concern. It is apparent, for example, in Westley's works, and in more general discussions such as that of Tappan (1959). But unlike the lawyers, the sociologists emphasized that malpractices are built into the policing situation. Within a police department the emphasis on results inevitably creates pressures for a relaxation in standards; the policeman is guided by expediency rather than abstract notions of justice. Analysis of this kind led Tappan to suggest more careful recruit selection as a reform measure. Skolnick (1966) took the issue a stage further. 'Malpractice' was endemic in the policeman's work situation not because policemen were of poor calibre and therefore yielded to temptation, but because society placed contradictory demands upon its policemen, namely, high production coupled with adherence to a set of formal procedures which make high production impossible. Output has high visibility; adherence to formal procedures has low visibility. The result is inevitable. The policeman's view of his role in society and occupational pride reinforce this tendency. The solution, if any, certainly lies outside police selection and training procedures or tinkerings with the law relating to police powers. This is not to deny the crucial importance of such safeguards: merely their centrality.

The scope of police discretion also gave rise to concern among the lawyers (e.g., Goldstein, 1960, 1963; Kadish, 1962; Osborough, 1965). Policemen must decide whether behaviours seen constitute an offence, what action if any to take at the time, and the offence with which to charge. Legal reform to introduce controls was again suggested. Goldstein in particular argued that the *fact* of police discretionary powers be acknowledged rather than denied, as a prerequisite to control or reform. Remington (1965) argued that discretion over these matters was intrinsic to police work, that it was not necessarily undesirable, and that in any case the courts could not function were discretion to let off curtailed. This suggested again that it was necessary to look outside of the police for the forces giving rise to the situation. It remained, from this standpoint, for La Fave (1965) to examine in detail the policies and practices governing one of these discretionary decisions, namely, whether or not to arrest a suspect.

Thus both sub-issues in the citizen rights area led ultimately to large-scale empirical investigations. La Fave's work is difficult to use because it is descriptive and because it is organized round discrete legal problems. Skolnick's contribution not only offered an explanation of police choices in sociological terms but also raised the larger question of what, and perhaps whom, the police are for.

Reasons for differences in police practice

Most of the studies discussed in this section take as their starting point that the police exercise discretion in apprehending or otherwise dealing with offenders. They are concerned in the main with initial encounters and with uniformed police work, so decisions about the nature of charges are not much discussed. This is partly because in this country there is as yet no research on the work of the CID, and in the United States, apart from the work of McIntyre *et al.* (1967), greater emphasis has been given to the part played by the legal profession in relation to such matters as plea and charge bargaining, than to the police (e.g., Newman, 1962, 1966; Blumberg, 1967).

Exceptions to the first point are the studies dealing with minority groups. Here researchers wanted to find out whether there was differential enforcement, and if so why (e.g., Wilson, 1968a and b; Bayley and Mendelsohn, 1969; Lambert, 1970). When differences on racial grounds were found, police practices were seen to be linked to wider systems of police behaviour, rather than to psychological phenomena such as 'prejudiced attitudes' which might have affected behaviour in relation only to one or more minorities. Both Bayley and Mendelsohn and Niederhoffer (1967) showed that neither police recruits nor serving policemen had personalities which were demonstrably more 'authoritarian'.

The distinction between enforcement and peace-keeping modes of operation has formed the basis of most of the studies which have sought the explanation of police behaviour in the structure of the community policed. Banton (1963, 1964a) argued that policing in a stable community is a reflection of the 'moral consensus' within that community. The policeman's authority is accepted because in a very real sense he represents what the collective regards as proper. He in turn conceives his task as maintaining the established order by persuasion and manipulation. When the moral consensus in the community at large is weak, this is not possible; the police must

15

resort to enforcement, and come to define their task in these terms. Yet Banton (1963) has also suggested that when the gap between policeman and policed is too great the policeman may *under*-enforce because of lack of understanding or indifference.

As long ago as 1945 Whyte found a 'peace-keeping' mode of operation by police in a stable Italian slum. The police were applying local rather than societal standards, when there was a clear difference between the two. Why? Goldman (1963) found a predominance of peace-keeping only in a relatively homogeneous middle-class suburb. Wilson's two low-enforcement areas—one operating with a 'watchman', the other with a 'service' style (1968a, 1968b)[2]—both had relatively stable populations, though only the 'service' style area was homogeneous and middle-class. Gardiner (1968), in his comparative study of the enforcement of traffic laws, makes a similar point. The latter two studies suggest, however, that the community affects police action in part through the mediation of the political system. The argument goes that people in unstable areas where there are no established power groups (or where there is no 'moral consensus'), must of necessity base their judgments on rational and universalistic criteria. They therefore require that their policemen should not discriminate on particularistic grounds, and so have a higher enforcement rate for juvenile offences and traffic offences, and in what Wilson calls 'law enforcement situations', including such offences as larceny and drunken driving. What is still unclear from these studies is the precise mechanism by means of which different groups in the population affect police activity. Nor has the existence of a recognizable moral consensus in some societies itself been explained.

Phenomenological insights suggest that there is no essential contradiction between explanations in terms of a common biography which gives rise to a shared world view (including ethical standards or a moral consensus), and an explanation of these same phenomena in terms of power. Certainly common experiences give rise to greater mutual recognition and shared understandings arising from a shared conceptual and evaluative framework which is partly linked to the experience, but the experience itself has meaning only in so far as it is reflected upon and interpreted. Thus even presumed 'crucial' life experiences—being at risk of death, childbirth, sexual desire and satisfaction, being hungry or thirsty—even such experiences gone through in company may not be shared. Their meaning varies from culture to culture, and they can be shared only when their meaning to the various actors is the same. Within a culture or shared-meaning system the interpretation depends on who has power to project his definition of a situation or experience on to others. A common biography as identified by an observer probably means exposure to

16

the same set of definitions. Therefore a common biography may be a necessary, but it is certainly not a sufficient, condition of high inter-subjectivity.

In chapter 4 I shall attempt to show how this understanding of the relationship between inter-subjectivity, common biographies, and power can help us to understand why policemen in certain homo-geneous and/or stable communities operate differently from those in heterogeneous and/or unstable areas.

Another point remains unclear in the approaches discussed, given that full enforcement is an admitted impossibility. Who specifically gets let off by the policeman, and, more important, which offences and offenders does the policeman not become aware of because his preconceptions prevent him from taking the necessary investigative action? (See, for example, Chapman, 1968.) This last problem could not be tackled entirely by work with the police, but knowledge of some of the assumptions which policemen make about others could be gained, and could throw some light on the issue. Demands for investigations of this kind follow from the phenomenological per-spective on deviance, discussed very briefly below.

Skolnick, 1966, Preiss and Ehrlich (1966), Cain (1968a), Mitchell (1966), Niederhoffer (1967), Clark (1965) and Wheeler (1968) have all in various ways explained police behaviour in terms of the nature of police organization. Skolnick has pointed to the importance for the policeman of departmental production goals. Preiss and Ehrlich, using a model of role conflict and a method of analysis very similar to those adopted in this study, argued that behaviour would be determined by perceived audience expectations, and found, like Skolnick from his very different standpoint, that audience groups within the police organization itself were most relevant. Yet although this research showed that the two variables postulated as primary by Gross *et al.* (1958), perceived legitimacy and sanctions, provided insufficient explanation of differences in effectiveness, the crucial 'why' question remained unanswered.

Clark showed that police officers were isolated from other agencies in the field, their attitudes being more akin to those of the general public than to those of other specialists. But whether the attitudes are cause or effect of the isolation is unknown.

Wilson, Cain and Wheeler, however, have all argued that the orientation to his client of the juvenile officer is affected by such organizational factors as the size of the department and the extent to which it is integrated with the rest of the police structure. Certain modes of organization may be necessary conditions for the develop-ment of orientations to young people atypical among policemen.

Niederhoffer, like Skolnick and the lawyers, noted the contra-dictions inherent in police work. He argued that they led to the development of a 'cynical' attitude. But cynicism is no help in explaining what policemen will do: it describes only their attitude to their own actions. Skolnick's look at the policeman's work situation found that danger and authority were the two overriding experiences, together with a professional certainty that they knew who was guilty and a clear orientation to catching criminals as a legitimation, both socially and organizationally, of their existence—a point also noted strongly by Lambert (1970) in this country. But who constitutes a criminal in police eyes is not treated as problematic.

Cressey and Elgesem (1968) measured police orientations towards enforcement or peace-keeping. They found the explanation of these in the immediate work situation. Thus there were predictable variations between officers in different branches. Here too organizational constraints could be considered as directing the policeman's attention towards one type of offender rather than another: the results suggest, however, that policemen regard types of offenders with whom they are in most frequent contact as more deserving of punishment: it is not simply that the organization constrains them to action only in these cases.

Effects of police action

The works gathered together in this section are perhaps more heterogeneous than in either of the others. The reaction against positivism in theories of crime and deviance, stemming largely from the works of Becker (1963) and Matza (1964) and given its most significant recent twist by the works of Garfinkel (1967) and Cicourel (1968), is well documented. In brief, it involves the recognition that deviant status is created by social control agencies, that becoming a deviant is a process involving consciousness and choice, and that allocation to deviant roles is not fortuitous. More recent still has been the growing recognition that the institutionalized rules themselves are problematic, leading to a new interest in the sociology of law. The law involves only one possible classification of behaviours, and even given that, only one set of selections from that classification for prohibition.

Thus, first, the nature of the interaction between the deviant and the social control agency is important, involving a negotiation of how the deviant's behaviour is to be interpreted and defined, as a result of which a decision will be made about what to do with him. This in turn can lead to further consequences in terms of the deviant's view of himself and others, and others' views of him.

Second, since deviant status is itself problematic, and since the action of social control agencies is no longer seen as neutral or in terms of its potential for 'reform' (itself a meaningless concept in the newer perspective) the initial selection of candidates for deviant roles has become a major focus of concern. So studies are needed which show in more detail which, among the people who come to their attention, the police themselves select for further action. How is police discretion exercised in particular cases? How much is it affected by specific situational factors? What cues in behaviour and appearance do the police regard as relevant?

But it is not just the conscious choice of the policeman with which the phenomenologists are concerned. There are many rule breakers—potential deviants—who do not come to the notice of the authorities at all. There may be structural reasons for this. But what concerns us here is that what policemen see is a function of what they look for which is a function of their assumptions about the world. Explanations of police choices required, therefore, include descriptions of the policeman's conceptual framework and assumptions, of the way he constructs his typologies of behaviours and of others, and of his orientations to such types as he identifies. At one further remove these variables are themselves linked causally with other structural properties, including, no doubt, some of those discussed in the previous section. The point of tangence is that such properties are not considered to exist in their own right: their relevance is in the way the actor, in this case the policeman, conceives them. The earlier studies discussed by and large ignored this point.

One study which deals with many of the problems thrown up by this approach is that by Young (1971). Here police conceptions of others and how these affect the law in action are both considered, and the effects on the career patterns of drug-users are traced.

Not perhaps wholly in response to these demands, but at least in part satisfying them, we have two studies by Bittner (1967a, 1967b) discussing the way police handle skid row residents and the mentally sick (as defined by policemen, the researcher and others in the situation), and two studies discussing the handling of juveniles (Werthman and Piliavin, 1967; Piliavin and Briar, 1964). From these we have learned, for example, that policemen give a fairly central place to economy in encounters; that their predictions as to whether there is likely to be further 'trouble' are based on fine particularistic knowledge of the circumstances of the case. We do not know what cues they use in the absence of such knowledge, though we have some suggestions. It could be that, in such situations, because their predictions are less likely to be accurate, policemen err on the safe side, and have a greater tendency towards enforcement. This could in part explain the finding of Banton and others that men regularly policing stable communities are less likely to adopt enforcement tactics than men in the converse situation.

19

The main problem with studies of this kind is that it is difficult to generalize their findings. We know that living or being in a certain geographical area, that being with certain others, that a particular mode of dress, constitute being in the 'area of suspicion' for some policemen; we know about the norms governing the interactions of some policemen and some groups of young people. Because such studies are by their nature local and particular (and this is prescribed by the methodological standpoint), many more are needed.

Finally here we have Steer's recent analysis (1970) of police formal cautions. This yields invaluable information about a section of those 'let off', but it cannot tell us enough about children informally warned, nor do we know whether young people, like adults, are ever let off in exchange for information or some other deal. We still do not know about those whom the police systematically do not become aware of.

What these studies have confirmed is that not only do police routinely under-enforce the law, but that many matters dealt with by policemen are not amenable to law at all. Thus Cumming *et al.* (1965) found in their analysis of incoming calls to one precinct station that 28·7 per cent could be classified as 'persistent personal problems'—matters such as health problems,[3] dealing with children or the incapacitated, and so on.

Linking this perspective with the problem of the genesis of law are works which indicate that certain laws are designed in such a way that only certain sections of the population are at risk of being convicted, regardless of the way in which the police exercise their discretion. Stinchcombe (1963) showed how restricted access to private places meant that laws prohibiting certain behaviours in public, such as being drunk and disorderly, necessarily affected predominantly working-class people. Skolnick and Woodworth (1967) showed how the fact that welfare departments made reporting a putative father to the police a condition of giving financial aid to under-age pregnant girls meant that the statutory rape laws were operated primarily against working-class males.

Beyond this we have studies and discussions of law-making (e.g. Hall, 1952; Chambliss, 1964; Jeffrey, 1957; Quinney, 1970) which show how particular interests are expressed in the law to the disadvantage of others.

Thus the choices made by the policemen are only one element in the differential impact of law, and the consequent allocation of deviant statuses and roles. Indeed, as Turk (1969) has argued, different levels of the social control process may operate in different directions. So the values and interests which colour the policeman's world view and enforcement decisions may be different from those of the legislators. Recognition of this has underlain many of the arguments for and against a national police force in this country. It is important to bear the possibilities of such discrepancies in mind, and to examine both the reasons for them and their consequences. This point is taken up in the next section.

The police and social order

That the police exist to maintain social order appears incontrovertible, but it is in fact a meaningless statement. For it to make sense one must pose the question, order from whose standpoint? For some people the risk of arrest may introduce an element of disorder into the predictable routine of getting drunk on a Saturday night. Some of the studies discussed here touch on this point, but none analyses it. The police themselves (with a few notable exceptions) operate with an essentially consensual model of society. Indeed, this is for them the prime legitimator of their role. They see themselves as protecting the mass of decent, respectable people from the few who are neither decent nor respectable (see also chapter 4, pp. 112–19).

The opposite view is of a fundamentally divided society wherein the police are agents of a dominant power group, enforcing its standards and order in the face of alternative sets of standards and definitions of order. Rosenberg (1971) presents this model, suggesting also that sociological work on the police to date (including that of Westley, Skolnick and myself (1971)) has disguised this issue by presenting the 'liberal' image of an heroic, indeed 'Hamlet like', policeman, exposed on all sides and valiantly trying to find an acceptable balance between different social pressures in the face of all the odds. The picture is overdrawn, but there is some truth in it. Law and its enforcement in the widest social and political context has largely been ignored by sociologists. And when a political scientist such as Chapman (1970) turns his attention to the police, the question is of the relationship between the police and the central organs of government, while the effects of this on the wider society are not dealt with in any depth.

Two works, those by Wenninger and Clark (1967) and Silver (1967) attempt to rectify this balance. Both air the major questions, and are sufficiently important and sophisticated studies to warrant detailed critical examination.

Basing their analysis on Parsonian systems theory, Wenninger and Clark argue that the police contribute to two of the essential functions of the social system, goal attainment and value maintenance. The police are an *instrumental* agency of social control on behalf of the government, and a *symbolic* agency of social control, representing established values. Their argument falls into four sections. I will comment on each of these and then raise some

21

general issues. I do not intend here to recapitulate the major arguments against Parsonian analysis (e.g., Lockwood, 1956; Black, 1962).

First, the authors argue that the two functions 'cannot be equally stressed during the same period of time within the same social structure', because goal attainment requires conscious transformation of one steady state of structure to another, and it is *after* this that value maintenance reassumes its importance.

Second, they present a discussion of the two positions. Having presented one polar model of a self-regulating, consensual society (in which they suggest that any kind of behaviour somehow or other reinforces the system, which after all tells us only that behaviour in a system is behaviour in a system), they very reasonably raise the question, why are policemen necessary in a society like this? The answer is a lot less than satisfactory. I quote it as given: 'the answer is, of course, that humans are somewhat recalcitrant. Socialisation and institutionalisation are not perfect or all pervasive processes, and rarely is the social "insulation" of the society sufficient to keep it from new ideas'. The first statement is reductionist, and tells us nothing; the second raises and begs 'why' questions—the fallibility of these processes in such a society is surely not something to be taken for granted; the third statement most obviously raises and begs questions of power, and of the mechanics of the social processes involved.

On goal attainment the discussion is happier. Law, like the police, serves two masters. It is an instrument of integration and also an instrument of goal attainment. In addition, allied to custom it can further serve to maintain values. However, because 'there is always [*sic*] an awareness by the members of a society that the law is being consciously used to attain given ends, and that it has potential physical force to sustain it', the authors state that for their purposes the law is best conceived as contributing to goal attainment. Thus when enforcing the law the police function as an agent of government in an instrumental capacity.

At risk of being unfair, this model posits (1) that laws are designed to achieve something and (2) that they operate on behalf of 'government', conceived as non-problematic and unitary.

In the third and most important section of their paper the authors develop a typology of deviant behaviour in four cells, based on whether customary and legal dictates are co-extensive or not, and to which the deviate does or does not conform. Their discussion of likely police action in each of these situations is often insightful and the issue of laws that lack a consensual base is always an important one. (It is possible for such laws to happen in Wenninger and Clark's world, because they seem to acknowledge that consensus in part results from the government pulling a con job on the populace.

They state that the government must provide and recreate justification for the norms and values whose 'original purpose' and legitimations may have been forgotten. But who pulls the government?) It is also important because they recognize the possibility of discrepancies between different levels of the social control process—police, law, government (see also Turk, 1969). Thus some oversimplifications are avoided but others remain.

The problems are, first, that the community and custom are conceived as single, homogeneous entities, give or take a few deviants. Second, that the autonomy of government is taken to the extreme. What can the interests of the government be when opposed to this wholly united community? Are they simply the interests of the bureaucracy? Do they not reflect the goals, values and 'customary morality' of some segments rather than others within the community? The *assumption* of homogeneity precludes subjecting this last question to empirical test. (If Wenninger and Clark are not intending to present a homogeneous community, but something more akin to homogeneous sub-cultures within the wider society, why do they state, for example, that the police usually operate according to custom? Does this apply to *every* sub-culture?) Third, the model does not suggest the *reasons* for police choice of actions. This is a danger, for example, when action is retrospectively described as *identifying* with government. This is treated as an explanation of police action, rather than a descriptive statement that the two coincide.

In the two cases in the typology where there is a discrepancy between custom and law, the deviate conflicting with either one or the other set of prescriptions, it seems that police action would be 'a function of their personal convictions and their relationship with one side or the other'. These are precisely the areas which need investigating. Wenninger and Clark claim to have presented a framework, rather than a theory, but as a framework it gives insufficient guidance as to where the investigation of these critical convictions and relationships should begin. However, like Bredemeier's similar work in the related field of the sociology of the courts, (1962) the work of Wenninger and Clark has the considerable value of *identifying* some crucial problems.

The last section of the paper includes the development of some ideas thrown up by the typology, and a theoretical proposition. In the discussion the empirical fact of a non-consensual community is admitted, though the question of what this does to a typology based on the notion of a *single* community is not raised. The authors argue that customary usually take precedence over legal dictates for policeman and citizen alike, though 'professionalization' of the police might limit this. They argue, that to the extent that there is a consensus (in their case an agreement between communal and legal norms) the role of the police would be more symbolic than instrumental. This reminds one of Banton's distinction (1964a) between peace-keeping and enforcement orientations. Like Banton, too, they argue that when consensus is less (in their case, the separation between customary and legal expectations is greater) 'the quantity of instrumental police action is increased'. This is their main proposition and I will link a discussion of it with my more general comments.

The main problems stem from the unitary notion of the community both directly and because this makes it possible to treat 'the government' as non-problematic. Is there such a unity? If not, which community's set of norms do the police apply? The framework does not, as the authors claim, contribute to an understanding of selective enforcement because these questions are not raised. Again, the authors seem to assume that the separation between law and custom on which they base their arguments is the same as the situation described by Goldman (1963), which they discuss, in which there is *no* consensus within the community. Instead of this we need to know which segments of the community agree with which laws; which laws and/or customs at a point of time the police agree with; the situation both when a segment agreeing or disagreeing with a law has power and when it lacks power to define the situation for the police. Once you acknowledge that differential power between segments of the community must be considered, the limitations of even a complex static model become apparent. A group with power over the police may, through time, re-define a situation for them so that police agreement with law and/or custom is changed; a powerful segment may get the law changed. Are segments with power over the police the same as segments with power over central government? What is the situation, through time, when they are not the same and when they are?

Although Silver analyses the genesis of police forces in terms of class struggle, he also argues that present-day society shows an unprecedented and extending value consensus. But for him this consensus is an observed empirical fact rather than an axiom. The similarity with Wenninger and Clark does not end there, however, for he too states that the police both symbolize consensual moral standards and act as the agents of legitimate coercion, especially when patrolling the 'periphery' of society.

With the establishment of industrial capitalism: 'Not only did the manufacturing class wish to avoid personal danger and inconvenience while protecting their property, but they also saw that . . . the use of social and economic superiors as police exacerbated class violence.' Thus they favoured a police system which 'insulated them from popular violence, drew attack and animosity upon itself and seemed to separate the assertion of "constitutional" authority from that of social and economic dominance' (Silver,

1967, pp. 10–12). Though this suggests conflict, Silver also argues that the development of a modern police force 'absolutely required the moral co-operation of civil society' in order for the benefits of bureaucratic policing to be maximized. Policemen symbolize moral standards, and by doing so continually re-create them. But a pre-existing moral consensus for symbolization is a necessary condition of such a display. The consensus, Silver hints, is a managed one, but no less real at a point in time for that. And it was, in the nineteenth century, as new a phenomenon as the police forces which simultaneously symbolized and created it.

Sadly for the police, their very effectiveness, Silver argues, raises expectations about the level of order which it is possible to attain. In the face of an ever-widening consensus 'criminal' and 'political activities' are re-defined as threats to the very foundations of social order, and once again, as at their inception, the police are seen as 'a garrison force against an internal enemy'.

Silver's analysis overcomes many of the difficulties inherent in that of Wenninger and Clark. It recognizes that understanding of an institution like the police requires an historical perspective, and explicitly documents changes through time; it does not assume a consensual community, or even a consensual majority, but explicitly documents dissensus and discusses the relevant bases of it, as well as describing changes in the range of consensus; it does not treat 'the government' as an autonomous or otherwise non-problematic concept (for Wenninger and Clark I think it is an *entity*), but is at pains to identify which interests are expressed in legislative processes. However, Silver does not attempt to analyse the nature of police actions, and in this area Wenninger and Clark do raise important issues. Even given scepticism about a general model and a typology which precludes the raising of major empirical questions about the nature of society and government, it is necessary to acknowledge that the very real problem of the relationship of the policeman with the community he polices, as opposed to his relationship with central organizations, is posed.

Rightly, they argue that we cannot presume correspondence with either the one or the other. It is necessary to spell out the conditions under which different kinds of police actions may be taken.

At this point the analyses and findings discussed in the second section here, concerning the influence of community structure and police organization on police actions, again become relevant.

The present research in context

This research is concerned with the relevance of different role-definers for police action and role conception. Because the focus is on the policeman and his organization, it falls (as chronologically might be predicted) into my second category. Readers interested in the third set of problems will find incidental information about, for example, the policeman's view of others. They will find considerable discussion of which groups have power to define reality for policemen. It may help to provide some necessary links between their problems and the fourth and final set of problems analysed above, although it was not designed to tackle these either.

This study, then, looks at the relationship between the policeman and the community he polices in terms of the power which that community has or does not have over him. It seeks to identify the bases of this power, and that of other groups. The policeman's world view and the negotiations of reality between a policeman and a particular client are capable of independent description, and it is important that such data should be available. But mental constructs are also social constructs, and each actor brings to a particular transaction a socially derived set of concepts and more complex mental constructs which shape and limit the encounter. The source of these and the extent of the actors' commitment to them are linked and relevant questions. Moreover, an analysis of the bases of community power, of the reasons for 'moral consensus' in some situations between policeman and policed, is a necessary counterweight to a too crudely simplified conflict model. Differences, both horizontally and vertically between social control agents are open to examination. To assume uniformity here is as dangerous as to assume it within the community. The question is of crucial importance in a divided society. Whom would a Welsh policeman support if there were a Welsh Nationalist secession? A similar question could be posed about a major withdrawal of legitimacy from central government along class, religious or ethnic lines. In Northern Ireland the question has been posed many times, in a rather bloody manner.[4] Imagining or analysing extreme situations of this kind sharpens the issues, but they remain within what may indeed be an increasingly consensual society. Here we must distinguish between types and bases of consensus. But bearing all these complexities in mind, it is still possible to approach an empirical answer to the questions, *whose law do the police enforce and why*?

Summary

The developments in role theory which shaped the research design have been presented, together with the practical problems with which the police were concerned at the time of the study. Following this the methods and scope of the study have been described and discussed.

In the second half of the chapter the monograph has been put in its contemporary context. The development of sociological thinking about police work has been traced under headings indicating four roughly chronological areas of concern, namely, (1) citizen rights, (2) reasons for differences in police practice, (3) the effects of police action and (4) the police and social order. It was suggested that this monograph falls under the second heading, though it also makes a contribution in the fourth and final area.

2 Rural police work

PC Smith said he had been on traffic duty at the evening
procession of the mayor to the chapel. He said that he had
stopped one car to let the Girl Guides go through. 'The people
of Yoxborough were amazed. They didn't think the old boy
could lift his arm so far.'

(Rural beat PC from field diary, 27 May 1962.)

The research division

At the time of the study, the nearest estimate of the population of
the division chosen for the research in the county was 46,374. The
area covered 19,355 acres. Four of the five sections comprising the
division were rural; the sub-divisional headquarters was a small
town, here called Hillbridge. Hillbridge section consisted of two
one-man rural beats as well as the town, which had a population of
7,235. Apart from this, the beats covered on average 3·8 parishes,
the largest number for any beat being six and the smallest two.
Average population on a one-man beat was 1,307. This calculation
includes one beat where the section station, situated in a village, was
operated by a sergeant and one beat PC. There were also three
small-town beats, two of which were policed from section stations
and one from divisional headquarters. These had populations of
2,204, 2,081 and 2,144 respectively. Each of these beats included an
extensive area of farmland as well as the town itself. One was
staffed by a sergeant and two constables, one by a sergeant and
three constables, and the DHQ section by a sergeant and constables
varying in number from two to four during the period of the research.
In Hillbridge there were six beat constables and a section sergeant.
A detective sergeant and constable were stationed at DHQ and a

DC at Hillbridge, which is a rapidly growing town situated on a trunk road from the Midlands to the coast.

The postings of the county men are shown in Table 3.

TABLE 3   *Type of work of county men interviewed*

Admin.	Patrol car	CID	Townbeat 6–20 men	Country beats 2–5 men	1 man	Total
2 (1)*	5	3 (1)	18 (5)	10 (3)	26	64 (10)

*Brackets indicate sergeants and senior ranks.

The work of a county policeman

A county policeman must be a jack of all trades, but also a master of many. He has to deal first with any eventuality on his beat from a stray dog, through outbreaks of fowl pest or swine fever, to traffic offences, crime, natural disasters, sudden death, murder and suicide. Moreover, he is used as an all-purpose public service agency by his parishioners, and is expected by them not only to be constantly on duty but also to have an intuitive knowledge of many details of their personal lives. But though the variety in the work of a rural policeman is undisputed, it is also true that the more spectacular of these events occur relatively rarely. What is needed is some closer approximation to what constitutes the daily round of the average beat PC.

Table 4 shows annual averages of various items of police work, based on records of the year prior to the research. The figure for movement of animal licences issued relates to a twenty-month period which includes 1961 and the first eight months of 1962. Figures not in brackets can be added to give a rough estimate of the total volume of recorded work.

To get the work of the beat policeman further into perspective it is necessary to look more closely at the facts behind these figures. Of the 269 crimes reported on one-man beats, 28·1 per cent were dealt with by the beat PC, 34·9 per cent by the beat PC together with his section sergeant, 3·4 per cent with the help also of the uniform inspector, and 32·2 per cent with the help of CID personnel in addition in some cases to uniform inspectors and others. Of the remaining two (1·4 per cent) crimes, one was cleared up by mobile patrol men and one by men outside the division. Thus well over half of the crimes on one-man beats were dealt with by the local uniform men.

TABLE 4   *Average annual recorded work load per constable*

	Country beat (1 man)	Small town (per PC)	Hillbridge (per PC)
Crimes reported	9·5	3·25	17·6
(Crimes recorded)	(7·2)	(2·45)	(14·4)
Injury accidents	6·0	4·9	6·4
Non-injury accidents	8·2	7·9	12·0
Traffic offences reported	17·2	31·5	41·8
(No. of reports)	(13·1)	(23·5)	(32·8)
Other non-indictable offences reported	4·3	3·75	2·0
(No of reports).	(2·8)	(2·4)	(1·5)
Coroner's enquiries: no inquest	1·4	1·9	0·7
Coroner's enquiries: inquest	0·4	0·9	0·0
Firearms enquiries, etc.	5·1	6·9	4·0
Enquiries other forces, etc.	6·2	4·25	7·0
* Movement of animal licences per month	12·1	9·7	7·4

*A number of beats where it was unclear as to whether a real count had been made were excluded.

In the analysis of indictable offences on one-man beats given in Table 5, only three of the five sections are included, since CID men were resident in the other two sections (DHQ and Hillbridge were section as well as sub-divisional stations) and tended to deal with crime reports. The 'purest', ideal typical form of one-man beat is found in those sections to which only a sergeant and a team of constables were posted. There were seventeen one-man beats in these sections. The uniform personnel available to deal with crimes on these beats was, therefore, seventeen constables and three sergeants. On average these men dealt with 5·1 reported crimes each per year, and 3·7 recorded crimes. The sergeant was, of course, responsible for the whole section, and in two of the three sections would have dealt also with crimes in the small town in which he and other constables were based. The one-man beat constable would also have worked on nearly all the crimes on his beat, together not only with his sergeant but also with CID men or more senior uniform staff. The figures are, therefore, an underestimate of his involvement with crime. The advantages of under- rather than over-estimating will be seen more clearly in the next chapter, where average work-loads per man are used to point up the contrast between rural and urban policing.

Details of the crimes reported on one-man beats in these three sections are shown in Table 5.

TABLE 5 *Indictable offences on one-man beats,* 1961*

	Larceny	Breaks	Other pro-perty	Sex off-ences	Against the person	Other	Total
Recorded:							
Uniform	62	5	—	—	1	7	75
CID	27	18	1	8	—	5	59
Other	—	1	—	—	—	—	1
Total	89	24	1	8	1	12	135
Reported and 'written off':							
Uniform	27	—	1	—	—	—	28
CID	3	—	—	1	—	—	4
Total	30	—	1	1	—	—	32
Grand total	119	24	2	9	1	12	167

*Excludes one-man beats in DHQ and Hillbridge sections.

Thus in these three 'ideal typical' sections uniform men dealt with 61·7 per cent of the crimes reported on one-man beats, and 55·7 per cent of the crimes recorded.

A large proportion of these crimes were of apparently trivial nature. One beat, the section beat which has also been counted here as a one-man station, can be taken as an example. In the three years preceding the research, fourteen of the twenty crimes were larcenies of an amount less than £2—including one larceny of plums valued at 4d.—and the remaining crimes were one false pretences, one assault occasioning actual bodily harm, one case of unlawful sexual intercourse, one attempted suicide, one larceny of a raincoat valued at 5 guineas, and one larceny of a cycle valued at £8.

The offences did not necessarily seem trivial to the men dealing with them. For many beat men clearing up crime was real police work, and brought intrinsic satisfaction as well as, possibly, recognition and prestige. 'I got a nice little crime up last week', a man might remark, contentedly. Moreover, to the victim on the beat the loss of a raincoat would be an important matter. He would know whether 'his' policeman was doing anything about it, and make his voice heard if he were not satisfied. Reciprocally, the policeman would know the victim, and what the loss of the raincoat really meant. *The members of the community defined for him what was trivial and what was important, what was real police work and what was not*—but that is prejudging my argument.

Any beat man would allow that crime was a small, albeit important, part of his work. Dealing with an accident could take up a considerable amount of time, for not only did the beat man have to attend the scene, get details of injuries, take measurements, take statements from those involved and any independent witnesses available—these might be taken in the days following and only the names and addresses taken at the time of the accident—arrange perhaps for a photographer to visit the scene, assess the situation, make out his own report in full (since *pro forma* accident books were not at this time used in the force), but also, in the event of an offence, he had subsequently to issue summonses and attend court. Contacts with other forces or divisions might also be required, since it was unlikely on a trunk road that those involved would live on the beat.

Again, the figure for non-indictable offences is an inadequate estimate of the amount of work involved for the beat man, and so is the number of reports which were submitted for a decision concerning prosecution.

Whether or not the offence was ultimately prosecuted, the beat man had to observe the behaviour, amass the appropriate evidence, and submit a full report of the behaviour with the correct heading for the offence, which, in the case of an unusual offence, had to be looked up in a legal reference book. The whole had to be typed out by the PC.

Some qualification is necessary, too, concerning the issue of licences for the movement of animals in infected areas. Monthly averages here, although a reasonable basis for comparison, do not present the whole picture. In an outbreak of swine fever, such as occurred during the research period, the men were exceptionally busy in this respect, and could scarcely expect a day to pass without being interrupted to issue one or more licences. On one beat, ten licences were issued during the whole year prior to the research, compared with 365 during the first eight months of 1962.

Rural beats

This was the work of the county policeman in so far as it was recorded. There remains much more. In a one-man station, gazettes—records of men wanted or arrested and other information—had to be brought up to date and cancelled, in theory each day. In a town this work was divided among the PCs.

In addition, the country beat man had to keep up to date a telephone book, a lost property book, a message book—'messages' were circulated to division only, to section stations, or to beats, according to their importance and relevance in a particular area—a list of stolen cars, and a 'beat book' giving such information as the addresses and telephone numbers of doctors, midwives, veterinary surgeons, etc., the situation of vulnerable property, and information concerning 'trouble-makers' and those known to have criminal records living on the 'patch'. In larger stations an 'occurrence book' was also kept in which were entered records of incidents and items of information which were deemed too important to go unrecorded, but which were not recorded elsewhere. On a one-man beat such entries might well be made in the policeman's pocket book.

Other routine work included a monthly (approximately) call at farms to sign the 'pig book'—recording movements of swine—and similar routine calls on scrap-metal dealers, though fewer of the beats had any of the latter resident. Vulnerable property had to be regularly checked, which often involved considerable travelling and possibly also the submission of a report. On the beats surrounding an approved school problems connected with escapes were not infrequent, involving night calls to recapture the absconder, and associated crimes reported. In the year prior to the research there were sixty-eight escapes, and the boys were found to be responsible for twenty-six crimes. Again, Diseases of Animals Regulations specify that swine bought from market in a fever area must be isolated for twenty-eight days, during which time the policeman should visit them twice. The beat men could not always get round to this at regular fortnightly intervals, but would probably go and see them when they arrived and again at the end of the period. A licence was sent to the station if pigs were to be purchased at a market, but the farmer was also supposed to notify the beat man himself. The burial of diseased pigs had also to be witnessed. Again, the PC had to be notified that sheep-dipping was to be carried out within the required period, though if the farmer did not take the

33

initiative the beat man would often give him a reminder. He also had to attend to observe that the dipping was done correctly.

Problems of communication have also to be considered. A divisional instruction 'enquiries at all farms' might involve some thirty or so visits, and contacting the farmer himself was not always easy when he was out working in the fields. In some sections the problem of internal communication was solved by a system of 'conference points' at which men on adjoining beats met for discussion at a point convenient to both, and stayed perhaps for half an hour. The sergeant might also attend.

Men on one-man beats worked discretionary duties, phoning in to the section station each morning the duties which they planned to work for the day, or had worked the previous day if there were any change from the plan. Thus hours of work could to some extent be adjusted to accommodate domestic needs, but this advantage was more than counterbalanced by the repeated intrusions on domestic privacy caused by callers at the station in off-duty hours. Figures already given for diseases of animals licences issued give some indication of the extent to which this happened, but there were many other reasons for local people to call at the police station. No count of callers at beat stations was possible, but in the course of one eight-hour beat patrol there were four calls at the beat station, dealt with by the policeman's wife. Two were for 'pig licences', one concerned a lorry load which had fallen on a child, and one was a telephone message which came from the division. While the family were having tea after the tour of duty two more people came for 'pig licences', and a bit later on a third came for the same reason. Many local callers came at inconvenient times, such as the very early morning prior to market; nor could callers be turned away with too much expedition. However trivial the item of business to be discussed, each expected a leisurely chat of ten minutes or so. This could not be recorded as overtime for which time off in lieu could be claimed.

A list is tedious, and it is in any case impossible to detail comprehensively the multifarious tasks to be performed. A quotation perhaps best indicates the diversity of work to be done: a section sergeant is talking.

Take last week now, we had that prisoner in and these three to come up to court. Well, I was up at half past six getting the court room ready (lighting the fire, etc.) then I had to come back and see to the prisoner's breakfast, then one of the men rang in and said there'd been a suicide on his beat and he was due at court so what should he do. Well, I told him to get the doctor there and come to court because there wasn't a lot he could do when the man was dead . . . Then (after doing the duty book) I had to go to court, and afterwards the inspector came along here . . .

Altogether there were fifteen over-night prisoners on the division in the year prior to the research, and a total of seventy-nine meals had to be provided—by the five section sergeants' wives.

Beat patrols

A beat patrol was usually a fairly leisurely affair, with ample time to stop and chat—and the men claimed, rightly, that this should be so. At this level it is impossible to isolate the work of the country policeman from his relationship with the community which he polices. Beat men saw their primary role as keepers of the peace. To have a 'quiet patch' was a sign of good policing, and this could only be achieved with the co-operation of the local people (Banton, 1964a). Chatting was, therefore, an intrinsic part of the job. The men tended to be possessive about their 'patch'. They developed individual characteristics in the way they set about their work and spoke with pride of their knowledge of the local people. (See also chapter 4, especially pp. 105–10.)

The patrol outlined below was not typical—no two were alike—but it does indicate some important aspects of the work. The extract is from the field diary, and names are fictitious.

Just after 2 p.m. . . . set off round the beat on bicycles. Delivered a circular about stolen bicycles to a garage—'Actually they don't have any bikes here, but I usually drop one in in any case.' Made a second visit. The owners of the house were out. PC Matherson had expected this as he knew the wife worked. A bicycle which the man who lived here had found on the main road had been found to have been stolen . . . 'I thought I'd better let him know about it, otherwise he'd be building up and thinking he could claim a bicycle in three months' time . . .' Matherson had a letter ready for the man so he slipped it through the box and carried on. We next called at the local hall. . . . Some new owners had recently moved in. Matherson had to see the man about his gun licence. Matherson and the man looked for the number on the gun, but couldn't find it . . . Before we left, the owner of the house thanked Matherson for keeping an eye on the place 'while we were moving in all that time'. . . . We called to deliver a pig licence. 'They asked me to bring it round. I always get a chicken from these people at Christmas actually.' The woman who took the

licence in said, 'Are you coming in for a glass of beer?' . . .
Matherson chatted to them about their family, and called them
by their Christian names . . . After leaving we passed another
man in his garden. 'We could call in there and I should get a
drink there too so I don't think we'd better. I don't go to these
places too often.' . . . The last visit was to deliver a statement
from Hillbridge about an offence. Matherson thought the
young man would be out but that he might see his mother.
When we got there no one was at home. A by-passer told us
that the mother was at a women's meeting in the chapel, and
we decided to wait. Then Matherson went down to the chapel
to ask where she was, and eventually found her in a shop. He
arranged with her that her son should call at the police station,
to save him another journey, and assured her that he wasn't
in trouble. She said that her husband had been coming down
anyway to get a pig licence, and Matherson said if he gave the
lad a message he would give the licence to him. Afterwards he
said, 'I thought I'd better just find the old girl and speak to
her, otherwise people would tell her "Oh, the policeman's
been down to your house", and she'd start worrying and
wonder what was wrong' . . . A man in a garden called, 'Good
afternoon, sir' as we went past . . . We passed a caravan where
Matherson said one of his real headaches lived . . . got back
to the station in time for tea and a game with the children . . .

Perks

This extract shows not only some of the tasks, the quality of the
relationship with the community, but also two aspects of the job
here called *perks* and *easing*, represented respectively by the chicken
and the beer. Both make life more pleasant for the beat man—and
this in itself is not unimportant—both are common, and both are
accepted as normal not only by the men but also by their senior
officers. Perks are advantages which accrue to an individual by
reason of being in a particular work situation, and which are not
part of the formal contract of employment. Perks, such as the
chicken, do not represent the policeman receiving bribes, nor, more
subtly, do they represent the policeman taking advantage of his
relatively high status in the community. Rather they are an intrinsic
part of the web of relationships which surround and support him.
Local farmers are pleased if the PC catches a poacher, and they
express due gratitude; or they are grateful for the convenience of
having their licences delivered—which might be done on odd
occasions in any case, but perhaps not regularly for nothing in
return. Reciprocally, the policeman needs their help both in order

to do his job effectively and in order to make life congenial for his family (cf. Chapters 4 and 5).

Easing

Easing can be defined as non-prescribed behaviour on the part of an employee designed to make his work or conditions more congenial. It can be either licit or illicit from the point of view of the senior members of the work organization.

The beer or the cider or the tea and home-made scones are *offered* in the same spirit as the perks, but their function is more directly connected with police tasks in three ways. First, a man will not be accepted by his local community if he does not to some extent comply with their standards and norms, and in this area the offering and acceptance of hospitality in the form of food and drink was an important ritual indicating both friendliness and a recognition of the status of the recipient. It was thus essential for the beat man to accept this offered hospitality in whatever form it was provided. Second, the easing behaviour provided the PC with an opportunity to talk with people and to exchange useful information about those living on the beat. Third, of course, it did fulfil the criteria required by the definition. In cold wet weather, having cycled some number of miles in the rain, the tea and fireside constituted a very welcome break for the beat man whose work at times could seem both uncomfortable and monotonous.

Official easing

Official easing falls within the general definition of easing behaviour, above. It has, however, the additional characteristic that opportunities for the behaviour are formally provided by the police force. Because the two concepts are so closely related, official easing is discussed here, although it is not related to the patrol just described.

In the county there were opportunities for participation in several types of sporting activity, and inter-division and inter-force contests occasioned widespread interest. In the country, beat men were expected to arrange their duties to allow of participation in these activities in off-duty time, and in the towns duties were usually so arranged as to make participation possible. Occasionally, however, the duty roster prevented town men from taking part. In Hillbridge, where easing facilities were in any case pared to a minimum, any difficulty of this kind gave rise to considerable ill feeling.

Work away from the beat

The type of easing behaviour indulged in varied according to the differing opportunities presented by various work situations. Dissatisfaction arose from those sources where no easing behaviour was possible: first, from the effects of the job on a man's domestic life, and, second, from those of his duties which took him off his own beat. (See also chapter 5 and Cain, 1964, chapter 6.) Even these last, if they did not occur too frequently, could serve as an added interest and a means of keeping the PC in touch with men and events outside his section. But at the time of the research men were called away from their beats in three of the five sections too often, by their own standards. They felt that their beats were 'neglected', not necessarily in the sense that essential duties went unperformed—though occasionally major incidents such as accidents had to be dealt with by 'outsiders' as a result—but in the sense that they did not have time to be 'seen about' which was essential for their peace-keeping role. Nor did they have time for the necessary chatting with the villagers. This both threatened their opportunities for future easing and for receiving perks and also made it more difficult for them to get help when they needed it, such as information to help solve a crime or volunteers to come forward as witnesses of an accident. It also limited their knowledge of what was going on. Since such knowledge was a sign of interest and belonging, knowing already was, paradoxically, a pre-requisite for being told more.

Events which took a man from his beat could be occasional, such as a royal visit or the County Show—for both of which men were drafted from throughout the force—or a 'watching job'. The 'watch' in which I participated required two men nightly for a week, drawn from a single division. Other occasional tasks for which men from a single division only were used were radar speed checks, a motor-cycle scramble, and a Ministry of Transport vehicle check.

Other tasks away from the beat had to be performed more regularly, such as being observer on the divisional night patrol car (10 p.m. to 6 a.m.) for either three or four consecutive nights. Each beat man did this once or twice a year.

Crime patrols

More frequently the men were called upon to be either driver or observer on the divisional night crime patrol. At the end of the research period the 'crime van' was going out on the 11 p.m.–3 a.m. shift nightly, covering the peak crime hours. In fact, the patrol usually ended an hour later than its scheduled time, since the observer had to be dropped at his beat station when the patrol had been completed, and this might be at a distance of some twenty miles from the divisional headquarters.

The main purpose of these patrols was to check vulnerable property on the division. In the course of fourteen patrols undertaken, one accident and one mysterious car, stolen from Scotland and found blazing on a disused airfield, were dealt with. The section sergeant and other beat men also attended the accident. One 'speeder' was reported. One earlier patrol of a similar kind was recalled to a town to watch some unruly youngsters leaving a dance. Otherwise the work was preventive.

Easing behaviour on the patrol took the form of an unofficial break for coffee, brought in flasks by those involved, or occasionally a call for tea with an ex-policeman from another force who had a night-watching job.

In all, over a three month period from May to July, the beat men in each of the five sections spent averages of 9·2 hours, 27·1 hours, 5·3 hours, 20·8 hours, and 16 hours per man on either the night car or the van, which represented a small proportion of something like 550 hours worked per man during the period. Unfortunately, however, the figures relate to a period before the *nightly* crime patrols were begun, and are therefore an underestimate.[1]

Section duties

A more serious threat to the beat man was presented by the requirement for him to do duties in his divisional, sub-divisional or section headquarters. To quote an earlier report of the study (Cain, 1964) in Hillbridge sub-division 'in a period of three months 37 per cent of the hours worked had been in sub-divisional headquarters'. This figure is a proportion of actual hours worked, and takes account of annual leave, sick leaves, etc. In Hillbridge the problem was at its worst. This was partly because the Hillbridge station was two men under strength, the full establishment being nine constables, partly because divisional and sub-divisional telephones and offices had to be manned all day from 9 a.m. until approximately 12.30 p.m. (though the closing down time varied) and this took two men off the outside strength daily, and finally because an order had been issued that two men instead of one should be on duty at night following a series of housebreaks. Beat men were therefore called in to supplement the strength, often on two or three and occasionally on as many as five days in succession. Full eight-hour tours of duty were worked in Hillbridge, plus travelling time, but only half-shifts were worked elsewhere. Duties away from home on Sundays and bank holidays were particularly resented for obvious reasons, but if the men could see a clear reason for their being needed, such as a serious crime, there were no complaints.

Variations between sections in respect of these duties are shown by

39

the figures in Table 6, which refer again to the same three-month period.

TABLE 6 *Mean number of hours worked in section headquarters per beat man in three months (total no. hours worked per man: 550)*

	DHQ *sub-division*			Hillbridge *sub-division*	
	A (DHQ)	B	C	D	E
Shifts ending after midnight	—	—	—	121	87·4
Total	17·7	25·6	26·2	188	131·4

Town police work

The work of the men in the small towns was in many respects similar to that of the country beat men. Their range of tasks was the same. They worked under closer direction from the section sergeant than men on one-man beats, but as five of the eight men involved had less than five years' service this was understandable. The three main differences were, first, that with the exception of DHQ men, they were called away from their sections less; second, they worked fixed hours, frequently split shifts; third, a certain amount of 'town work'—checking property at night and dealing with occasional traffic problems in two of the towns—had also to be done. The main problem was presented by the hours of work. Split shifts in themselves were not unduly inconvenient for men, all but one of whom lived within a few minutes' walk of the station; what was unsatisfactory was the *unpredictability* of the duties from week to week compared with a regular rota of eight-hour shifts or even with discretionary duties, where provisional arrangements at least could be made. The men did not normally work after 2 a.m. Moreover, the section sergeant was on hand and open to persuasion if any man wished to alter a duty.

Hillbridge

In Hillbridge the situation was different. There crime work was taken out of the hands of the PCs almost completely; nor did they very frequently come up against the more specifically rural tasks. A lot of time was spent dealing with traffic flow and parking problems, serving summonses and delivering other messages. Newspapers had to be collected from the railway station. The morning and afternoon were taken up with such tasks, the men on duty taking turns to patrol and to remain in the station. A third man would most probably also be on duty riding the station motor-cycle. This man would be controlled from headquarters once he had left the Hillbridge station and was on the air. He would frequently have to handle matters not directly related to the work of the Hillbridge station, such as a wide-load conduct. Two of the PCs were qualified to ride the motor-cycle.

In the evenings pub visits had to be made, and 'unruly' youngsters who congregated in the town centre watched and controlled as necessary. At night property had to be checked—some of it four or five miles from the town centre and the PC had only a bike for transport—and late trains watched in and out of the station. The night man kept hourly telephone 'points' with headquarters control room after 2 or 3 a.m. when the man on the 'late' shift in the town went off duty. The work was tedious, for the town was generally a quiet one. Opportunities for easing were limited. The men brewed tea in the station by day, and were occasionally able to do so at night at the back of a public building where there were night-shift workers. At night even the meal break had to be taken in solitude. There were few places, apart from a disused police station in the town, where the men could go for ten minutes' warmth and a quiet smoke. Most patrols in the town were on foot, but at night a bicycle was used.

A major source of complaint was the hours which the men had to work both because they were thought to be unfairly distributed and because the station carried insufficient men to cover all the night shifts. Many of the duties were chopped and changed about from day to day, although officially there was only one relief shift. A man whose duties were 5 p.m. to 1 a.m. might find himself actually working these hours on only one occasion. Only three shifts were normally worked for a full week at a stretch, by one man each. These were the 9 a.m.–5 p.m., the 10 a.m.–6 p.m., and the 10 p.m.–6 a.m. shifts. Thus four men each week had erratic duties. As in the other towns, a man could not predict what shift he could be on, so it was totally impossible to make private plans of any kind.

Country beat men were called in to assist with all the shifts except for 10 p.m.–6 a.m. nights. They stopped working this shift immediately before the research began.

The statement often made by the men that they were on nights 50 per cent of the time was shown by analysis to be an under- rather than an over-estimate of late shifts. Table 7 shows the average proportions of early and late shifts worked by the seven Hillbridge PCs, together with the total number of shifts worked by the men in the time.

TABLE 7 *Hours of duty of Hillbridge constables*

	Time of ending shift			Number of shifts worked
Days (*up to 8p.m.*)*	Evenings (*up to midnight*)*	Short nights (*up to 3 a.m.*)	Nights (*up to 6 a.m. or 7 a.m.*)	
37·4%	12·3%	24·6%	25·7%	390

*Includes all shifts ending after previous time stated.

These late hours of work further disrupted the domestic pattern, already made difficult by the unpredictability of the shift postings. Together with the intrinsic unpleasantness of night duty in this town, this gave rise to considerable dissatisfaction.

Mobile patrols

The division had one patrol car which operated from DHQ. The four drivers arranged their duties on a rota between themselves to fit in with the requirements of headquarters control. Once on the air the men were directed from headquarters, where their route for the shift was decided upon. The main problem of patrol-car crews was their dual responsibility to control and to the division. Although on the divisional strength, they were insistent on their status as mobile men, and themselves regarded the control chief inspector as their immediate superior. They felt the need of someone above the rank of constable to act as a buffer between their two authorities and to negotiate for them when they were subjected to conflicting requirements. But their small numbers did not warrant an established post of mobile sergeant on the division.

The men worked three consecutive eight-hour shifts, the duty rota starting at 6 a.m. There were also two overlapping shifts of 8 a.m.–4 p.m. and 4 p.m. to midnight. Night duties had to be worked only one week in thirteen. One driver was deputed to the night car with a beat observer; the divisional car was required to patrol on alternate, weeks, when it covered half the county area.

As in Hillbridge, abrupt changes of shift were resented, but they happened less frequently. The men tended to be enthusiastic, and would if necessary service the cars and write up reports in their own time. For men who had no immediate superior the visible end product of offence reports assumed considerable importance. Moreover, returns of offences per car had to be submitted to the Home Office, so the men were under pressure from their senior officers to submit as many reports as possible. The mean number of offence reports per mobile man per annum was 56·2.[2]

In an eleven-month period prior to the research (figures for one month were unaccountably missing) the work of the divisional patrol-car crew was as shown in Table 8. In addition, seven 999 calls

TABLE 8 *Recorded work of research division patrol car in eleven months*

	Total	Average per regular driver*
Offences reported (own division)	164	41
(No. of reports)	(149)	(37·25)
Offences reported (other division)	96	24
(No. of reports)	(76)	(19)
Fires	11	2·75
Accidents	44	11
Checked persons	158	439·5
Arrests	7	1·75
Suspicious persons or intruders	9	2·25

* Because night cars had beat men as observers, this is an overestimate of the number of reports, etc., dealt with by each driver.

were attended, five messages delivered, two wide-load conducts carried out, two air crashes attended and a considerable number of other matters, such as a road check, a domestic dispute and a flooded house, were attended to. Cars were operated not only as emergency but also as preventive patrols. Vulnerable property and AA and RAC boxes were regularly checked. Patrol cars attended the scene of all major crimes and were usually deputed to carry out a search of the surrounding area.

Patrol-car drivers received no perks, apart from facilities at the police station for the servicing of their own cars. Easing took the form of a break for a flask of coffee, though this was not usual on the afternoon shift. Mileage was closely watched, so the break served the additional purposes of keeping this to a minimum and providing the men with an opportunity to 'make up the books'. A few day patrols and all night patrols were conducted in pairs, which helped to prevent boredom. A patrol is described below.

> Picked up beat observer from a station twelve miles from DHQ. It was a slack night. Only three vehicles were stopped, two motor-cycles and a car. At one point the observer thought he saw a shadow moving on the wall of a garage where there were a lot of cars for sale, and the driver had just turned the car round to investigate this when two motor-cyclists with pillion riders—rather scruffy youths—were seen. He stopped the car and checked up on the youths before investigating the garage. Everything at the garage was in order. Various AA and RAC boxes were checked *en route*, but there were no other incidents. Called into Headquarters [not DHQ] for refreshment break at 2 a.m. There were no calls after the meal break. About 4.15 a.m. pulled up at the roadside for coffee, and the observer made up his pocket book for the previous five days. Dropped the observer off around 5.30 a.m. and drove back to DHQ. Booked off at 6 a.m.

Administration

One sergeant and one PC were responsible for administration. They worked regular 9 a.m.–5 p.m. days. Their tasks included the preparation of cases for court as well as administration concerned with personnel. Neither was involved in beat work.

CID

Each of the three CID officers was accompanied on at least one occasion, though rather more 'crime work' was done by the researcher in the company of the beat men. One of the officers, transferred to the uniform branch in the course of the research and not replaced, was responsible for fingerprint and photographic work, and also did much of the 'paper work' for the sergeant.

CID work carried high status in the force, in particular as promotions from the CID were thought to be more frequent than from the uniform branch. CID and uniform personnel were interchangeable, though to be transferred back into uniform other than on promotion was considered a sign of failure.

In the county it was possible when attempting to solve a crime to operate on the assumption that someone was bound to have seen or heard something relevant. If sufficient people were questioned the field of suspicion could be narrowed down until ultimately only the guilty party were contained within it (Skolnick and Woodworth, 1967). This approximated to the traditional detective thriller practice of looking for clues *at the scene of the crime*. In a large city criminal investigations in the main do not start here, but with informers and known criminals and those who are permanently within the 'area of suspicion' (Skolnick, 1966; Werthman and Piliavin, 1967; Laurie, 1970). CID personnel on the division used a combination of the two approaches, though beat men, who knew the people on their beats intimately, tended to stick to the traditional approach.

Summary

In this chapter the work of the policeman in a rural division of a county force has been described. His recorded tasks have been listed as far as possible, and an attempt has been made in addition to show something of the quality of the work. Similarities and differences between men posted to towns and villages, mobile patrols and the CID, have been indicated.

In addition three concepts have been introduced and defined in order to facilitate the analysis. These are *perks, easing behaviour* and *official easing*. Their critical relevance for understanding the work of a policeman in a large city force is shown in the next chapter.

3 City police work

The aim here is to pass things over rather than keep them. It's the same all through. If a 'Z' Division car, say, comes over here [i.e., to 'R' Division] and knocks someone off we say: 'Good oh, saves us the work', rather than anything else. It's the same with the CID. The idea is that that's their province, crime, and to hand it over right away . . . (Inspector in city force).

Introduction

The city force was divided into seven divisions, six of them being based on geographical areas, and one being comprised of members of various specialist departments.[1] Some of these specialisms operated on a regional basis (e.g., crime squad, records), others functioned at force level (e.g., fingerprints, Coroner's Office, the 'lock-up', and much administration). CID personnel worked permanently within the boundaries of the geographical divisions, but counted as members of the Specialist ('S') Division. Mounted policemen were in a similar situation. Other specialists working on the geographical divisions, such as dog-handlers, were counted as part of the normal divisional personnel, although their senior officers were on the 'S' Division strength. The traffic department covered the whole city and worked from a central garage and headquarters. These men too were 'S' Division personnel. Problems arising from these complexities of organizational structure will be discussed later; but in general the task boundaries were clearly defined, and problems were not only few but affected small numbers of men.

The research division

The geographical division selected for the research was the largest and the busiest in the force. Personnel of the Research ('R') Division at the time of the study numbered one chief superintendent, one superintendent, three chief inspectors, twelve inspectors, thirty-five sergeants, and 193 constables. The population of the division was estimated at approximately 214,700, representing a considerably higher ratio of citizens to policemen than in the county. Although partly as a result of specialization there were fewer patrol men per head of population, those patrol men who did exist were theoretically, at least, more efficient, and had less to do than the county men when dealing with almost any situation because of the specialist support available to them. The division was divided into three sub-divisions, to which men were permanently posted.

Central sub-division The density of the population varied as between sub-divisions and sections, though as police boundaries did not correspond with ward boundaries exact estimation was not possible. 'Central' sub-division was a typical 'interstitial area', which had already in 1962 housed a large number of immigrants, both coloured and white. Re-development had taken place in parts, though population remained dense as re-housing in flats was carried out on the site. Elsewhere small shops and pubs were mixed with warehouses, railway lines, new trunk road schemes and factories, from one of which came an all-pervading smell of burnt coffee. The shops on the two main shopping streets—on either side of the sub-division which was roughly V-shaped—sold cheap goods; the shoppers were drab. Except in the re-developed area there was an atmosphere of dereliction, at least by day. Most of the homes were small terraced houses, though there were a few larger Victorian terraced homes, in the main converted to other uses of varying reputability. Criminals and prostitutes abounded in the area, which was described, among others, by Colin McGlashan in the *Observer* in 1967 as an area 'of appalling housing conditions, overcrowding and exorbitant rents, of drug pushers, prostitution and delinquency. Every conceivable index of deprivation is well above the national average; from infant mortality and malnutrition to absenteeism or mental illness . . .'.

From the administrative point of view, Central sub-division was divided into two sections, one operating from Central police station —the sub-divisional HQ where the chief inspector of the sub-division also lived—and the other from Walker Street police station, where one of the four inspectors who worked on the sub-division was in residence. One inspector was on duty to cover each of the three shifts, and was responsible for the whole of the sub-division; the fourth inspector would be on relief, covering the leave days of the chief inspector as well as of his colleagues of the same rank. Sergeants and constables were not permanently posted to either one or the other section but were simply counted as being on the sub-divisional strength. In practice, however, semi-permanent postings to work from either Central or Walker Street stations were common. Eleven sergeants were posted to the sub-division. Three were required for each of the three shifts—one in the office at Central police station and two as 'outside men' working one each from Central and Walker Street stations. The sergeants worked a complete cycle of duties—a fortnight on each of the three shifts—followed by a fortnight on relief. This meant that they worked a six-week period with each 'turn' of men followed by an eighteen-week period when they would have contact with this group of men only occasionally when relieving for the regular sergeant on the turn. Inspectors worked to the same system (cf. also pp. 142–3). There were seventy-nine constables on the sub-divisional strength.

Rushbridge (DHQ) *sub-division* Both the remaining sub-divisions covered more socially heterogeneous areas. Rushbridge station, the divisional headquarters, was situated in a well-established suburb. Its area covered mainly housing estates and terraced housing, though there were some larger properties. Two section stations were attached to the sub-division. The Hope Street station was nearer to the city centre and adjoined the Walker Street area. One of the Central sub-division inspectors lived in at Hope Street. The more outlying parts of the sub-division were covered by Maypole section station. Here were larger private properties, many of them built in the early part of the century, some council housing, and less industrial or commercial development than in the other two sections—on the whole a pleasant, leafy area. A sub-divisional inspector lived in at Maypole station.

Administrative offices for the division were situated at Rushbridge, which boosts the figures for sub-divisional personnel. The chief superintendent and superintendent had their offices there. Other senior officers were the same as in other sub-divisions—one chief inspector and four watch inspectors. There were ten sergeants plus a dog sergeant, an administration sergeant and a road-safety sergeant. There were sixty-three constables, approximately ten of whom were posted to Rushbridge by reason of its being the DHQ.[2] These latter included men involved in record-keeping and administration, drivers for the chief superintendent, carpenters and a plan-drawer. As in Central sub-division, a habit of posting particular officers to particular section stations had developed. Office constables in particular tended to have worked regularly in the section before being posted to the section office—itself only a temporary appointment.

In addition, a number of 'S' Division personnel were also posted to Rushbridge by virtue of its being the DHQ, in particular the detective chief inspector. The detective inspector was also frequently seen there. The stables for the mounted branch were in the yard,[3] which was also used by police vehicles. The police woman inspector (who was responsible for two divisions) and the police woman sergeant responsible for the 'R' Division also had Rushbridge as their base.

Brockborough sub-division The third sub-division, here called Brockborough, was the smallest of the three. Diagrammatically, Rushbridge and Brockborough side by side occupied the wide part of the V-shaped division, while Central sub-division occupied the point. Brockborough, too, was a socially mixed area. Its most central part, covered from Brockborough police station, had acute immigrant problems. Most of the area was covered by 'respectable' terraced and some semi-detached housing. There was one sizeable light industrial trading estate. The sub-division was divided longitudinally by a trunk road from the city boundary to the city centre. A number of shopping areas were built along this road. The sub-division also had one section station, here called Outpost, situated just inside the city boundary at the side of a large and busy traffic island on the trunk road. The Outpost area was characterized mainly by prosperous detached and semi-detached housing built in the 1930s or later, plus council housing. Both Outpost and Brockborough stations had to deal with a considerable number of casual enquiries from passing motorists as a result of being situated on the trunk road.

TABLE 9 *Distribution of manpower by sub-division*

	Central	Rushbridge	Brockborough	Total
Sergeants	11	10 + 3	10	34*
Constables	79	53 + 10	51	193

*One sergeant on the divisional strength was away at the police college.

The chief inspector of the sub-division lived in at Brockborough station. Outpost had no residential accommodation, so none of the inspectors on the sub-division was required to live in. The manpower of the sub-division was ten sergeants and fifty-one constables.

The distribution of manpower in the division is shown in Table 9.

CID work

For a large specialized force such as this there can be no overall description of 'police work' as such. The work must be described in terms of the particular tasks on which the men were engaged. Although CID personnel were not formally on the strength of the research division, some description of the work of the CID is necessary, both because the crime pattern of the division puts into context the work of the beat men and also because dealing with 'criminals' tends to be regarded by both uniform and non-uniform men as their key function (Skolnick and Woodworth, 1967; Lambert, 1970).

Indictable offences on the division for the year 1962 are shown in Table 10. Of these, 1,811 (41·5 per cent of those recorded) were

TABLE 10 *Indictable offences on the division for the year 1962*

	Central	Rushbridge	Brockborough	Total
Crimes recorded	1,960	1,173	1,232	4,365
No crimes	60	127	96	283
Total reported	2,020	1,300	1,328	4,648

detected, giving an overall 'clear-up' rate of 45·1 per cent. The rate of crime per 1,000 population for the whole city in 1962 was 25·8 and for the 'R' Division 20·3 approximately. The city rate is higher because city centre crimes are included yet there is relatively little city centre population.

The detective strength of the division numbered sixteen—a detective sergeant (DS) and a detective constable (DC) at each station, plus a detective inspector (DI) and a detective chief inspector (Chief DI) responsible for the whole division. In addition there was at each station an 'attached man', on loan from the uniform branch for four months. This system served the purposes of boosting the CID strength by seven men, of giving senior CID officers the opportunity to assess and choose between uniform officers with a view to taking them on to the permanent strength of the department, of giving the attached men the opportunity to decide whether they would want full-time CID work should the opportunity arise, and of giving a cross-section of uniform men some insight into CID tasks and their modes of operation. It also had the effect, for men not qualified for promotion, of relieving the monotony of twenty-five or thirty years 'pounding the beat'.

CID personnel organized their own duties at station level. Hours, as always in this branch of police work, were long. Three or four times a week the men worked split shifts—8 a.m. to lunch time and then on duty again at 5 p.m. or thereabouts with no fixed finishing time. But an advantage of the job was that the men usually had Sundays free. Once in seven weeks a DC was required to do a night shift, nominally from 10 p.m. to 7 a.m., though after a busy night he might have to stay on later and get the 'paper work' resulting from the night's events up to date for the officers on duty at 8 a.m.

One CID night man covered the whole division. His role was reactive rather than initiative. He would be summoned to the scene of a reported crime, usually following attendance by uniform men; or he would be summoned by uniform men to assist them with the interrogation of suspects or 'prisoners'.

Both these tasks were also part of normal CID routine. But officers on duty at other hours were mainly involved—apart from record-keeping and the preparing of cases for court—in 'detecting' crimes. As indicated in the previous chapter, this rarely involved the traditional crime fiction procedure of starting *at the scene of the crime* with clues and possibly a range of suspects to be narrowed down; rather the city CID men started at some distance from the crime and operated in a reverse manner,[4] with a broad spectrum of people who were more or less permanently in the 'area of suspicion' (Werthman and Piliavin, 1967) and with information purchased from regular informants, known as *sarbuts* or *sarbs*.[5] When sufficient information had been gathered by direct purchase or in the course of casual conversation with members or fringe members of the criminal sub-culture for a CID man to feel convinced that he knew who had committed a particular offence, there were broadly three courses of action open to him. Which he took would depend partly on the characteristics of the offence, and even more on his knowledge of the suspect's character and habits. In order to make the correct decision in this and other respects the CID man must have in his mind a mass of such particularistic knowledge, much of it useless most of the time, but all of it stored and docketed. The long evenings spent in pubs and sleazy clubs are justified by the men on the grounds that there is no other way of building up such a store of information[6]—and this may well be true, wasteful though the procedure is.[7] The CID man may also attempt to keep track of those criminals living on his pitch (not a 'patch' as in the county) and their movements. When a new family of known criminals arrives they will be watched[8] closely for a time to see whether they intend to be 'quiet' and what their pattern of movements is. Records of local criminals are kept at the central lock-up. When a known criminal moves into or returns to the city his full record is obtained from Scotland Yard and filed, in readiness for his first court appearance.

The three choices open to a CID man, then, when he 'knows' who has committed an offence, are first, to get evidence against the suspect sufficient to prove a case in court; second, he may bring the suspect into the police station for 'questioning' and by one means or another elicit from him a statement or admission of guilt, piecing together extra evidence required for a court case retrospectively; third, he might decide to wait until the suspect 'came again', and then arrange for him to 'wear' the first offence also as an offence to be taken into consideration (TIC).

In practice, the first and second of these choices are often partially combined; even if the officer has evidence he will want an admission in support of it if possible, if only because a plea of guilty involves a lot less work; if he decides to call the suspect in for questioning he will usually either have some evidence or pretend he has in order the more easily to convince the suspect that he has nothing to lose by making a statement.[9] The getting of evidence is also important because the suspect may change his mind and plead not guilty at the last moment and police would then have either to withdraw the charge or to prove their case. Evidence can be, and no doubt usually is, collected legitimately. Decision 1 is unlikely to be taken unless a considerable amount of evidence is already available however it may have been obtained.

> ... And then sometimes you find things, like they might have been using a van and you could take a vacuum cleaner to the van when we get it so we get the forensic science people down, but you couldn't take a vacuum cleaner to it when they come. Something's happened to it in the meanwhile that just clinches it. A wonderful thing, forensic science. (City officer)

Illegal methods are also used in the carrying out of decision 2. A man is not brought 'voluntarily' to the police station for questioning unless the officer concerned has 'reasonable grounds for suspecting that [he] has committed an offence' (Home Office, 1964), in which case he should be cautioned at once and due procedure followed. It is very difficult for a CID officer not to infringe the Judges' Rules and also to maintain a high clear-up rate. The effects of such infringements on relationships with colleagues and senior officers will be dealt with in more detail in later chapters.

Decision 3 is the 'safest' of the courses of action open to the CID man, but he will get no great credit for it, only an absence of censure. Another officer may even get the case when it does come up, or the offender may not be caught in the future. Moreover, with a travelling criminal such a course of action is not possible. Lambert (1969) has estimated the proportion of 'detected' crimes which are in fact cleared up by being taken into consideration as 40 per cent. Unpublished research by Cain and Hall Williams (1963) showed that in 1956 breaking offenders appearing in a group of higher courts[10] including this city had a mean of 2·96 offences TIC per court appearance. But breakers may not be typical of other offenders, particularly of those appearing on lesser charges at magistrates' courts; also this is an average per court appearance rather than per conviction. However, for some classes of offender the number of 'clear-ups' by TIC may be higher than the overall figure of 40 per cent.

It is clear, as Lambert points out, that CID men have good grounds for regarding the getting of admissions of TICs as an important part of the interrogator's skill. In this respect they are in a good bargaining position with the offenders, for research has shown (Hammond and Chayen, 1963; Cain and Hall Williams, 1963) that although offences TIC do have an effect on sentence, this is not so in every court. For the offender, to run the risk of a slightly more serious penalty now may seem preferable to being called before the court again at a later date, particularly if the CID officer offers in return for such admissions to get bail for the offender or even to 'reduce' the charge, say from housebreaking to shopbreaking. For the CID man, the savings in time and effort from getting an offence TIC are considerable.

But the meaning of CID work for the men involved may be best summed up in the words of one attached man:

> It surprised me when I came onto this, you know, because
> I thought it would be all knocking people off. But it isn't.
> There's a lot more to it than that. There's a hell of a lot of
> paper work on this job that I hadn't realized, because when
> you're in uniform you just put your hand down a bloke's
> collar and that's it, isn't it? You hand it all over to the CID
> and don't think any more about it. And like this morning,
> I've got all that bucketful [of paper] to get through, and all
> these bills to settle with, and dealers to go and see.

There is every day the bureaucratic routine; but it is compensated for by the knowledge of being part of an élite corps within the police. Outsiders do think that CID men spend their time 'knocking people off', which carries high status.

Uniform men

The distribution of the research sample by the type of work on which the men were currently engaged is shown in Table 11. The distribution by rank is indicated in Table 12.

Probationary constables were all engaged in straightforward beat work; training attachments in this period were in any case of only a fortnight's duration, and were discounted for research classification purposes. Of the sergeants, one was responsible for road safety

TABLE 11   *Type of work of respondents*

Uniform patrol		Patrol and cars		Station office		Administration, etc.		Plain clothes		Dog section		Attached CID		Total	
%	n	%	n	%	n	%	n	%	n	%	n	%	n	%	n
58·2	32	18·2	10	7·3	4	5·5	3	3·6	2	3·6	2	3·6	2	100	55

(coded as admin.), two were in the station office and the remainder were engaged on outside supervision of the beat men. The remaining variations in the types of post were within the group of established constables.

TABLE 12   *Rank of respondent*

Probationary constables		Constables		Sergeants		Total	
%	n	%	n	%	n	%	n
12·7	7	69·1	38	18·2	10	100	55

Foot patrol work

There was a tendency in the city for beat men[11] to be engaged on residual tasks which no specialist department had as yet taken over, and their work can be understood only within this context. However, the work of the beat man varied considerably from shift to shift, or, in the language of the men, from turn to turn.[12] Even within shifts no specific patrol could be described as typical. The frequent encounters with the unexpected constituted the main intrinsic interest of the job. Before describing beat patrols it must be pointed out that the research was carried out during a particularly severe winter and this may to some extent have modified the behaviour of the beat men.

First watch   On first watch (6 a.m.–2 p.m.) the men reported for duty at 5.45 a.m., when they would 'parade' with the inspector, who would outline to them any important events or matters requiring special attention and allocate tasks. Extracts from General Orders including announcements of awards would be made at this time. Parade was always taken formally, with the men standing in a line and the inspector facing them. The inspectors usually took parades at the sub-divisional stations. At the smaller section stations, although the men were still required to arrive a quarter of an hour before their tour of duty started (for which they were not paid) it was not customary to have any formal ceremony to mark the beginning of a shift. The men were expected, however, to glance through the 'minor occurrence book' (MOB) and catch up on the events of the sixteen hours since they were last on duty. Office sergeants and constables did not parade, and in places they operated an informal system of relieving each other a quarter of an hour early on each turn.

After parade it was customary for the men to go to the canteen for a cup of tea. The duration of this break varied between subdivisional and section stations, i.e., as a function of proximity to the watch inspector. One watch inspector, however, transmuted this unofficial into official 'easing', by formally instructing the men to go out for an hour immediately after parade and then to return at 7 a.m. for a permitted 'tea warmer'. Always, however, the first task of the men when they did go out was to have a preliminary look round the beat to check for overnight breaks and damage. Then there were the children to see into school on crossings deemed too busy to be dealt with by a warden, or where for some other reason the crossing-keeper was absent. Since absenteeism of crossing-keepers tended to be greatest in the coldest weather, the beat men had this task thrust upon them most frequently when it was most unpleasant to perform. This would take from 8.30 a.m. to 9.0 a.m. Breakfast breaks ($\frac{3}{4}$ hour) were at 9.0 a.m. and 10.0 a.m. A man on crossing duty would have 10 o'clock breakfast, and so would have to patrol after leaving the crossing until breakfast time. If he had no specific task he might well try to find some means of getting warm again. After breakfast there would be summonses and messages—from the hospital, notifications of men in custody, and so on—to deliver, and enquiries such as the checking of addresses given by prisoners to be made. Homes and shops where overnight crime had been reported would have to be visited unless the report had been made by a 999 call, in which case a car would go. Then school crossings would again have to be manned for the lunch-time exit from and re-entry to school. Between times 'on patrol' there would be casual conversations with shopkeepers, questions from passers by, and possibly traffic problems to deal with. On the more outlying areas none of these events occurred so frequently and patrols could become monotonous. However, those conducted in outlying areas during the research period were atypical, since in better weather patrol work here would have been done on a low-powered motorcycle. In addition, of course, the patrol man might at any time meet with one of the more macabre or spectacular aspects of the job—a suicide or a road death, or a daylight smash and grab thief; or he might receive a complaint from a resident about noise in the street, or a request to assist with frozen or burst pipes.

On each patrol, points had to be kept. Keeping a point involved standing at a call-box for up to twenty minutes—ten before and ten after the time of the point. A man might be visited by the sergeant or the inspector while keeping a point, or he might be contacted by phone. Often none of these things happened. Four points were arranged for each shift, but usually only one or two were kept. One would be made unnecessary by the meal break, and at least one more would usually be made unnecessary by a fortuitous meeting with the sergeant or inspector or by a call back to the police station for other purposes. Points served the three purposes of communication, supervision and a safety check.[13]

On average there were 1·75 items of compulsory police duty per first watch patrol. This figure includes the keeping of school crossings but excludes matters internal to the police force such as the keeping of points or relieving the office. Between dealing with these incidents the time was spent 'patrolling'—walking about and not necessarily speaking to anyone. Contacts with members of the community could, however, be initiated by the policeman. In the outlying districts opportunities to initiate contacts were limited; in the central area it was easier to make the work interesting in this way. In the course of one eight-hour patrol from Walker Street, for example, six such contacts were made with either shopkeepers or people whom the PC met on the road. Usually all that resulted was a friendly conversation, though one man was advised to move his car. In addition on this patrol there were three items of easing behaviour; one was a call back to Walker Street station for tea, between the beginning of the patrol and breakfast time; the second was a call to a local pub for a quick drink with some plain clothes policemen; the third was a break for a cup of tea in a cafeteria attached to a local public building. *On this patrol there was one item of compulsory police duty*—a call to see whether a man intended to plead guilty to a traffic summons.

Not only were contacts more difficult to initiate in the outlying areas, but easing behaviour was also less varied. There were fewer shops and cafés to visit. Easing, therefore, most commonly took the form of unofficial calls back to the police station for tea. Usually there would be one such call on each half of the shift. Easing was more noticeable in the smaller section stations than in the sub-divisional stations, where the presence of the inspector and chief inspector was inhibiting.

Details of one routine first watch patrol from Central station are cited below.

Patrolled first watch at Central (working with a different PC for each half shift). For the first half we were on the 'straight'.

He said he had spent the whole of the previous day thawing out people's pipes. 'If we didn't do things like that it [the straight] would be a terrible pitch.' We stopped for a smoke round the back of one of the churches. There were few people about . . . We went in to tea at seven, and afterwards the inspector got them all on clearing the snow from outside the station and car park for about an hour . . . We then went round the pitch again, to sort out a bus supposed to be stuck, but we couldn't find it. On the way back we called in at a cake shop and spent a few minutes and had a word or two with the girls working there and promised to call back again later. The inspector asked where we had been when we got back and said that he had been out himself directing traffic and moving a vehicle stuck in the snow. We had noticed this one but decided to leave it. We went back to the station at 9 a.m. The PC relieved the office for an hour, and then had breakfast at 10 a.m. . . . After breakfast patrolled with another PC. It was snowing hard and bitterly cold. We called in at a cycle shop for a warm and a smoke and there we met my former companion and a colleague. After keeping a point we walked back to the station. All the plain clothes men came into the office. We stayed in the station about ¾ hour—a Brockborough sergeant was covering the office—and then went out again with two messages to deliver. The first people were out. The second message was to notify a family that a bicycle which had been stolen from their back shed had not been returned or found . . . The woman asked us in and offered tea. By the time we left we were able to walk straight back to the station and book off . . . (Central).

Second watch The work for the part of a second watch patrol before tea was similar to the work on first watch, with messages to deliver, children to see out of school, and in some areas a traffic rush around five o'clock. However, there were generally more people about and it was usually less cold than on the first part of first watch.

After tea (usually 5.30 p.m. or 6.30 p.m.) the work took on a different character. Shops and factories were closed, and required checking to see if they were secure or if there had been intruders; in the more central areas people were out bent on pleasure, and pubs, coffee bars, cheap cafés and the streets, as well as the clubs and more specialized haunts, began to be filled with a lively if dowdy cosmopolitan crowd.

In forty-four hours of foot patrolling on second watch four crossings, involving five schools, were manned, two messages were delivered, one lorry was moved on, one burst pipe was

57

attended to, and one man was arrested for larceny. *This is an average of 1·6 tasks per patrol.* The last three tasks were initiated by the PC.

There were the same differences between the suburbs and the central areas in both the work and the easing behaviour as were observed on first watch. However, there was one addition to the easing facilities. The drinking of alcohol whilst on duty (an offence against the Discipline Code) was a popular form of easing. This was done only once while the researcher was actually patrolling on second watch (more frequently at night), but uniform PCs on second watch were seen to come into a pub for a drink on a number of other occasions. The custom was for the men to call at a rear door of the premises and have their drink in a quiet room, usually the private living-quarters of the establishment. The frequency of this sort of easing was probably greater in the central areas—where in any case there were more pubs and, even given similar proportions, a greater number of landlords who 'knew the form', i.e., to keep quiet about what went on even as between one policeman and another unless they had actually been drinking together. Also easing facilities of this type were easier to organize when patrolling a limited area on foot, as in the central districts. On the basis of the evidence available categorical statements about frequency are impossible; but easing of some kind took place on every patrol.

Patrolled two beats near to the station. Went to an Indian restaurant for coffee, round the back way. The PC said they were friends of his and he regarded the place as his personal haunt . . . He made a point at the box after patrolling the main shopping street. The PC said, 'Hang on a minute, I'll just have a look in here'. It was an unoccupied pub and he pulled open the side door. There was an Irishman in there with a home-made hand cart full of coal. He asked him whether he had permission to get it and the man said he always got his coal from there. He had been stopped before and told by a policeman that as it didn't belong to anybody, it was alright. The PC said, 'We'd better take him up to the station', and told the chap to push his cart. There were about six cwt in it and he was puffing. The PC said, 'Wait, till he gets to Walker Street' (a very steep hill). He took him into the station and left the cart in the road. Two of the men later moved it. There was a great deal of hilarity about the cart. 'You didn't make him push it all the way up there did you . . .?' The man was charged and put in the cell and later collected by the lock-up van . . . The CID questioned him regarding 'form'. One for drunk was all, they thought. The matter was handed over to them. One of them had said to the prisoner, 'Haven't I seen you in here before?', and he had then admitted the drunkenness. The PC was off duty at 6 p.m. For the second half of the shift patrolled with another PC. We covered the whole section for the first hour (6 p.m.–7 p.m.) as the other man on duty was at 6 p.m. tea. Then we did three beats—the same two plus an extra one. We walked round and then went back to the station for tea. The PC was asked to go round and test the address of a drunk taken earlier in the day; this visit also served the purpose of informing the relatives. He had to call back later in the evening and tell them that the man in custody had been granted bail. The original message was incomplete. One further message was delivered. We went off duty at 10 p.m. (Walker Street).

Nights Work on night duty customarily consisted of a brief period —two hours at most—of fairly feverish activity, dealing with people coming out of public houses and other places of entertainment, and giving lock-up property a preliminary security check. After this there was little to do. Remaining property would still have to be checked, and all of it was usually given a second look over in the last hour before going off duty. Points were fairly diligently kept as there were fewer interruptions which conflicted with their appointed times. There were few people about to talk to even in the more densely populated areas, and few specific police tasks to undertake.

There was less variation as between the men in the types of easing behaviour indulged in, although the cold and monotony made it more necessary; it took the forms of more prolonged periods in the police station, of after-hours visits to public houses, or of finding a fairly warm 'put-up' where the policeman could while away an hour in relative comfort. The first form was more common in the outlying districts where there were relatively few opportunities for any other type of easing. It must be emphasized that without any form of easing behaviour night shifts would have been virtually intolerable.

In the course of seven routine night foot patrols conducted (fifty-six hours), there were only six items of police work, excluding points, and three of these only involved insecure properties. Part patrols, 'incidents attended' and other motorized or miscellaneous aspects of the research work are excluded from these as from all other calculations of police work-load on foot patrol duty.

The easing behaviour which was indulged in as a result of the monotony had two main effects: first, it was one factor which increased the solidarity of the beat men—they had to protect each other against being found out by senior officers; second, the men developed a protectiveness about their beats similar to that of county men. Although city men were less dependent on the goodwill of the community than county men, either for the carrying out of their work or in relation to their private lives, they were more dependent on certain members of the community for the provision of easing facilities, and contacts with these people had to be maintained.

A patrol at one of the outlying stations (Outpost) is described below.

On nights with very talkative PC. Tried to knock up newly made inspector for celebration tot but no success. Kept point on main road—acting sergeant surprisingly didn't come. Afterwards walked back to the station for refreshments and played fives and threes at dominoes. Then we sat talking by the coal fire in the canteen. Another PC on the beat said 'Sit down, have a rest. You mustn't be too eager'. The area car crew had called in while we were having supper and told us that the night stick[14] had gone off at 2 a.m. as it was his day off the following day. We stayed by the fire for the rest of the night. At 3 o'clock we were meant to have a point. The other PC said, 'No, Sid (acting sgt.) won't be there, not at this time of night'. My companion phoned the point. A third PC was making it at the same time, and Sid wasn't there. At 5.30 a.m. Sid came in and remarked, 'It's all right for some people being in the canteen all night'. PC: 'We haven't been in all night. I made a point. We waited for you, but you didn't come'. Sid: 'Oh no, I was there.[15] John told me. I got there just after you phoned'. Off duty at 6 a.m.

Night crime patrol In addition to the 'ordinary' night patrols there was also the Special Night Crime Patrol, known as 'Commandos'. The Commandos consisted of a body of thirty men drawn from among those who would normally have been on night duty on every division. The purposes of the patrol were, first, to facilitate speedy collection and transportation of a strong body of men so that they could readily be available at the scene of any major event or catastrophe; and second, to provide in the meantime intensive coverage of particular trouble spots. The men moved nightly from area to area and division to division, where they patrolled very small beats over a limited area in pairs.

From the research point of view the system was fortunate, since it provided a ready-made control situation of men patrolling beats which they had not had the opportunity to 'work up' and of regular beat men threatened by having strangers on their pitch, strangers who had nothing to lose in terms of easing opportunities or perks by antagonizing 'good' landlords and other useful citizens, and nothing to gain by making an effort to keep them sweet. In fact, the boredom of having to carry out a patrol with even less work than usual because of the greater number of men—plus regular beat men—patrolling the area, and with no opportunities for easing because of inadequate knowledge, meant that, in the view of the regular patrol men at least, Commandos were anxious for any form of activity and tended to 'look for trouble', thereby antagonizing the regular beat men even further. Contact with the regular men was rarely long enough for them to find out who among the Commandos could or could not be trusted, a pre-requisite for the passing on of information about 'put-ups'.

No easing behaviour was indulged in on the Commando patrol conducted by the researcher; one of the officers involved, who was, according to his colleague, 'looking for trouble', finally baited a drunken man sufficiently for the latter to respond and be taken into custody. The PC concerned then went off duty at 2 a.m. for court; the other made few comments about the arrest, but remarked (these are not his words) that he found going off at 2 a.m. inadequate as a form of easing since it disrupted one's sleep routine and in the long run made things more difficult.

Details of two 'ordinary' night shifts are given below, the first from Walker Street and the second from Brockborough. They indicate further the nature of normal night work and, more importantly, both patrols show the effects of the introduction of strangers—the Commandos—to the beat. The relevant passages are italicized.

1. Went out after parade with Maitland and walked round until about ten or quarter past eleven. We made a point at the box on the main shopping street. We met the inspector by the pillar. Maitland said, 'I hope he met the other two', meaning he hoped they weren't in anywhere drinking. He said, 'I never bother to check locks on nights because I look at it this way. I might be walking down there checking the locks on one side and then just go round the corner and someone could go back and break in on the other'. . . . *He spoke about the Commandos spoiling the pitch. They had turned people out from one pub at 10. 35 p.m. 'Don't they know there's ten minutes drinking up time? I always give them until quarter to eleven and* then *you give them a bit of leeway if it's a good licensee.'* . . . We were walking up the road and Maitland called in and asked the landlord of one pub if he wanted it clearing. He said yes. We then went in and got rid of the customers. We didn't stay there. Maitland just had a few words with the licensee. *We had hoped to call in at the Dog's Head on our way back to the station, but hadn't been able to as there were four Commandos standing outside on the other side of the road. 'They're probably wanting the same thing*

and trying to stay each other out,' said Maitland. . . . We went
in at 11.15 p.m. and at 11.30 p.m. we went into the canteen to
help the canteen man, Jones. Maitland left me for part of the
time I was in the canteen, and certainly the prolonged stay
of three hours here was a bias introduced by the presence of
the researcher—an obvious choice for cook, waitress and washer
up. Jones said he usually found himself in the canteen when
there were a lot to cook for. . . . The men came in at half-
hourly intervals, one, one-thirty and two o'clock. The
Commandos came in at one and two. There were about
fourteen altogether with the inspector, and the rest went to
Central. . . Maitland stayed in waiting for me although his
meal-time had been one o'clock, we went out again about two-
thirty or so . . . We walked back down the road. Maitland
said he had a bottle in his pocket, just in case. He didn't
usually do it but he thought that otherwise I wouldn't be able
to get a drink (another major bias). There was still the sound of
voices from the Dog's Head and he tapped the window and we
went in the outdoor. The family were there and a couple of
others in the bar. We were later followed by a Walker Street
PC and his Commando mate, and then even later by the others
who had heard our voices. The barman was very good and
went to the door so that we could all get round the back in
case it was the stick [inspector]. *Maitland said that the local
beat PC who was drafted to the Commandos had been before
and that this was probably how they [the Commandos] knew about
it . . .* We left about 3.45 a.m. and Maitland commented that
we had better walk round a bit. At the bottom of the road
we went to check a garage. Then we walked on a bit,
skidding on the ice, and had a warm by a night watchman's
brazier. Maitland said he liked talking to these old boys;
they were often philosophers in their own way. This
particular one was asleep . . . We crept up a passage to
one of four clubs which Maitland had pointed out. There
was a noise from this one and it must have been 4.30 a.m.
He said they had already been done once. We met the
stick and the sergeant in the car outside the club and told
them about the noise. Later the inspector said he had had a
look and although they were making a row they were all right,
mainly the family. It would be unwise to do anything in case
the plain clothes were concerned. Maitland said to the
inspector, 'We'll have a little walk back in now, if that's
all right, sir.' We went the long way round and then went
in. The inspector let them all go home about 5.30 a.m. or so.
[Commados go off at 5.30 a.m.].

2. At night patrolled with a young PC (Judd) . . . We went round
the trading estate (a considerable walk from the station) and
found a factory insecure. The PC phoned the office sergeant,
using the factory phone. Judd said, 'Some of the chaps won't
come up here on nights, they get dead scared because there's
no way of getting any help . . . nobody would ever come up
here to find you and there's no phone here.' The station then
gave us the name of the keyholder, and the PC phoned him
also after searching the premises. Eventually the keyholder
came and locked the rear door and checked the premises. This
gave us the chance for a warm and a smoke inside. We moved
on and checked the rest of the estate in some detail, and then
found the door of a factory just left undone. Judd said,
'No, it can't be . . .' We went in and had a wander round.
There was a noise of running water which was a bit nerve
racking in the silence. Judd said, 'We won't tell the office
sergeant about this one, I think. He'll do his nut.' Then, after
searching the premises he apparently changed his mind, because
he went back into the office and attempted to phone, but we
couldn't work the switchboard so we sat for some time and
had a smoke. Finally we left the premises. Judd put a match
in the door. We finished checking the estate, then went to the
nightwatchman at the end of the lane leading up to it and
phoned up the station from there. The watchman and the PC
remembered some incidents in common, but we didn't stay
there long. He told me that the inspector was coming down
with a padlock and chain. 'He said could the door be fixed by
this. It can, can't it?' Neither of us could remember exactly
what the door was like. Then we went back and waited. Judd
commented, 'We went the right way to work with this one,
didn't we? Let it wait a bit before we phoned and had a good
look round. All that foam rubber would make a wonderful
mattress wouldn't it? But I'd never find the place open if I
went there by myself. It would make a wonderful put-up.' The
inspector (Mayhew) came and said, 'There isn't anything more
than coincidence in this is there? I thought we might have had
a mass break in with two factories open in one night.' We told
him that everything was in order and the door was secured.
There are instructions on the padlock about calling at the
station for the key. The inspector said, 'Where are you going
next?' Judd replied, 'I was just going to check Copdock's
garage, sir, then we're in for coffee.' Mayhew: 'Come on then,
I'll drive you up there. I've never driven this van before, so
I'm not very sure of it.' He and Judd checked the garage
together, then Mayhew drove off. Judd said, 'That's made his

night, that has, we can take it easy now. I usually find myself
a put-up and have a kip down after coffee anyway. Let's see
if we can find one of these cars undone . . .' There was an
unlocked car parked behind the garage. We sat in there for a
while, leaving just time to walk back to the station for 2 a.m.
refreshments. Two PCs, one of whom was meant to have been
off at 2 a.m., were in the kitchen. *The Commandos were there.*
After the meal Inspector Mayhew said to Judd, 'Come on—
I'm going to give you a game of snooker.' (In the canteen
kitchen there were complaints that the meal served up for
the Commandos was better than that normally provided for
the night men . . .) We were in the station for quite a time as
Judd was typing out the report about the insecure property.
The sergeant asked where we had got to. Judd explained. . . .
Sgt.: 'Well in a case like that you should tell the office men to
ring your last point, because I've been standing twenty minutes
in the cold with the two points you didn't keep. Anyway, you've
got another one at 5.15 so you'd better make that.' . . . We
went out again and had a quick look round the pitch, then
Judd said, 'Let's go to the laundry. I always go there,
whatever beat I'm on. It's lovely. You know, you can lie down
there in all the piles of laundry along the side, and it's soft,
and they always have it warm.' Judd looked at the place next
door where they were working extra early and saw that everything was in order, then tried the various doors of the laundry
with a knife, but they were all locked. He said he had never
known this before. You could always get in somewhere.
Eventually we settled down in some bundled laundry in an
adjoining garage. Judd: 'This place is always undone. What we
usually do is bung an insecure in on it every so often. We have
to do that just to cover ourselves in case anything goes wrong.
*But we don't put them in too often or else our gaffers would get
on to it, and then they'd get on to the insurance people and they'd
put the premium up if he didn't lock it.' I said perhaps the
Commandos had put one in on it, and he said, 'Oh, I hope they
haven't because if they do that will be two this week.'* . . . He
kept the point at 5.15 a.m. and after that walked back to the
station. We went down to the boiler room at the back of the
station to wait until 6 a.m. to book off as we were back early . . .
Judd said there was a fuss if you got in only a minute or two
before your time. We were joined there by three other PCs.

Foot patrols—The need for 'action'

Two questions arise from the foregoing analysis of foot patrol work.

The first is, why is it so dull? The second is, what have the authorities done to correct these tendencies?

The answer to the first question is, quite simply, scale and specialization, with the ill results of these exacerbated by shortage of manpower. As new departments were created to deal with new or growing problems the beat was denuded not only of its traditional tasks but also of its men. The result was that a 'peace-keeping' role as in the county was impossible.[16] One or two men could not effectively deal in this way with a section with between 30,000 and 40,000 inhabitants.[17] They started their tour of duty knowing that their task was impossible, with the consequent ill effects on morale (Cain, 1964). A number of men claimed 'you can make it interesting' or 'the job is what you make it'—by easing behaviour, by being prepared to approach and talk to members of the public, by being on the watch for 'interesting' offences (not minor road traffic offences, though a man with this attitude would probably approach and verbally caution a motorist), in fact by approaching each situation with some zest. But these men would have been at least as keen had the work had more intrinsic interest; they in no way compensated for the many who decided to see their time out as comfortably as possible, making sure only that they did not 'cross' anyone in authority.

For all the men, however, the 'event', the prisoner caught in the act or, more commonly, the street brawl, assumed an overriding importance, because these things broke into the dull routine and also because the men had no other clearly defined role as the county men had. These events told them who they were. They became their justification and *raison d'être*. Thus a 'good pitch' to work was one on which crime and fights were frequent. One such had been 'lost' to the division shortly before the beginning of the research period, to the great chagrin of the beat men who reported with some glee that the pitch had now been 'spoilt' by the rival division (i.e., cleared of crime and the more obvious breaches of public order, and made quiet). As with the premises which must not too frequently be reported as insecure, so too if the publicans and brawlers are cracked down on too hard the former will not yield information or co-operate with after-hours easing facilities and the latter will go and do their drinking elsewhere, thereby still further increasing the monotony of the average patrol. The pitch must be kept 'good'.

The 'best' pitch on the division from this point of view was Central sub-division. Men working there regarded themselves as something of an élite, and probationary constables especially who worked at other stations were either defensive about their own work *vis-à-vis* that of their Central colleagues, or were openly envious. 52·7 per cent of the arrests (prisoners) on the division were made on

Central sub-division in 1963, almost a third (31·8 per cent) of the divisional 'prisoners'[18] being 'booked' at Central station itself (Table 12).

TABLE 13   *Divisional arrests, 1963*

	Number of 'prisoners'
Central	693*
Walker Street	455*
Rushbridge	207
Hope Street	105
Maypole	437
Brockborough	231
Outpost	48
Total	2,176

*These totals are not identical with those presented on pp. 67–8. These are the official figures for each station, and I have used them in these calculations because they are undoubtedly correct. The totals of 687 and 445 for Central and Walker Street respectively, given on pp. 67–8 are based on my own transcription and subsequent analysis of data from the 'prisoners books'. A return visit to the research division to 'find' the sixteen lost cases was not possible. I can only hope that their absence causes no bias, and state that to the best of my knowledge this is the case.

At Central station uniform men made 611 of the 687 analysed arrests (88·8 per cent). At Walker Street they made 325 of the 445 analysed arrests, or 254 of 445 (57·1 per cent) if the 'plain clothes' offences are excluded.[19] The last figure may be the best estimate of the work of uniform men, for the Central figure is an overestimate. At Central there was no way of distinguishing arrests made by the attached CID man from arrests made by ordinary uniform constables, and they are therefore lumped together as uniform arrests. At Walker Street this distinction was recorded, and I have, therefore, treated arrests made by the attached CID man as a separate category.

Using the figures as cited above, this yields an average of 11·1 arrests per man during 1963. This calculation assumes a total of ninety constables and sergeants, less eight office and four attached men. Because of the inclusion of the work of the Central attached CID man the average represents an overestimate of the work-load per man.

The data for the rural and urban areas are not strictly comparable. City figures refer to arrests; the rural figures given on pages 30–1 refer to offences reported and recorded. An arrest pretty well every month would be inconceivable on a one-man beat. Yet we have the paradox that it was predominantly in the city that the beat men felt themselves to be under-used as well as under-valued. This feeling was even more marked on the less busy sub-divisions.

The reasons for this become clear when the content of the arrest figures is examined (Table 14). Over half the 'prisoners' on the sub-division were arrested for offences against public order (defined in key to Table 14), that is police initiated activities where the policeman had the widest discretion as to whether or not to take action, as well as the decision about what action to take. Exact figures are 73·7 per cent of the 'prisoners' dealt with by uniform men (including the attached CID man) at Central station, and 53·5 per cent of the prisoners taken at Walker Street by uniform men (excluding the attached CID man and plain clothes personnel, to whom all arrests on charges relating to drugs or prostitution have been attributed).[20]

The similarity of these distributions with those of Wilson's (1968a) watchman style forces is marked. I would argue, too, that the same low morale and disillusion, the same sense of having a rough job to do with inadequate equipment or recognition, the same sense that promotion had little to do with 'real police work' were apparent in the city I investigated, in the days before panda cars and pocket radios. Yet despite these similarities a different explanation of these arrest practices is offered for the research division, based more on what the men thought and said about their work. Characteristics of the community policed are also important: they made the chosen mode of action possible. On the other hand, it is not the characteristics of the community in any absolute sense which matter. Explanation of police action must be in terms of how policemen interpreted and made sense of this structure, in terms of the community structure which they created and lived with. This aspect of the explanation of these policemen's behaviour is dealt with in the next chapter. Here the part of some internal factors is considered.

On central sub-division the men were 'making the work interesting' (their expression) and incidentally legitimating themselves, by initiating prisoner-getting activity against the most vulnerable section of the population. Of those arrested for drunkenness and other 'public order' offences by uniform men at Central station, 26·2 per cent (118) had no fixed abode.[21] Central men boasted of having more prisoners than any other station in the city. Potential prisoners were not available in such numbers on the other two sub-divisions in the research area.

So, the paradox is explained. While deriving their status from

TABLE 14   *Arrests, 1963*

Main charge	Central station				Walker Street* station				
	Uni-form†	CID	Specials	Total	Uni-form	Attached CID	Other CID	Other‡	Total
1 Against the person	7	9	—	16	5	3	4	—	12
2 Property with violence	2	—	—	2	1	—	4	—	5
3 Breaks	51	27	—	78	43	11	24	2	80
4 Larceny	55	26	—	81	35	9	33	—	77
5 Other property	11	—	—	11	10	—	—	—	10
6 Drunken driving	16	—	—	16	9	—	—	—	9
7 Drunk and public order	451	7	4	462	136	—	—	6	142
8 Soliciting, etc.	1	—	—	1	54	—	—	—	54
9 Drugs	1	—	—	1	17	1	—	—	18
10 Other	16	3	—	19	15	5	16	2	38
Total	611	72	4	687	325	29	81	10	445

*The data are derived from Walker Street 'prisoners book'. They relate to 'prisoners' brought into Walker Street police station, rather than to arrests by Walker Street personnel.

†Includes attached CID.

‡Special constables and one probation officer.

Key to 'main charge' headings in Table 14

1 includes murder, woundings (sections 18 and 20), and indecent assaults;
2 includes robbery;
3 includes burglary, all breaks, attempts, and breaking with intent;
4 includes all larcenies and attempts;
5 includes malicious and wilful damage and taking and driving away;
6 includes being drunk in charge of a motor vehicle and driving while under the influence of drink;
7 includes drunk and disorderly, found drunk, committing a disorderly act, being found wandering, loitering with intent, drunkenness when coupled with malicious damage or assault upon police, but not the latter two categories when no charge of drunkenness was lodged. (The assumption here is that it was the drunkenness which attracted the policeman's attention.) Loitering is excluded when coupled with a charge of being in possession of housebreaking implements;
8 includes soliciting and living on immoral earnings. One entry simply read 'prostitution';
9 includes being in possession. There were no other drugs charges;
10 includes, *inter alia*, all arrests on warrant whatever the charge.

their prisoners, Central and Walker Street men were yet aware that running in the drunks[22] was not quite the same as thief-taking, the core of 'real police work'. Official bodies, judges, all ranks within the police service and, as far as one can tell, a sizable proportion of the rest of the population share the view that policemen should devote their energies to the catching of 'real criminals', rather than to various other tasks, which change with the context of the discussion.[23] The content of the 'real criminal' category probably changes too, through time and between groups. The problem for the men on the research division was that they doubted whether their 'drunks' fell into the 'real criminal' category, as defined by those outside the police force. Policemen need to believe in a largely consensual populace whose values and standards they represent and enforce. *It is by reference to this that they legitimate their activities.* They are intermediaries who bring forward for punishment those whom 'most people' deem to deserve it. To bring forward for punishment those who do not deserve it by this criterion could not 'make sense'. Even if it were allowed (as it was) it could not legitimate the policeman's whole career choice as thief-taking could. The more policemen are convinced of the consensual support for their activity, the more obvious and self-evident it is that they are 'right'. Men will voluntarily give up off-duty time to join in a search for a murderer or the attacker of a child. As this book goes to press, the massive search for the killer of Blackpool's Superintendent Richardson, the scale of inter-force co-operation in that hunt, the 100,000 people who turned out to watch the civic funeral, the plaintive letter in *The Times* (28 August 1971) saying then even 'do gooders' disapprove of such 'thugs', bear out this point. These activities, and thief-taking, are so obviously 'right' to 'everyone' that they give a blanket legitimation to police work, and *the more an activity has this legitimating effect the higher its status among policemen.*

Thus, although the Central beat men, busying themselves with picking up the drunks, could get satisfaction from engaging in 'the symbolic rights of search, chase, and capture' which form the ideal image of policing for policemen (Skolnick and Woodworth, 1967), although this activity carried some status because it was analogous to thief-taking, yet still they knew that they were kidding themselves, that these 'prisoners' were not *real* criminals. Their work only made sense if they could feel that those captured deserved to be punished, and their notions of who deserved to be punished, they needed to feel, were the same as those of the 'silent majority'. As a group of ordinary working-class men they had their doubts about this in the case of the drunks (see p. 101 for an analysis of social class background). Some men openly disapproved of 'unnecessarily' picking up 'poor old drunks'. For others it was fun, quite simply. For

69

another, more detached group it was an opportunity to be used, when necessary. 'My God, you needed one', remarked the office sergeant when a PC who had recently been in trouble 'wheeled in' a drunk. Yet the mythology of Central, the exploits of which some of the older constables and sergeants boasted, the 'good old days', included nights when all the cells were full and drunks were laid out in the corridors, when the confusion was so great that some drunks were counted twice, 'before he went out into the yard for a leak and on his way in', and when drunks' heads were flushed in lavatories. To ask whether or not such tales were 'true' is to miss the point, which is not even whether anyone actually believed them. The point is that they represented to the men the ideal of the 'good pitch' to work, the pitch where something was always going on. Thus, despite their doubts and their persistent sense that even they, the élite of the beat men at Central, were not doing real police work, despite this for all the men a 'good' night meant a busy night for prisoners.

Rural and city definitions of police work

So far as arrests go, and non-indictable offences, the city patrol man had more visible, recorded work than his country colleague. The crime picture is different. Of the persons proceeded against for indictable offences on the whole 'R' Division (not just Central sub-division) in 1963, 44 per cent were dealt with by uniform personnel. This gives an average of roughly 2·3 persons proceeded against for an indictable offence per uniform constable.[24] (See Table 15).

TABLE 15   *Persons proceeded against for indictable offences, 1963*

Offence	Uniform	Branch of officer Policewomen	CID	Total
Breaks	180	—	180	360
Other	236	8	341	585
	416	8	521	945

The higher proportion of 'breaks' dealt with by uniform men results from attendance of patrol-car crews at premises where burglar alarms had been set off.

Rural constables on one-man beats, it will be recalled, had an annual average of 7·2 recorded crimes (p. 30) or, for one-man beat men in the three ideal typical sections, 3·75 per per man if sergeants are included in the calculation, and 4·4 per man if they are not (pp. 30–1). However the calculation is done, each rural constable appears to have more crime work than his city colleague with his average of 2·3 persons per annum proceeded against for crime.

An exact comparison is not possible. However, it does seem that country policemen, for all the quiet, sedate patrols round scented clover fields and cosy chats in ancient farmhouses, none the less had more 'real police work' than the city men, despite their apparent busy-work with the drunks in the central areas. This conclusion is suggested by the figures; when one thinks about their meaning it is reinforced. City uniform men did not deal with crime unless there was a prosecution. By and large they dealt only with crimes cleared up by on the spot arrest. They would have done little 'crime work' apart from that concerned with persons proceeded against. The country man, on the other hand, would have had a fair amount of investigative work on each of his crimes (even, indeed, on those subsequently written off). The station sergeant would have prepared the lesser cases for himself or the inspector to prosecute. The constable would have been involved in rounding up witnesses and taking statements. He would have devoted several days to enquiries about even undetected crime. So although there are always more crimes than persons who commit them the comparison is not altogether unfair.

The argument is finally confirmed when one looks at the two situations from the standpoint of the men involved. According to their own definition of 'real police work', rural one-man beat men thought that that was just what they were doing. For one thing, crime work carried high status and, they suspected, other more tangible rewards. They dealt with more than half their own crime, and were usually involved in the work generated by the rest of it. The crimes may have been defined as 'petty' by city men, but they were defined as important by the rural men who had to deal with them. *The people of the community defined them as important, and had power to define them for their policeman.* Because the community defined them as important, dealing with these crimes had the legitimating effect from which I have argued the high status of crime work is derived. Moreover, the rural man did not define his task purely in terms of crime. He would say that people 'liked to see him about'. It reassured them, perhaps, that the world was as it should be. We, no less than the beat men, struggle for a way to express and conceptualize this—peace-keeping, symbolic or representational function, value maintenance—none quite catches it, but the beat man 'knew' that whatever it was, that was what he was *about*. Country men felt that the main limitations on their doing 'real police work' resulted from attempts to rationalize their task

71

and render it calculable, as when they were instructed to report *all* offences, leaving the action decision with the superintendent, or when they were taken away from their beats to do more visible work elsewhere. They also resented 'intrusions' from CID men, or senior officers 'stealing' their crimes and 'upsetting' their parishoners. They never questioned that the 'real police work' was there to be done, if only they were allowed to get on with it.

City men defined 'real police work' rather differently. Some had an inkling that a satisfying 'peace-keeping' role could be possible for a policeman, but was not possible for them. 'On the cars you never get to talk to the people.' Nor do you when there is only one man out for each 26,838 members of the population. They felt that shortage of manpower denied them this role: in my view the more divided structure of the community itself made it less possible. Reactive work to emergency calls was obviously useful, but the men only had work of this type when posted to the cars. Even then, it was not a real alternative to 'peace-keeping'. City men fell back on crime work as their defining task. It legitimated their career, by making them feel at one with a community which was highly consensual in this very narrow and specific area. Crime work was not only a legitimator: it was perhaps also a meeting point with outsiders who were otherwise not there, as a unity, to be met, let alone symbolically represented. Yet beat men did not have much crime work. They made out with analogous prisoner-getting activity, but they did not make do. The feeling that something in police work had eluded them was compensated for by action. Action as a way out certainly took precedence over easing behaviour. All the men emphasized that they did not engage in illicit easing activities when there was work to be done. But because 'peace-keeping' was denied them, work had to be defined in terms of specific tasks. Police-initiated action could bump up the number of these. *But once the work had perforce been defined in this way the periods between specific tasks inevitably became periods when there was no work to be done.* From the patrol man's standpoint there was therefore no conflict between working hard and engaging in easing behaviour. The patent impossibility of systematic prevention with a force of only a few (at that time) ill-equipped men encouraged the beat man in this view. But what he *really* wanted, often, was not a good put-up but some real police work to do.

Official responses

The official response to this situation was to provide various forms of legitimate 'official easing' as in the county. Unfortunately the two main forms which this took both aggravated the already serious manpower problem. These two main forms were attachments and gimmicks.[25] Others, such as the toleration of the early morning tea break or the lengthy stay at the station to write up a report, could be classed as semi-official. These were tolerated at inspector level and were therefore official as far as PCs were concerned, but senior officers were not *formally* aware that they took place.

Attachments No constable or sergeant interviewed in the city had been in his present post for more than five years without a break of some kind. Thus the policy of attachments served among other things to mitigate the monotony. These attachments were of varying periods; twelve months to the plain clothes section, four months to the CID, and six months to the traffic department were the main ones. In addition there were occasional attachments involving only one man from the division at a time to the vice squad, to the regional crime squad as driver, to the regional Criminal Record Office and to headquarters administration. These were usually of twelve months' duration, though the man in administration did six months on the beat and six in the office each year. Other variations in the work which did not count as attachments were spells of six months as office constable in section offices and postings to patrol cars. Men who were qualified as drivers alternated frequently between periods of foot and mobile patrol. The hours of the shifts were similar, so this was possible without disturbing the system of regular 'turns'. All these men remained on the divisional strength. In addition, there were pro-con (probationary constable) training attachments of a fortnight each to each of the major departments. Excluding the pro-cons, some forty men would be permanently detached in each twenty-four hours. Refresher courses and training courses of between two and four weeks' duration had similar purposes and effects.

Gimmicks Sickness, leave, court attendances, manning up of specialist departments and higher ranks to cover leaves and sickness, overtime owing and taken off, and occasional special tasks such as keeping observations, all operated further to reduce the manpower. Furthermore, there would be men involved in 'gimmicks'. In the city this term was used to cover not only sport but any pastime or task which took a man away from normal duties at regular intervals. There was a very high toleration of these activities by senior officers. Once they were officially recognized by the chief the allowance of time off to indulge in any of them was at the discretion of the watch inspectors, and most inspectors felt that if time were allowed for one activity it had to be allowed for all (Cain, 1964). In addition to

73

various sports the force boasted a concert party, a choir and a pipe band. At least half the personnel for the first and last of these were from the 'R' Division. Time off for these activities was usually required on either second watch or nights. It led not only to low staffing in an overall sense but also to a number of annoying inconveniences, like having four different observers on one patrol-car shift, or another man having to change his duties with only twenty-four hours' notice. There were diverse opinions about the gimmicks among the men. Broadly it seemed perhaps that those who took advantage of the facilities were in favour and the rest against, and it must be remembered that there were good enough reasons for not taking part, in that a man would be expected to give his own spare time to the pursuit of his choice as well as some of the force's time, and time to spend with one's family was for many men at a premium.[26] Most people recognized the need for some system making such social activities possible, since shift work precluded participation in civilian organizations, but there was a feeling that the thing might have got out of hand. One man known to the researcher indulged in three gimmick activities, and another in four. There was perhaps too much inhibition about refusing a man time off even when the situation warranted it. But official reasons given for the perpetuation of the system claimed that the man who took advantage of the facilities returned to work more keen as a result, or, in the terminology used here, the gimmicks were officially recognized as easing behaviour which operated so as to prevent boredom and low morale. Thirty-one of the officers interviewed had at least one gimmick.

A headquarters study of four selected gimmicks—the pipe band, choir, dance orchestra, and athletic and football associations—showed that over a twelve-month period beginning 1 November 1962, 982 *working days* (7,856 hours) were lost by constables alone as a result of these activities. Two hundred and seventy-eight days (2,224 hours) were lost in this way by constables and sergeants on the 'R' Division. A study carried out on the division during 1965 suggests that a figure of 100 hours lost per week would be a more accurate estimate of the total divisional loss as a result of *all* gimmicks—one day a fortnight per man—which would not be altogether unreasonable if the time off were evenly distributed among the men. The same study showed that in a four-week period 296 shifts or part shifts were lost through non-availability, apart from semi-permanent 'detachment'. The average number of men for a twenty-four-hour tour of duty during the period was 53·08. Of these, twelve would be posted to the area cars and a further four to the landrover, one would be 'gaffer's driver' on nights, and twelve more would be office constables at section stations. The remainder would leave an average of 2⅗ men 'on the ground' per shift per sub-division, or eight men to cover the division, or eight men to cover seven sections, or one man for every 26,838 members of the civilian population. However one chooses to phrase it, there were plainly not enough policemen to fulfil any of the roles which have at times been suggested for them, from nightwatchmen through emergency service to the intensive, empathetic peace-keeping role of the ideal-typical country policeman. And the figures above represent an average. Not infrequently there was only one man out on Rushbridge subdivision. But the problem was highlighted on the cars:

On the 7 a.m.–3 p.m. car with A and B. 8.30 a.m. B for breakfast, had to parade for court at 9.45 a.m. C relieved him. 1.0 p.m. A off for football. D came as driver. C was a beat man, therefore off at 2.0 p.m. E relieved him. As he went off C commented that his watch was short of drivers . . .

Such complexities of organization made necessary by the shortages, and the difficulties of knowing exactly which men would be available when (made worse by the gimmicks), increased the administrative work-load and thus may have reduced even further the number of hours which could be given to 'straight' policing.

Attempts were made in several directions to improve the working conditions of the men. The canteens were subsidized by the watch committee to the extent of provision of heating and lighting and staff. Snooker tables were available at four of the seven stations and the men made regular use of them during meal breaks. There was a newly-built social club on a division adjacent to the 'R' Division at which dances were held every Saturday—in addition to other functions through the week—and the bar there was well furnished and comfortable. But these things do not compensate for or solve the real problem. Nor did the perks, which in the city were limited to being able to get most things at cost price by means of contacts, and being able to use pubs after hours. The researcher was also told of money gifts by members of the public to policemen, but never witnessed this take place or heard tell of a recent, specific and verifiable case.

Specialist work

Mobile patrols (area cars)

The main purpose of these patrols was to provide an immediate 'first aid' response to any urgent situation. It was the proud claim of the then chief constable that any point in the city could be reached within four minutes, though the drivers felt that this was something of an exaggeration. Area-car crews dealt with all 999 calls and other messages sent via the information room. Messages first received by the local station might be dealt with by either a local beat man or an area car, depending on the urgency. Once on the air the car crews were under the direction of information room rather than the local station. Area-car crews attended all the more spectacular events, though some of the situations which they dealt with were more trivial, such as minor accidents or domestic disputes which could have been handled by beat men had the complainant used an alternative method of communication via the local station, or if the local station had had a man available. Many men liked the opportunity to 'be where things are doing', though they were often irked by their inability to follow cases through. This was highlighted on the cars because the cases were often of greater intrinsic interest. Moreover, because 'you can't hide a car' there were fewer opportunities for easing, though the warmth and the increased activity made this somewhat less necessary. But since a large part of the policeman's cultural system had been built round 'easing', the desire for this sort of behaviour persisted even when the need for it was partially removed.

Two patrol cars operated on each division throughout the twenty-four hours. In addition there was coverage by a landrover between 8 a.m. and 4 p.m. and 4 p.m. and midnight. The landrover most usually operated on the outskirts of the city and tended to be used as a reserve vehicle which was called upon only when the two 'area cars' were engaged elsewhere. Incidents dealt with on the landrover were therefore fewer and are separately calculated.

Immediately upon going on the air the cars received instructions as to which route they would be on and at which station and at what time they would be having their refreshment break. Other points in common between the shifts concern the incidents dealt with. Although ostensibly rendering a 'first aid' service, area-car drivers in many cases had more work to do in connection with an incident attended than their colleagues on the beat. Accidents provide a good example. Injured persons would frequently be taken to hospital and the crew would then have to attend the hospital to learn the degree of the injury, possibly to take statements, and also on occasion to transport other people involved. Immediately following this it was usual for the crew to drive to the section station concerned and leave the report, having previously taken the necessary measurements, got names of witnesses and statements where possible from the people concerned. This typing up of reports in the station and calling at stations to deliver accident books or other records—and every major incident had to be reported or recorded in the MOB (minor occurrence book) or the complaints book—obviated the need for easing in many cases, since the men could have a cup of tea at the same time. Also, although only one-fifth of the police tasks dealt with in the course of area-car patrols were initiated by the crew, there was often an opportunity for 'secondary initiation', i.e., an opportunity for the men to take further actions not specifically instructed by information room following a call to an event. Relatives could be informed, bystanders questioned, and people required to 'tie the case together' tracked down. Information room had to be informed of the activity, and could, though this was not observed, give contrary instructions.

The nature of the work varied but slightly from shift to shift; on first watch there would be more reported breaks to deal with, on second watch more brawls. The evening and early part of the night were the busiest times. For this reason the second watch figures are an overestimate of actual activity over complete shifts since the men were accompanied mainly after the supper break.

Easing behaviour on a slack shift took the form of calls at one of the smaller section stations for tea, the observer remaining in the vehicle with the radio. Also on first watch and in the early part of the afternoon the drivers would make calls at their own homes and at private houses for refreshments or to deliver personal messages. Again, the observer would be left in the vehicle on these occasions so that the crew remained on the air and available. In the late evening chips or beer could be purchased and consumed in the vehicle. During the quiet part of the night, around 4 a.m., the crew might well pull up in a quiet area so that the driver and observer could have a nap by turns.

The average number of incidents dealt with in each eight hours is shown in Table 16. These figures include incidents initiated by the

TABLE 16 *Mean number of incidents dealt with on a mobile patrol*

	First watch	Second watch	Nights	Second watch (landrover)
Incidents (per 8-hour shift)	2·0	5·7	3·8	1·75
No. of hours patrolled	24	64	56	36

men which were usually trivial in nature such as warning a cyclist without lights or pedestrians walking in the road. The most serious incidents initiated by the men were reports of drivers for speeding, though in most cases these offenders were simply warned. Less specific actions, such as cruising around an area to look for stolen cars, have not been included. The range of incidents was wide, from suicides and attempted suicides through a burnt baby, breaking offences, accidents, and domestic disputes, to pub and street brawls or children causing a nuisance.

Station officer

A sergeant manned the office at the sub-divisional stations and an experienced PC at the section stations. A previous intra-force training course was necessary for both. The posting was a responsible one because, apart from dealing with callers at the desk who had a wide range of queries and complaints, the office man was responsible for accepting the charge whenever a 'prisoner' was brought in. He tended to be something of a pivotal point, responsible for feeding information from headquarters and elsewhere to the men, and for informing the men of tasks which needed to be performed and despatching them accordingly, and giving advice to less experienced men on the most appropriate method of dealing with situations. Moreover, since all the men at some stage passed through the office he alone would have a complete picture of what was happening on the shift, and he was responsible for seeing that this was accurately recorded.

Plain clothes

The mode of operation of plain clothes was similar to that of the CID in that they had their own regular informers, but many more of their tasks involved either the slow accumulation of evidence—as when watching a club for illegal sales, or a brothel—or the catching of offenders ostensibly 'in the act' as in the case of soliciting for prostitution. The main distinction between CID work and plain clothes work is that plain clothes men must seek out their own offences (Skolnick, 1966). The section was supervised by a sergeant, also posted for a year. Posting overlapped so that there was never a complete change of personnel. Thus newcomers could be shown the ropes. Hours, split shifts or days, were organized between the men and were flexible. There were many complaints from wives about the irregularity and the lateness of hours on plain clothes. As in CID, men might officially 'book off' some time before they actually finished work.

Dog section

One dog sergeant was posted to the division, and one dog-handler (constable) to each station. Handlers had an hour allowed for grooming and feeding, so were only on patrol for seven. They also booked off duty at home, rather than at the station, and worked mainly first and second watch. When possible they trained fortnightly. At night the city would be covered by two dog vans which would be summoned by information room to any incident where there was likely to be a 'prisoner' to track down, but they often had considerable distances to travel so area cars were always sent as well. Patrols from the stations during the day were the same as for normal uniform men.

Administration

The work in this section was not examined in detail. It differed from administration in the county mainly in scale and the degree of internal specialization—for example, the city force had a man specifically appointed as a plan-drawer.

Summary

The characteristics of the research division and of the work involved in policing it have been described. CID work was discussed first, and then the work of foot patrol men. Easing behaviour is seen as an intrinsic part of all patrols, and it has been shown that such behaviour was made necessary largely by the fact that much of what they considered to be 'real police work' was denied the beat men and that police work was defined in terms of *specific tasks*, so that there was 'nothing to do' in the gaps between these. Some consequences of easing behaviour have also been identified. These are:

(a) the need to keep such behaviour invisible from senior officers;
(b) the need to maintain easing facilities;
(c) the consequent dependence of the men on each other with resulting solidarity in the face to face working group;
(d) the exclusion of unknown and untried men from this group.

These points are taken up more fully in chapters 6 and 7.

It was also shown that uniform officers 'made their work interesting' where possible by engaging in prisoner-getting activity against vulnerable sections of the population, namely the 'old drunks', a high proportion of whom were homeless. This gave status to officers on the busy sub-divisions, but was recognized as being not quite the same as 'real police work' directed against 'criminals', although analogous to it in many respects. The figures suggest that despite the appearance of being busy which this gives, city men in fact had less high status crime work than their country colleagues. And this conclusion is reinforced by the different definitions of 'important' crimes and 'real police work' in the two areas.

It was argued that policemen can only legitmate their work by appealing to the consensual community whose standards are being enforced. Areas of work where they can feel relatively sure of such general support carry higher status, and provide a blanket legitimation for other police tasks. This is why 'crime work' carries such high status, especially in the city. 'Evidence' of such consensual support also underlies the distinction between 'real crimes' and other criminal offences. (In the rural area evidence of communal support was available for a wider range of activities, because policing standards *derived from* the community.)

Official provision of easing facilities was seen to exacerbate the problems, though it provided a short-term panacea for certain individual officers. The difficulties of the beat men stemmed largely from the fact that the area and population to be covered per man was too large to make a peace-keeping role possible; on the other hand there was not enough work to make a role of reacting to specific incidents interesting. Most work of this type was hived off by specialist departments, while the absence of officers who were participating in official easing behaviours made an effective, pro-active, peace-keeping function even less possible.

In the final section the work of some of the specialists on the division was briefly described.

4 Interdependence with the community

I heard them having a dust with a group of Jamaicans . . .
so I thought to myself, 'Well, I can't get involved or the
watching will be finished,' so I dialled 999 . . . I looked really
scruffy, you know, old jacket and boots and that, and I was
standing on the corner there and as the area car came along he
slowed down, and I forgot how I looked and how I was dressed
and I pulled open the door and started climbing in to tell them
where to go when thump, right on my ear hole. 'Well', I
thought, 'what a way to treat the public!' (City police sergeant).

Introduction

Few policemen have the same opportunity as the sergeant quoted
above to experience what it is like to be part of that down-at-heel
fringe-criminal sub-culture which forms the main butt of police
activity in a large city, partly because its members have restricted
access to private places wherein to carry on their activities without
intervention, and partly because the logic of policing leads one to
look for trouble where one has found it before, and where one seeks,
one finds (e.g., Werthman and Piliavin, 1967; Stinchcombe, 1963).

The seedy characteristics of the sergeant quoted above led his
colleagues to suppose that he was of this group, and they responded
accordingly. Such a response is known in euphemistic police terms
as 'talking to these people in the only way they can understand'.

But the passage is not quoted in order to emphasize police use of
physical violence: the researcher was not permitted to observe this,
and did not press to do so for fear of damaging *rapport*. What the
passage does indicate is that city policemen tend to divide society
into the police and the rest, the public. And the public, too, was
broadly sub-divided into the 'rough' and the 'respectable', and

within these categories by race and sex. The respectable were alternatively referred to as being 'a nice class of people'. This was descriptive of their behaviour patterns rather than their socio-economic group, relationship to the means of production, or any other sociological definition of class.

The division of the public into these categories enhances the *possibility* of police violence. Identification and therefore empathy is with certain categories only; the corresponding distancing of the other categories could enhance their vulnerability to rough treatment.

In the county there was no such complex classification of the public, and the main distinction both for the police and the residents appeared to be that between locals and newcomers. 'Yobs' or 'trouble-makers' were an unwelcome part of the community but a part of it none the less.

In this chapter a number of factors influencing the relationship of the policeman with the members of the public are dealt with. Differences between county and city men are considered first, and then differences in the position of rural and urban wives. The bases of interdependence between policeman and policed are discussed, showing how the power structure influences the development of consensus. Finally the relationship with the community at work is considered, first for the county and then for the city men.

Influences of police organization on relationships with the general public

Differences in police organization in response to the work situation —the amount and characteristics of law-breaking, the characteristics of the area to be policed—were revealed in the previous two chapters. One major difference was that the large majority of county men lived in or adjoining the police station from which they worked, whereas in the city no one below the rank of inspector lived in at a police station. Even these more senior officers were not involved in the work of the station unless, in the case of inspectors, it was their shift in any case or, in the case of duty chief inspectors, an emergency arose. Policemen in the city could therefore leave the job behind, both spatially and in terms of responsibility, when they went off duty; their rural counterparts could not. The second major difference was the greater degree of specialization in the city in response to the multitude and variety of police tasks.

The result of these two differences was that the county policeman, spatially isolated from his colleagues but not from his work, had to interact with non-policemen *as a policeman* even when he was off duty, or forego social interaction. The city policeman off duty could without too much difficulty interact with his colleagues if he wished, or again he could more easily cast off the police mantle and interact socially with non-policemen as one of themselves. The non-policemen with whom he interacted socially would not be the same people with whom he had to work, partly because his home would in many cases be at some distance from the area to which he was posted, and partly because in his work he did not deal with a total cross-section of the population.

Specialization was one factor which limited the range of people the city policeman met in the course of his work. Men in one specialist department might meet a disproportionate number of prostitutes; another department might deal mainly with a particular type of criminal. Specialization enhanced the tendency of city men to perceive the population not as a total community but as divided into specific groups—motorists, drug-pushers, informers, nice people whose homes get broken into, drunks, and poor old ladies and children who needed help, among others (see also Skolnick, 1966). Because he thought in these terms a city man might be more cautious about the category of the people he met socially. The rough/respectable distinction was more important to him than distinctions in terms of social class. In this last respect there was little difference between the city and the county. Among men who specified their friends and their occupations, in the city 92 per cent (n39) had friends mainly in social classes 2 and 3 (Registrar General's Classification) and 100 per cent (n47) in the county. Men who answered in general terms are not included in the analysis in Table 17.

TABLE 17   *Social class of friends**

	1	2	3	4	5	Business/† Professional	Ordinary working/* ordinary	All sorts	No ans. DK	No. of respond- ents
County	—	21	26	—	—	2	1	9	5	64
City	2	17	19	1	—	—	5	2	9	55

*General Register Office Classification of Occupations.
†General description rather than specific examples given.

Segregation of the police role

Banton (1964a) has offered an important explanation of why the 'problem' of the relationship between the police and the public exists, for example (p. 197):

It would seem, therefore, that the contamination of the policeman's private roles by his occupation is accentuated by

83

two factors. First, in respect of income he lives at a class level which offers him less protection [i.e., than other authority figures have]. Secondly, the authority vested in the police evokes a distinctive response from the public such that they find it harder to accept him (the policeman) as an ordinary sort of person.

On the other hand Banton points out that effective segregation of the policeman's role is necessary not only for his social satisfaction but also in some cases for the effective performance of his duty. For at work the patrol man operates constantly on the boundary of his social system; he will to a large extent be judged by the effectiveness of his contacts with those *outside* his work organization, as a salesman would (Kahn *et al*, 1964). There are thus two areas in which the policeman's relationship with the community is important, his private life and his work.

Relationship with the community—social

There was little difference in the mean scores on the 'desire for integration with the community'[1] scales between the two forces. The figures were 15·8 in the county and 17·6 in the city (significance 0·05). The modal scores were 15 in the county and 18 and 19 in the city. The slightly lower scores in the county could perhaps be explained by the fact that the country policeman's role is less segregated and the men therefore felt an element of distancing to be necessary to support their authority. This interpretation is suggested by many comments made in the course of informal conversations (see p. 88).

Contact

In the measures of actual integration or interdependence a rather different picture emerged. Scores for actual contact with the community (social)[2] in the course of the fortnight prior to the date of interview were as shown in Table 18. 'Contact' in the sense used here was plainly greater for the county than the city men, and from

TABLE 18   *Index of contact with the community scores*

	0	%	2	%	3	%	4	%	5	%	6	%	No. of respond- ents	No answer
County	11	17·5	10	15·9	5	7·9	16	25·4	12	19·0	9	14·3	63	1
City	16	29·6	11	20·4	5	9·3	10	18·5	8	14·8	4	7·4	54	1

this it might be deduced that their dependence on the community for the provision of these social contacts was also greater.

A more detailed look at the content of the 'contact scale' is perhaps in order. County policemen on average met non-policemen socially on 4·2 occasions and the average number of people present on these occasions was 5·7. City policemen had on average met non-policemen socially on only 3·4 occasions, the average number of people present being 4·0.[3] City policemen's spontaneous remarks in this connection suggested that the hours of their duties were in many cases the main factor inhibiting their social contacts. This is linked with their greater desire than county men for integration, which they were prevented from achieving by the formal requirements of their work, rather than by distancing behaviour engaged in either by themselves or by non-policemen.

Thus an essential ambiguity becomes apparent. County men were heavily dependent on the community for their social contacts yet they perceived too close a contact with the people among whom they worked as threatening to them in the exercise of their authority. City men were often geographically separated from those among whom they worked when they were off duty. So although city men had less social contacts they claimed to have more 'friends' living near to them than did county men, friendship being deemed to imply a social relationship involving the possibility of legitimate and non-specific mutual demands. The mean number of friends living near was 3·7 in the city and 2·4 in the county.[4] Seventy-four per cent of county men felt that they had fewer friends in their area of residence than if they had a different occupation, compared with 44 per cent of city men.[5] The reverse held true for friendships outside the immediate area of residence, county men here claiming to have 6·5 friends each on average and city men 4·2. (See analysis in Table 19.)

TABLE 19 *Number of friends in the area of residence compared with non-policemen*

	County		City	
	No.	%	No.	%
More	4	4·8	7	13·0
Less	46	74·2	24	44·4
Same	13	21·0	23	42·6
Total respondents	63	100·0	54	100·0
No answer	2		1	

Accessibility of relatives

The distance of relatives, in difficulty of access if not in miles, further increased the county man's dependence on the local community. County men had seen relatives on an average of 2·2 occasions in the previous fortnight compared with 3·3 occasions for men in the city, and this despite the fact that 50 per cent of county men came from the same town or county as that in which they worked compared with 40 per cent of city men (Table 34, p. 100). However, this difference in birthplace is reflected in the fact that a higher proportion of city men (33·3 per cent compared with 23·8 per cent) had had *no* meeting with a relative in the previous fortnight. But for city men whose relatives lived in the same town, frequency of visiting was high. Only one county man had his place of birth, and therefore his family of origin, within a five-mile radius of his present home. (See Table 20 for total number of occasions when relatives were seen.)

TABLE 20 *Number of occasions on which relatives seen in the previous two weeks*

			Occasions							No. of respondents	No answer
	0	1	2	3	4	5	6	7–10	11+		
County	15	15	11	6	7	3	3	0	3	63	1
City	18	6	4	5	5	3	4	6	3	54	1

Accommodation

Not only did county policemen live in or adjoining the police station in most cases, making the segregation of their role difficult; they were also isolated from other policemen. This limited the range of alternative social contacts open to the county men. Of the county men for whom I had information, 65·1 per cent (n63) lived in a house or flat or 'digs' which was entirely separate from any other police dwelling so that even if there were other policemen in the town or village, the man's immediate neighbours would be non-policemen. Only 27·5 per cent of city men who were interviewed lived in accommodation of this type (n40). Of the eleven city men who lived separate from other policemen, five were living in their parents' house (see Table 21).

Interdependence

Replies to the question 'what are your main activities and hobbies

TABLE 21   *Type of accommodation**

	County	City
Own house	1	5
Single beat station	27	—
Other single house/flat	9	1
2–5 police homes together	11	11
6–10 police homes together	11	13
11+ police homes together	—	1
'Digs'	4	—
Single men's quarters	—	4
With parents	—	5
Unknown*	1	15
Total	64	55

*This question was not specifically asked, therefore information could often only be obtained when the wife was visited at home.

in your off duty hours?' served as an additional indicator of inter-dependence with the local community. Responses, when classified in terms of who else would be involved in the leisure activity are shown in Table 22. Thus while almost one-third of the county men were involved with non-police groups this applied to only one-sixth of the city men. This group participation indicates *inter*dependence with the community; not only does the man get personal satisfaction from it but the community is dependent on the policeman also in so far as he runs the Cub Scout pack or youth club or is a member of the photographic society. In other social relationships described so far the dependence has been much more one way.

TABLE 22   *Other people involved in main activity or hobby*

	Involving self and family only		Involving other police-men or police families		Involving non-police groups		Other/ unknown		No. of respondents	
		%		%		%		%		%
County	23	35·9	16	25·0	20	31·3	5	7·8	64	100·0
City	24	43·6	18	32·7	9	16·4	4	7·3	55	100·0

Supportive evidence concerning the policeman's social relationship with the community

Social relationships between the police and the community could only be observed by living in turn with a series of police families. This was not done, and the illustrative remarks below make no pretence of being unselected or random. They have in fact been selected from 445 recorded remarks offered gratuitously in the course of the research.

Lack of role, segregation, and consequent isolation: county

I'd never go and have a drink in a pub on my own beat. Once you start doing that you might get involved. There's the problem when other people insist on buying you one and you can't get out of it . . . people like to get friendly with the policeman and then take advantage of it . . . There's a certain barrier between you and other members of the public, and if you break it awkward situations can arise.

I'm friendly with a lot of people but you can't regard them as friends so much as on a friendly basis . . .

I don't find people are unwilling to make friends. If they feel that way they're not worth making friends of anyway, but you can't be too friendly, because then people would take advantage of it . . .

It's important not to get too friendly with people in the country. My wife and I have plenty of friends at . . . [town where previously posted], so we don't need any more. [There] if someone you knew was involved in something you could pass it over to someone else, but this isn't possible in the country so it's wiser not to get involved . . .

When you're going to have to book them you can explain the consequences to a real friend, so you pick your friends with that in mind. . .

You make a barrier yourself, in the country it's essential.

These statements are selected, but not deliberately biased. An opposite view was rarely expressed. Some men were better at performing the balancing act than others; those who could not perhaps tended to emphasize more their social distance and relatively high status. In this way they were often supported by the community, but it made for loneliness.

Role segregation—and lack of it; perceived fragmentation of the community: city

You'd find if you were in the job long you'd get suspicious, you know. Your friends wouldn't want to know you. They have a different attitude to you when you've been in a long while . . .

I haven't made any civilian friends since I joined, but I keep up with those I made before . . . but I'm not made for a social life . . . The police force has got no say who I have for friends. That's up to me . . . If a chap does know [I'm a policeman] he'll be very careful sometimes what he'll say to you because he's got the impression that you'll go round shopping him all the time.

You can't exist without some sort of social life outside the force. It makes a nice change to get away from it . . . It's impossible to be accepted by the community just like that, as just one of themselves . . . You've got to have some authority over them so that if necessary you can put your foot down and separate them out as being members of the public which if you didn't do sometimes they'd run riot.

I suppose I've got as many friends as people in other jobs . . . It's because they're mainly coloured people round this way and they wouldn't be my friends in any case, whatever my job was . . .

All my friends are motorists and have a little grumble but we treat it as a joke . . .

I used to have a lot of friends but the hours on this job cut it down . . .

I think you'll find that most of a policeman's friends are out of the job. I don't like to be thought of as a policeman when I'm off duty . . .

The impression given by these remarks is of greater diversity between the men in the city, and of isolation, where it exists, stemming from the community rather than being voluntarily imposed by the policemen themselves, as in the county. The greater desire for integration in the city may reflect this barrier. City men verbally separated non-policemen by dubbing them 'civilians' or 'the public'; in the county it was never implied that together or in groups non-policemen would run riot unless checked!

Public expectations for the policemen—off duty Being *the* policeman (not just *a* policeman) gave the county man an institutionalized status in the more tightly-knit rural community, as it did not in the city. As a result, possibly, the community had more clear expectations as to how he should behave, though this could not be tested. But certainly since there was more contact between the local community and the policeman in the county the local people there had more opportunities to make the policeman aware of their expectations. He would as a result of this be not only more aware of these expectations but also more accurate in his perception of them. Certain expectations attached to the policeman *qua* policeman, but he was also known personally by the local people, with the result that although their normative expectations might remain the same, their actual expectations of how Mr Smith, the PC, would behave would be based on knowledge of his previous behaviours. The pressures to which he was subjected would thus in the course of time be modified to fit more closely the actual situation, while the policeman in his turn would at least know enough of what the public expected of him to be able to modify his behaviour in the direction of their expectations if he so wished. It is my contention that if his interdependence with the local community is high he will be more likely to come to see things their way and conform to their expectations and wishes. But contact is a pre-requisite of this, or else he will not know what these wishes are.

Most of the community expectations for them mentioned by the men related to the work. Few said that they felt unduly constrained in the manner of conducting their private lives, apart from the problem of not getting too closely involved. Young men seemed more concerned about these pressures, but the evidence here is slight and unreliable. On the whole it is fairly safe to conclude that the problem was not a serious one for the men, although it was for some of the wives. How the man behaved as a policeman, whether on or off duty officially, was what counted.

Public expectations concerning off-duty behaviour were rarely mentioned in the city. On the whole, men were sheltered from such expectations by the spatial separation of their home and work place and by the partly resultant role segregation.

> The public don't realize that policemen are human [i.e., those the police work with]. They never think that we've got homes and families the same as them, and we're expected to know everything. (City constable.)

Interdependence of wives and families with the community

The nature of the interdependence between policemen's wives and the local community proved more complex than that of the men. The problem was enhanced by the fact that measures of actual contact give no indication of the quality of the contacts. Nor was it simple in comparative terms to assess difficulties and isolation caused by an established position in the community which carried a *high* status, for this phenomenon was unknown in the city. But an examination of the position of the policemen's wives throws light on the position of the policemen themselves. The social position of the wives also affects the men's interdependence with the two counterpositions of community and family and their consequent behaviour in particular situations. Interdependence with both colleagues and superiors is also indirectly affected. A man whose wife and family are thoroughly absorbed in the local community will most probably not wish for a transfer, and he will therefore need to satisfy his senior officers in relation to his work. To do this he may need the support of his colleagues, while on the other hand for the sake of his family's contentment he will need to keep on good terms with the local people.

Wives' contacts with the community

Desire for integration with the community scores for wives were identical in both areas, 16·7 in each case. Nor was there any difference in the number of friends claimed by the wives in their area of residence, mean scores being 1·8 (n55) in the county and 1·1 (n25) in the city. Mean scores for numbers of civilian friends further away were 4·7 (n55) in the county and 5·6 (n23) in the city, again an insignificant difference (see appendix IV, Tables F, G and H). There was no difference in the number of occasions on which non-policemen had been met in the previous fortnight, mean scores being 4·6 (n56) and 4·3 (n30), with the county force again given first. City wives, however, tended to score higher on the overall contact with non-police scale because on average they saw more people on each occasion when contact was made than the city

TABLE 23   *Wives: number of occasions in previous two weeks on which non-police 'seen' socially*

	Occasions										No. of res- pondents	No answer
	0	1	2	3	4	5	6	7–10	11–15	16+		
County	14	7	10	2	4	1	3	7	5	3	56	1
City	7	5	3	2	2	1	1	5	4	—	30	—

wives, means being 6·5 (n23) in the city and 4·8 (n42) in the county. Data on the number of occasions of contact and people seen are presented in Tables 23 and 24. Scores on the index of contact with non-police are presented in appendix IV, Table I.

TABLE 24   *Wives: number of non-police seen in previous two weeks*

| | No. of people | | | | | | | | | | No. of res- | No |
	0	1	2	3	4	5	6	7–10	11–15	16+	pondents	answer
County	14	16	7	3	4	0	0	4	6	2	56	1
City	7	4	3	4	0	2	3	2	3	2	30	—

The difference in the number of people seen on each occasion can be readily explained, for 36·7 per cent of city wives were in paid employment outside the home compared with only 15·7 per cent of county wives (see Table 25). The difference was mainly in part-time working since even aside from the differential availability of this type of work, travelling distances involved in the country made a few hours' work not worth the effort.

In Tables 23 and 24 working wives were scored for ten occasions of contact over the previous fortnight unless otherwise stated, and an arbitrary number of five people involved on each occasion was allowed in the scoring.

TABLE 25   *Current work of wives**

	Full-time	*Part-time*	*None*	*Total*
County	1	8	48	57
City	6	5	19	30

*From interviews with wives.

For an estimation of the *nature* of interdependence what is important is that county wives had as many occasions of contact with non-police families as city wives despite the fact that fewer of them went out to work. They had in fact more purely social contacts. Moreover, although both types of contact are useful indices of interdependence, the social relationships in the county would be more difficult to reproduce elsewhere than would a satisfactory work situation in the city. Thus dependence on the particular contemporary formation of relationships was probably greater in the county.

Other differences in the pattern of contact with the community follow from this one. County wives both visited and were visited relatively more frequently than wives in the city, despite the limited catchment area for this kind of relationship in terms of the size of the immediate local population. On average 53 per cent of 'civilians' seen visited the county wives at their homes (the police station) and 32 per cent were visited at home by the police wives (see Tables 26 and 27). In the city the equivalent figures were 42 per cent and 27 per cent. Wives who work have both less time and less need for a high frequency of inter-visiting.

TABLE 26 *Wives—proportion of non-police 'seen' socially in own home (of wives who had 'seen' one or more)*

	Under 10	10–19	Percentage 20–9	30–9	40–9	50–9	60+	No. of respondents	Not applicable
County	6	3	3	2	3	11	14	42	15
City	7	1	2	3	0	3	7	23	7

TABLE 27 *Wives—proportion of non-police 'seen' in home of non-police family (of wives who had 'seen' one or more)*

	Under 10	10–19	20–9	Percentage 30–9	40–9	50–9	60+	No. of respondents	Not applicable
County	14	2	4	6	2	11	3	42	15
City	10	3	2	2	1	3	2	23	7

Also to be expected on the same grounds was the slightly higher proportion of 'activities and hobbies' involving non-police families in the county, though the difference in 'integration' here is much less than for the men, and is not statistically significant. The absence of involvement with other police families is striking (see Table 28).

TABLE 28 *Wives—main activities and hobbies*

	Involving self and family only No. %	Involving other non-police groups No. %	Other No. %	None No. %	No. of respondents
County	35 61·4	21 36·8	— —	1 1·75	57
City	20 66·7	9 30·0	1 3·3	— —	30

Perceived situation—rural isolation

But in spite of the similarity in actual contact and the greater frequency of inter-home visiting in the county, many more county wives *thought* that their husband's job affected their friendship patterns in the area in which they lived (see Table 29). All but one of the wives who felt this believed that she had fewer friends than she would have if her husband were in a different job. Approximately the same proportions of wives in the two forces felt that their patterns of friendship beyond the immediate local area were affected, though three (5·3 per cent) of the county wives felt that they had *more* widely scattered friends as a result of the frequent moves which formed part of their husbands' work patterns.

TABLE 29 *Perceived effect of husband's job on wife's number of friends*

No. of friends compared with non-police	Area lived in				Further away			
	County		City		County		City	
	No.	%	No.	%	No.	%	No.	%
More	1	1·7	0	—	3	5·3	—	—
Fewer	29	50·9	10	35·7	19	33·3	9	36·7
Same	27	47·4	18	64·3	35	61·4	17	57·7
Don't know	0	—	0	—	—	—	2	6·6
	57	100·0	28	100·0	57	100·0	28	100·0
No answer	—	—	2	—	—	—	2	—

This differential perception of a situation which was in fact very similar can be explained by the distinction drawn by the men in the county force between 'being friends with' and 'being on a friendly basis with'. If more of the county wives were only 'on a friendly basis with' the people they contacted they might well perceive themselves as having fewer friends in their immediate area. But their free comments and some measured attitudes indicate that for the wives, unlike the men, this was not their own choice. They were only 'on a friendly basis' because this was the sort of relationship which the rest of the community *thrust* upon them. The men *opted* for a measure of social distance.

The wives were asked a question concerning the attitude of local people to them. Subsequently coded responses are given in Table 30.

The largest single group of wives in each force claimed that the attitude to them of the local people was not affected by their

TABLE 30 *Attitude to policeman's wife of local people*

	County		City	
	No.	%	No.	%
Job no difference/friendly	19	33·3	7	24·1
On very good terms—no reason	5	8·8	5	17·2
Casually friendly—no reason	—	—	2	6·9
Friendly once they get used to you	8	14·0	2	6·9
Little contact with them, so makes no difference	1	1·8	5	17·2
Status isolation—distant but friendly	14	24·5	—	—
Suspicion/fear/mistrust, etc.	7	12·2	3	6·9
Some friendly and not concerned with the others	1	1·8	2	6·9
Don't live with the sort of people would want to mix with	1	1·8	1	3·5
Not in area long enough	—	—	1	3·5
Don't know	1	1·8	2	6·9
Total	57	100·0	30	100·0

husband's job. The wives' free comments make possible some further elucidation of the other answers.

Status isolation Of the rural wives, 24·5 per cent experienced status isolation as the main community response to them. No wife in the city gave this answer. Positions in the rural community are fixed by highly institutionalized sets of expectations. The policeman's wife is accorded high status because this has always been so. This involved the village people in maintaining social distance and even taboo. Phrases used frequently to describe the phenomenon were:

They're all friendly, but they treat you with a sort of reserve . . .

or

The trouble with the villagers is that they treat me like a lady, and I don't want that. I don't consider myself any better than they are, and I should like to mix in. It just embarrasses me, like if I go into a shop and there's a queue of people and then the shopkeeper leaves off serving and attends to me first, even if I say, 'This lady was before me' or whatever . . .

D*

Suspicion Second, the community kept its distance because of the very real power of the policeman in the country. Informal social controls were strong: gossip was an important medium of social control; any public infringement of the law was known and reprehensible to everyone; the policeman was the visible embodiment of all this. Therefore people were guarded in his or his family's company.

In its manifestation it is not always possible to distinguish suspicion from status isolation. Such things as a sudden hush or a change in conversation when the policeman's wife approached could be interpreted as evidence of either or both. For the seven county wives coded in this category, however, suspicion was definitely seen as the dominant response. However, suspicion in this sense must not be confused with hostility. The following responses are typical.

> You can't talk to them the same can you? I mean, other people, they always seem to be on their guard a bit because you're the policeman's wife.

> You hear, 'Oh, be careful what you say to her, her husband's a policeman' . . . You never quite know where you are with people except close friends.

Strangers In the rural community social change was slow and detailed knowledge of family background and character were the accepted bases for interaction. The status of 'policeman' ensured continuity between successive officers in their interaction *qua* policemen with members of the public. For the wives there was no such established pattern of communication, and they had to live in the area some considerable time, or else have considerable social skills, before they could create a satisfactory one.

One-fifth of the county wives had lived in their current house for less than a year. A total of 61·1 per cent had lived there for less than three years, and 79·6 per cent for less than four years. Many

TABLE 31 *Wives—length of time in present house*

		Length of time						
	Under 6 months	*6 months to 1 year*	*1 to 2 years*	*2 to 3 years*	*3 to 5 years*	*5 years and over*	*No answers*	*Total*
County	11	3	11	9	14	9	—	57
City	1	2	2	2	8	6	9	30

of them were thus newcomers by any standards, and most of them were by rural standards (see Table 31).

Not only were the police wives newcomers to the village, but a considerable minority of them were also newcomers to the county. A fifth of them came from a neighbouring county (Table 34), but even so for the village people they were strangers. (City wives who had not been born in the same city tended to come from much farther afield.) Buses to the local town from these villages often ran only once or twice a day, sometimes only on two or three days of the week, and then at inconvenient times and by long, tortuous routes. Police wives complained of this but the local people were accustomed to it. Twentieth-century concepts of distance formed little part of their thinking.

Accessibility of parents[6]

The fact of their being strangers affected the attitude of local people to the police wives in the country, but the fact that by car they were not really distant from their birthplaces, or from the current homes of their parents, eased the lot of the rural wives. Those who found friendliness without friendship insufficient could turn to their families in the manner often traditional for English women (Young and Willmott, 1957; Willmott and Young, 1960). Eighty-five per cent of rural wives lived within 'day trip' distance from their parents' home (this figure excludes those whose parents were dead), that is to say, their parents lived in the same or a neighbouring county. But only two women had parents within five miles of their present home. City wives, on the other hand, had parents within five miles in 70 per cent of cases. But the remaining parents of city wives all lived further than convenient day trip distance (see Table 32). This diverse pattern in fact produced almost identical mean figures

TABLE 32   *Residence of wife's parents (if living)*

	County		City	
	No.	%	No.	%
Same town/county	25	62·5	10	55·55
Neighbouring county	9	22·5	1	5·55
Other English county	6	15·0	3	16·7
Wales/Scotland/Ireland	—	—	4	22·2
Other	—	—	—	—
No. of respondents	40	100·0	18	100·0
Unknown, dead, etc.	17		12	

for the average number of occasions on which relatives had been seen in the previous fortnight. This includes all relatives, not simply parents as in the previous figures. Means were 1·8 in the county and 2·2 in the city.

When asked their opinion on the distance of their posting from their parents, 31·3 per cent of county wives said they would be unable to visit them if they had no car. Only four of the respondents (12·5 per cent) said that their present post was convenient for visiting parents. Responses are given in Table 33. The compensatory factors mentioned were the alternative proximity of husband's parents and the regular hours of work in the current post which made other difficulties pale into insignificance.

TABLE 33 *Wives' opinions of distance from parents, county**

	No.	%
Difficult to reach, regretted	6	18·8
Difficult to reach, don't mind	5	15·6
Difficult to reach, compensatory factors	2	6·2
Accessible only because run car	10	31·3
Convenient post for seeing them	4	12·5
Left home before married, therefore 'can't blame police'	5	15·6
	32	100·0
No answer/not applicable	25	

*This question was not pursued with city wives, who regarded their choice of place to live as quite unconnected with their husbands' work.

Characteristics of wives' friendships

Thus the picture emerges of city wives having contacts with the community through their work and being involved in a loose network of selected friendships and of county wives with a much tighter web of relationships in the local community but fewer 'real friends' there. Women accustomed to the rural pattern would be able to enjoy their high status in it; 'town girls' seeking a looser web of *confidante* relationships could feel isolated and unhappy. In this situation, families were a support, and despite transport problems frequency of contact was as great as in the city.

Biographical indicators of a shared reality

For the policeman some degree of value consensus—often the result of shared background and experiences—is a pre-requisite not only for satisfactory social relationships but also for effective policing, especially given the way the rural policemen defined their role. Authors with standpoints as widely diverse as Banton (1964a) and Silver (1967) have argued that some consensus is a necessity before anything recognizable as a police force can operate.

I have already argued that contact is a necessary preliminary to understanding of another's views, and even to knowledge of what these opinions are. It has been suggested, too, that where frequency of contact is high mutual understanding, a consensus of values and a shared world view, is more likely to be arrived at, though this need not necessarily be so.

Contact, exposure to a world view, is a necessary pre-requisite to adopting it. Another necessary condition is an imbalance in the power structure, so that one of the parties in the contact through time adopts the way of thinking of the other. I want to argue here that country policemen were not only more exposed to the world view of the people they policed, as has been shown, but also that they had, to a greater extent than city men, already been exposed to, and perhaps adopted, these thought patterns, values and opinions. In the first chapter (pp. 16–17) it was argued that evidence of a common biography is a useful indicator of a probable consensus, since the odds are that the parties with a common biography will have been in a similar position in a power structure, and will have been exposed to similar definitions of the world. They will have learned to think the same way, so that their objectively similar experiences will in fact have been the same. In the case of country policemen and the people they policed this cannot be proven. The men were not asked about their subjective experiences of events in their past, and in any event there were no interviews with members of the community. Allowing for this, it will simply be noted in the following pages that country policemen had more biographical experiences in common with those they policed than did city men. This probably indicated that a definition of reality was shared between policemen and policed.

The third reason for rural policemen to share the definition of reality and the values of their parishioners to a greater extent than city men is that the members of the community had power to project their definition, so that their policeman would come to adopt it. Further aspects of community power will be analysed when the relationships of the country policeman in his work are examined. Again, the contrast with city men will be drawn.

A final reason for the greater consensus between the rural policemen and his 'parishioners' is then considered: namely, that within the rural populace there was a shared definition of the world to be projected. This was probably not the case in the city.

Birthplace

Rather fewer of the men than of their wives were born in the area in which they currently worked (Table 34). This reflects simply the fact that many of them travelled from home to join the police force at the age of nineteen and met their wives some years later. Apart from this, the distribution of birthplaces for the county men is similar to that for their wives. In the city another pattern cuts across this tendency for more of the wives to have come from the area of the work. Nearly a quarter of the women had come from Scotland, Wales, the Six Counties, or Eire. For the men the equivalent proportion was only 16·4 per cent, but many more of them came from the more distant English counties. Thus where the wives had travelled to the city, they tended to have travelled further than the men.

TABLE 34   *Place of birth*

	County				City			
	Men		Wives		Men		Wives	
	No.	*%*	*No.*	*%*	*No.*	*%*	*No.*	*%*
Same town/county	32	50·00	34	59·16	22	40·00	16	53·30
Neighbouring county	17	26·60	12	21·00	4	7·30	2	6·70
Other English county	13	20·20	9	15·80	19	34·50	3	10·00
Wales	2	3·20	—	—	4	7·30	2	6·70
Scotland	—	—	—	—	4	7·30	3	10·00
Ireland	—	—	1	1·80	1	1·80	2	6·70
Other	—	—	1	1·80	1	1·80	2	6·70
No. of respondents	64	100·00	57	100·00	55	100·00	30	100·00

On this basis the county men were in a better position than the city men to develop common understanding and perhaps a value consensus with the people among whom they worked.

Social class

There were differences between the city and the county men in the reported social class of their fathers (Table 35). Three-quarters of the county men came from social class 3 compared with 58 per cent of city men. These figures include 10·9 per cent of men whose fathers were policemen in the county and the equivalent 5·5 per cent in the city. Almost a third of the men in the city claimed to come from social class 2. If they remained in local authority housing this could have limited their social contacts, and may be part of the reason why 12·5 per cent of respondents lived in their own houses, and many more expressed a desire to do so. Certainly this claiming of middle-class status could have enhanced the difference between the police in the city and those from the unskilled working classes—the 'drunks', the 'criminals', the immigrant Irish and others—with whom they had to deal. If the status of origin is accurately reported then there will be a genuine difficulty in achieving consensus: the world will have been understood differently by the different groups from childhood; if the reporting is inaccurate then the dissociation is deliberate and the lack of understanding and value consensus may be even greater.

TABLE 35 *Social class of father**

	1 %	2 %	3 %	Police %	4 %	5 %	No. of respondents
County	— —	9 14·1	41 64·1	7	10·9	6 9·4 1 1·5	64
City	— —	18 32·7	29 52·7	3	5·5	4 7·3 1 1·8	55

*General Register Office. Classification of Occupations, London; HMSO, 1960. According to this, policemen are social class 3.

The reported class of origin of the men differed slightly from that of the wives in both forces. The large number of men from social class 3 in the county had drawn wives from the two adjoining classes, 2 and 4, as well as from their own class. In the city men tended to claim a higher class of origin than their wives, which could be related to the fact that more of them were migrants (appendix IV, Table K).

Educational background

The educational background of city policemen compared with that of county men suggests that they were fairly accurate in their reporting of class of origin. Significantly more of them had remained at school beyond the age of sixteen (Table 36).

TABLE 36 *Age of leaving school*

	14 No.	14 %	15 No.	15 %	Age 16 No.	Age 16 %	17 No.	17 %	18+ No.	18+ %	No. of respondents
County	24	37·6	27	42·2	11	17·2	1	1·5	1	1·5	64
City	23	41·8	18	32·8	8	14·5	4	7·3	2	3·6	55

Previous occupational experience

A factor frequently mentioned by the men as being important for both understanding and being able to communicate with members of 'the public' was experience in other occupations. They did not speak in terms of a shared world view or of knowing the concepts in which the other thought, but this is what they implied. Many men said that the problem with the increase in cadet entry was that cadets had had no contact with people in any walk of life apart from the police force. Sending them to work in factories for short periods as part of their training was not sufficient, these men felt, particularly as they usually went in groups and were not, therefore, forced to interact to any great extent with others of their workmates. Twenty-nine per cent (n142) of the recruits to the city force in 1962 were from the Cadet Corps. Only half as many county men as city men had joined direct from the cadets.

In Table 37 being a police cadet or a period in the armed services are each counted as one previous job. Even so, county men had had a slightly wider range of experience when they joined the force, and on this basis too were in a better position to achieve an understanding of the people they policed.

TABLE 37   *Number of previous jobs*

	1		2		3		4		5		6		Total	
	No.	%	No.	%	No.	%	No.	%	No.	%	No.	%	No.	%
County	12	18·75	22	34·40	12	18·75	13	20·30	3	4·70	2	3·10	64	100·00
City	14	25·50	19	34·59	12	21·90	7	12·70	2	3·60	1	1·80	55	100·00

Immediately previous jobs were classified by social class except in the case of police cadetship. If the last occupation had been National Serviceman, the social class of the next immediately previous occupation was recorded. Results indicated that relatively few men had used the police service as an avenue of upward mobility (Table 38). Less than 2 per cent of men in the city had had a lower occupational status before joining. But though this may be satis-

TABLE 38   *Social class of last job*

	1		2		3		4		5		Police Cadet		Total	
	No.	%	No.	%	No.	%	No.	%	No.	%	No.	%	No.	%
County	—	—	3	4·7	48	75·0	7	10·9	—	—	6	9·4	64	100·0
City	—	—	2	1·8	35	65·5	6	10·9	1	1·8	11	20·0	55	100·0

factory from the point of view of the quality of police recruits it indicates that for most of the men the pattern of life of unskilled and semi-skilled workers would be a completely unknown field.

Many policemen suggested that a period in the armed services was of great value for the development of an understanding of 'people at large'. Only 23·4 per cent of men in the county and 32·7 per cent in the city had no service experience. 54·7 per cent of county men and 45·5 per cent of city men had been in the regular services, the remainder in each case having done two years National Service only (Table 39). County men in the sample tended to be older—

TABLE 39 *Experience in armed services*

| | *None* | | *National Service* | | *Regular or enlisted service* | | *Total* | |
	No.	*%*	*No.*	*%*	*No.*	*%*	*No.*	*%*
County	15	23·4	14	21·9	35	54·7	64	100·0
City	18	32·7	12	21·8	25	45·5	55	100·0

39 per cent of them being forty or over compared with 20 per cent in the city—which accounts for the difference between the two forces (appendix IV, Table L). Most of the older men would have been on active service during the 1939–45 war. The mean length of military service, excluding those who had no such experience, was 5·0 years in the county and 4·6 years in the city (Table 40).

TABLE 40 *Number of years in Armed Services*

| | *Years* | | | | | | | *No. of respondents* |
	0	*2*	*3*	*4*	*5*	*6–9*	*10+*	
County	15	14	15	2	5	8	5	64
City	18	12	9	4	3	6	3	55

Conclusion

In so far as common biographical features suggest the probability of a common conceptual framework and system of values, these data suggest that rural policemen were more likely than city men to see the world the same way as the people they policed. They were born and bred in the same area in many cases, and had had a fairly

103

wide experience of ordinary working life. On the other hand, in the county as well as in the city the men's social class backgrounds and previous job histories suggest that few men had any direct experience of the life style of semi-skilled or unskilled workers. A quarter of the city men had stayed at school beyond the age of fifteen. For the most part the men were similarly ignorant of the life styles of upper- and upper-middle-class people.

Work relationships with the community

Background to the work situation

We have seen that county men were in a better position than city men, both in terms of their numbers of contacts and in terms of their previous life experiences, to develop an understanding with the members of the community. Moreover, because of their greater dependence on the community, their world would be more likely to be defined for them by community members. Their similar biographies to those of their 'parishioners' indicate that they probably shared a world with these people before they arrived—we expect that understanding and liking will ensue when people 'have a lot in common'. In addition, however, the fact that the community had power over them, that they were dependent on the local people in a wide variety of ways, suggests that through time they would come to see the world even more as their parishioners saw it, and to enter their world as opposed to understanding it in a detached way. The dependence of county men on the local community was increased by the fact that their wives too were dependent on it for social satisfaction in terms of contacts, even if they were not as fully accepted as some of them would wish. The men were aware that the acceptance of their wives and families was to a considerable extent contingent upon their own acceptability as policemen.

In the city the men had less contact with the local community and were less dependent on it. Nor was there much evidence of the community being in its turn dependent upon them. Wives too were less dependent, for many of their social contacts were at work and they were in a better position to select and maintain loose networks of 'real' friendships. Physical and social separation meant that the men's behaviour at work would have no effect on their wives' social lives. Yet whereas county men and their families felt themselves to be absorbed into a system which, though at times demanding and claustrophobic, was generally friendly disposed towards them, city men and their wives often perceived either the general public as a whole or fragments of it as positively hostile. And whereas county men felt it necessary to withdraw from too close relationships (which their wives would have liked) with members of the community in order to shelter themselves from conflict situations in performance of their police tasks, city men rarely saw such conflict potential inherent in social relationships. Rather they felt circumscribed in their friendships by the number of the 'right kind of people' who would be willing to be friends. In the county, men said, 'I'm friendly with everyone but . . .' In the city certain categories of the public were excluded from friendship, and sometimes even from friendliness. These were the people who were not respectable—often the people who lived near the workplace but whom one did not want to live near oneself. With the 'respectable' one had by definition a value consensus and common understandings—that was why they were defined as respectable—and some of the respectable were chosen as friends on the basis of this; with the 'rough' there was no point of contact and nothing in the policeman's life experience —even to the point of being born in the same town—which could provide a starting point for real communication. Moreover, the organization of the force into specialist units and sections reinforced, or perhaps partially caused, a fragmented picture of the community.

Largely as a result of these differences the work relationship between the policemen and members of the public in the two areas studied was so different that they cannot fruitfully be examined side by side. Accordingly, the pattern of relationships in the county force will be dealt with first and that in the city force subsequently.

Interdependence with the community at work—county

For the county man with his unsegregated role, interdependence with the community at work was very closely linked with social interdependence. Much of his success, both socially and as a policeman, depended on his being regarded as a 'good old boy'. Contact was necessary before this opinion of him could be formed and before he could learn what he must do to acquire the appellation. The need of himself and his family for social relationships with the community has been shown, as has also to a lesser extent the community's need for his participation. His dependence on the community in the work situation has been hinted at in chapter 2. The role which the county policeman defined for himself, peace-keeping when there is only one definition of peace, policing to a consensus which he himself symbolizes, being about, such a role cannot be conceived of without reciprocal dependence. The fact that the men wanted to police this way itself implies that the common understanding already existed.

County men also regarded clearing up crime as a major part of their role. In order to do this they were also dependent on the community, though this time in a more instrumental way for assistance and information. Two-thirds of the crime on one-man beats was dealt with by local uniform personnel without the assistance of CID. The method of solving crime in the more rural areas approximated closely to the traditional procedures of looking for 'clues' at the scene of the crime and following these up by narrowing down the range of suspects until the identity of the guilty person became obvious. 'Clues' sometimes took the form of fingerprints and hard data of this kind, but more usually it was a matter of enquiring among the local people as to what they had seen or heard. It was frequently stated that county people would talk to their beat PC, who was a familiar figure, more readily than to an outsider. It was not possible to verify this, but in any case it was true as far as the beat men were concerned. The beat man was dependent upon the co-operation of the local people in solving reported crimes. Even where he used the alternative procedure of starting at some distance from the scene of the crime with information given by people not connected with it, he was dependent on the people of the community. Rural beat men did not have a separate category of informers. Country people might, if they thought sufficiently highly of their policeman or if they regarded the offence as a serious matter, voluntarily come to their policeman with relevant information without being approached first by him. For this unsolicited information to be given the policeman had to be well accepted by the local people. He had no system of monetary rewards at his disposal with which he could buy such information, and these might in any case have been inappropriate within the setting of non-specific and particularistic relationships. Beat men wanted to clear up crime because they shared the views of their parishioners about what was heinous and what was not. Moreover, the men felt that senior officers judged them by the two criteria of the number of offence reports they put in and the proportion of their crimes they cleared up, and that in the promotion 'race' the latter was of particular importance. They were thus highly motivated to clear up their crimes and to gain the co-operation of the local people as a prerequisite for doing this. There was, however, some conflict between the two criteria, for instead of monetary payments the policeman might 'let off' a useful or potentially useful member of the community for a minor offence. But again, this was not so much a reward for services rendered or to be rendered as an attempt to behave in the way which the community would find acceptable. Opportunities actually to observe relevant situations were rare, but it is worthy of note that in the course of one set of crime enquiries in which headquarters CID were also involved it was the *local* sergeant who had a quiet word with the landlord of a public house, while the CID men stayed in the background. In this case the 'tip off' given by the landlord led to the identification of the culprits.

In the absence of further concrete evidence some examples quoted by the men and other comments serve as the best illustration of interdependence in the work situation. First a concrete example of give and take: a young PC on a one-man beat is talking to a farmer whom he has just asked for help in identifying some photographs:

> 'Can I see your pig book while I'm here?' Pause. 'Oh well, it's all right if you can't find it then, only if you've got it handy.'
> 'Well, that isn't right made up. Here. Can you leave me a few spaces to fill in afore you sign it?'
> 'How many spaces do you want then?'
> 'Er . . . five if you please.'
> PC signed the book, leaving the blank spaces, muttering, 'Seeing as it's you.'

A beat PC is talking while out on a cycle patrol:

> If you're in a place a long time you get to know the people. Like that boy I spoke to just now . . . he'll always help. There's this chap who's disqualified around here, and I know for certain that he drives a tractor . . . Well, this boy is getting married soon and I said to him if you help me with this I'll see you have a nice wedding present so he said . . . 'I'll keep you to that Mr Atkins', so I said, 'Right-o, boy', and that was that. Well, a bit later he phoned me and told me this chap had got the tractor out and was driving it along and told me where he was going, see . . . so I rang up one of my specials . . . and I said to him, 'Can you get the old car out, boy, I've got something on'. Well, he was down there right away and I was all rough, I'd been gardening, but we went down there and I got right down behind the dashboard and we got where we should meet him. Then this other chap cycled past and gave us a look. He couldn't see me and that wasn't a police car but there isn't much traffic along there . . . When we got up there the other bloke had left the tractor and gone. I know what happened, you see, this other bloke had warned him. But I shall get him, I'm sure of that.

Again a PC working a one-man beat is talking. The incidents may seem trivial but every crime and every offence had importance in the county because of the relative scarcity of each.

> It's important to know the people on your beat. Now take this example. There was this old chap, over eighty he was, and I met him one night and he was a bit the worse for drink.

Well, I said to him, 'Good evening, Mr Henry. How are you?
You be careful', and all that, and then he went to go and I
noticed that he hadn't got a rear light . . . Well, I know that
old boy. He come up there every night and he was as straight
as a die . . . Well, I called to him and said, 'What's happened
to your rear light then, boy?' 'What,' he said, 'isn't that on?'
'No, boy,' I said, 'let's have a look at it.' So I took it to pieces
and there wasn't a battery in it at all. 'Well, boy,' he said,
'I reckon that's these boys a' bin playing tricks on me again
then.' Well, I know that was what had probably happened . . .
'Well, boy,' he said, 'have I got to walk home then?' Well, I
knew he didn't live that far up the road, but he was a poor
old boy and that was a fair way. 'Well,' I said to him, 'I'm
going the other way and what you do when you get away
from me I shan't see', so I left him. 'Thank you, sir', he said,
but then you see that paid. A bit later on this brass fitting went
from a field on my beat and we couldn't get a lead on it and I
went down to have a look, you see . . . Then I was just going
home, you see, on the edge of the field when this old boy cycles
past, and I was looking round, you see, to see if that had got
hidden anywhere. Well, he calls out to me, 'Looking for
something, sir?' And I said yes and I told him. 'Well,' he said,
'I'm in a hurry and I don't want to be seen standing around
here talking to you but there's just one word I've got to say
to you, steamroller,' and off he went. Well, I stood there
scratching me head . . . when I looked down and saw that the
tar on the road was fresh . . . so I got on to the CID and they
checked up on it and found which company it was you see,
and it turned out that one of the drivers had got it.

Consensus in operation County men responded more favourably
than city men to an item on the job satisfaction scale concerning
whether or not they received adequate recognition from the community for the work they did. The proportionate distribution of
responses is shown in Table 41. County men could not have operated

TABLE 41 *Community recognition*

	Very well satisfied		Fairly well satisfied		Neither satisfied nor dissatisfied		Not very well satisfied		Very dis- satisfied		Total
	No.	%	No.	%	No.	%	No.	%	No.	%	%
County	36	56·2	16	25·0	9	14·1	2	3·1	1	1·6	100·0
City	7	12·8	23	41·8	6	10·9	5	9·1	14	25·4	100·0

effectively without this 'recognition' nor would their private lives have been very satisfactory.

This sort of recognition implies acceptance of the legitimacy of the policeman's authority. And this is basic to rule by consensus. Consensus implies that in certain cases the policeman is expected to act, just as in other cases he is expected to 'turn a blind eye'. Mutual understanding was evident in almost every contact between beat men and members of the community observed, though it was not always apparent in contacts between patrol-car crews and the public.

Attempts to achieve acceptance by the community were evident with beat men in many small ways. Several instances were noted of a beat man's accent lapsing into a more broad dialect when speaking to this 'parishioners', as they were often called. The men would chat to farmers about their cattle and crops, showing on all occasions some knowledge of the subject as well as an interest. Often they would explain that they had consciously to adjust their pace to that of country people, and not try and rush them. Country men might be addressed as 'boy', the local form of greeting. One man said:

> I've got one poultry dealer on my beat but I'm able to tell
> him beforehand when I'm day off, so if he wants any licences
> for the next day he can get them then.

Another, speaking of sheep dipping, remarked:

> She was pouring the stuff over them with a saucepan, but
> really they were doing a much more thorough job than a lot
> who do comply [with the regulations].

Another discussed with a boy to whom he had just delivered a witness summons how he could best arrange with his teacher to get time off from school. The PC advised him not to go to school at all that morning, and also told the lad to ask his father to phone him and discuss the best way of arranging transport with him. Finally, as an example of consensus and mutual help based upon understanding and thinking in the same concepts:

> A farmer came in here the other day, a nice old boy, as straight
> as you please, and I know he's crammed right up, he's got to
> get the stores out because he's got fifteen sows all in litter and
> he's got to have room for them so I gave him a licence, but
> I gave it to him on a condition. I said, 'I'll give you this on
> condition you don't sell to X', because he's a dealer you see
> and he robs these people, he really does . . . so he says,
> 'Right-o, boy.'

In two of the rural towns men were observed to bundle drunks into a taxi, having first ascertained that they had either money or a cheque book—('I shouldn't tell him [the driver] that you've got no money until you get there. There's nothing he can do about it then.')—and send them home. This was double-edged, in that it not only kept the people concerned happy that they had not been charged, but also avoided the problem of having a man on duty in the police station all night guarding the prisoner. The men said too that on special occasions, as both these were, drunken behaviour was understandable.

Acceptance of legitimate police authority was shown in two verified cases of beat men who had had to report friends of theirs from the beat for offences. One of the victims, a farmer, good-humouredly remarked, in the hearing of the PC, 'He's a right swine you know, took me to court and all.' The PC laughed.

Mobile crews and the community One example will be sufficient to illustrate the rather different approach of the mobile men:

A van had been stopped for travelling faster than the permitted 40 m.p.h. in a restricted vehicle. The driver remarked that this was getting a favourite place for stopping people, and then, after the business of producing documents was complete, went on, 'You must admit it's a stupid law,' etc. The PC then cited the law and said that the man was doing 60 m.p.h. 'As you haven't got your book out I'll tell you, I thought it was my mate running me up.' He then continued talking about the law. The observer, a beat man, remarked, 'That isn't our job,' meaning to judge the laws. The man said: 'Well, go on then, report me if you want to.' Mobile man: 'That's just what I'm going to do. . . .' Afterwards the beat man remarked that what the man had said about the law was right. The mobile man said defensively that after what the van driver had said he had had no alternative but to report him 'when he turned out like that'. The beat man did not answer this directly but remarked: 'The thing is, he shouldn't get caught. I've got a restricted vehicle and I haven't been caught. . . .'

Mobile patrol crews were a special case in the county force. They lived in a cluster of police houses in the DHQ town, so were less dependent on the community for their social relationships; they did not need public co-operation in order to do their work. Many of the people they dealt with in the course of their work were unknown to them. They were expected to 'get offences', and those offences which they did report resulted from their own observations. They made their own evidence, and needed little external assistance in making out a case.

The county man's view of criminals Informers in the county are part of the community rather than a separate category (cf. chapter 2, for example). Beat men in fact spoke of a CID man who had cleared up a series of breaks by means of an informant in the more usual sense of the word, a man who received payment for his information, as if this officer were not really deserving of praise for his success. This was not police work as the beat men knew it. Likewise offenders, although often undesirable, were part of the community.

A beat PC went to great lengths to talk to a boy who had been brought in for questioning and had admitted a number of offences of malicious damage and nuisance. He discussed with him his job and his problems with his girlfriend, which he already knew about. Later he gave the researcher a full biography of the boy whom he had known for a number of years, and said, 'I feel sorry for the kid in a way.' Later the boy was involved in an assault, again, as it turned out, resulting from his relationship with his fickle girlfriend. The beat PC remarked:

> I shall bring him [to court] actual bodily harm rather than
> grievous bodily harm, which I could do, as that has to go to
> Assizes and I think that will be bad for the boy.

Adult criminals too were responded to as individuals, and with understanding if not sympathy. The policemen were almost unanimously in favour of relatively more severe penalties, and referred to a court which imposed these as a 'good court' and vice versa. But the offenders remained individual people rather than part of a category.[7] Indeed, there did not seem to be fixed *types*, conceptually, into which 'criminals' could be put. If they were not known to the policeman before the offence, as the lad discussed above, then the policeman had to fall back on his ideas about people in *general* as a basis of interaction.

> I said: 'Did he eat it all,' and he said, 'Well, he kept one bun
> for the evening, poor chap.' Then my husband took pity on
> him and took over this great thick slice of bread and cheese
> and a mug of cocoa later on . . . This morning, too, I said to
> my husband when he kept putting all this into the pan,
> 'Whatever do you think he's going to eat?' (A sergeant's wife.)

Only two clear *types* of offender were apparent in the county beat men's thinking ten years ago. One of these was labelled 'yobs' or 'tear-aways'. These were young men who were expected to fight, swear, and generally 'make trouble' outside dance halls, and to 'hang around' on the pavement outside the fish-and-chip shop which might be found in the larger villages and small towns. Tear-aways might also ride motor-bikes and it was thought that they were the sort of people who might 'do' (break into) AA and RAC boxes along the main roads. But these last were not defining characteristics. My impression was that a lack of deference to the local policeman and an exaggerated having nothing in particular to do, together with youth and maleness, were the qualifying features of the 'type'.

The second general type of person who might be presumed, in the beat man's thinking, to commit offences, was the gipsy. To gipsies were attributed the characteristics of all having among the same few surnames, of changing the name frequently when in trouble, of banding together, sticking up for each other, lying, inconsistency, and never knowing anything. They were expected to engage in dubious trading, for example in old vehicles, and to steal or pilfer (as opposed to breaking and stealing) easily disposable objects. Their reputed loyalty and skills at evasion were almost admired. It was 'recognized' that they had a code of ethics of some sort, albeit a different one. The yobs, by contrast, were presumed to be amoral.

It was also claimed that most rural beats had their trouble family, the sons of which would grow up to be yobs. But here the family name itself was used as a concept to identify the type. When a remark was made such as 'Oh yes, we all have our Robinsons' it indicated a family which was regarded as shiftless to a man, un-reliable, and liable to steal. But I am less certain of the characteristics attributed to this type, possibly in part because each beat man knew the characteristics specific to his trouble family, so the concept was not completely shared even among the men.

People subsumed under these types would probably be recorded in the 'beat book', together with the local vet., doctor, health visitor and so on. Despite this institutionalization of roles, it was possible for individuals to be re-defined. Thus 'You'd never think she was a Robinson . . .' or 'He was a right tear-away when he was sixteen but . . .'

Interdependence with the community at work—city

As in social life so at work interdependence for the city men was lower than for their county colleagues. In the first place the areas they policed were so large that it was often impossible for them to get to know the people on the beat. Offences of a trivial kind were frequent and all about them, and, as in the case of the mobile men in the county, the securing of offence reports was simply a matter of putting their own observations on paper. That relatively few of them chose to operate in this way is a different problem. Second, the uniform men were not responsible for dealing with crime except in the case of offenders who were caught in the act. Even for the CID men the mode of operation was different from the county and involved interdependence only with a small fringe-criminal subculture rather than the whole community (pp. 50–3).

It was shown in the previous chapter (pp. 67–70) that a high proportion of the 'prisoners' attributed to uniform patrol men were arrested for offences of drunkenness or other offences against the public order. These arrests resulted from initiatives taken by the policeman in a situation where he has a choice of doing nothing, cautioning, taking some 'unofficial' preventative measure (such as county men took when they called a taxi in which to send a drunken man home) or going through formal arrest procedures. Those at risk of being drunk in the street in any case represented a small proportion of the population (Stinchcombe, 1963 and chapter 3, p. 67).

In one respect, however, that of provision of facilities for easing behaviour, the city men were more dependent on the local community. The chill and potential boredom of the job made easing necessary behaviour for the city men. With publicans and café proprietors there was high interdependence, for the police could offer support in times of difficulty with customers and turn a blind eye to certain stretchings of the law. In return they received easing facilities, and also services. These were the people to whom the plain clothes and CID staff often had recourse for information in addition to their paid informers. Thus what for the county men was a relationship with a whole community ofr the city men became a relationship with a small group within the community. The same is true of consensus. Any urban sociologist will point out that this phenomenon is not unique to policemen (Wirth, 1957, is a good and early example), what is important for us is to understand how city policemen constructed, or reconstructed, this fragmented community.

Consensus in the city In the city consensus was observed between beat men and patrol-car crews and those of similar estimated class background to the men themselves, though in general these 'respectable' citizens only came into contact with the police as either motorists or complainants.[8] Minor infringements were let pass without even a warning, and a man might remark at an accident, 'I don't think I'll do him for anything', if there were not a flagrant case of a breach of the law. In another case the PC spoke to the driver of the vehicle about his insurance: 'I'm not advising your or anything, but I'm just telling you that I know what has happened and what will happen in case you didn't know.' He told the driver that he would lose his no claims bonus if the case went to court, even if it were proven not his fault. In another situation when a passenger appeared unwilling to 'shop' the driver following an accident, the PC told him: 'The best thing is to say you don't know if you're not certain. You know what I think? You weren't really looking then and couldn't say.'

Again, in the case of an accident in which a man's wife was injured, the PC recommended the least of the possible alternative charges, saying, 'He's been punished enough already.'

But even with the 'respectable' section of the public a common world view did not always exist. One man said that he had no time for the landrover mobile police station idea 'because it encourages them to come with petty things they wouldn't normally take the effort to go to the police station with'—referring to people of 'respectable' disposition on the outskirts of the town. Another man said that he would like CID work because in the CID 'you don't have to be bothered with the stupid public; you know, little Johnny who's found a sixpence'. These demands were too far removed from the high status thief-catching self-image. They pose again the question, if their role was not defined for them by the section of the community which they labelled 'respectable', with which they had some sympathy and shared meanings and values, and whose imputed approval legitimated their existence, then by whom was the police role defined? It seems plain that many of the 'respectable' would have welcomed more than a narrowly defined thief-taking role.

Rural policemen, as I have shown, would chase up a larceny of plums or (in one case) pea sticks if the complainant considered that this was important. By contrast with city men, they tended almost to boast that in the country people came with every little thing, help with a tax form, a domestic problem, and so on. They were irritated that their domestic life was interrupted when they were off duty, but it was always the timing of the intrusions rather than the fact of them about which they complained. The 'parishioners' defined the policeman's role, and their coming with 'petty things' was a reassuring sign to him that he was playing it satisfactorily, apart from the more important fact that he accepted that this was what he was for. In the city, members of the community, even those whom the police labelled 'respectable', lacked power to get their definition of the policeman's job across.

The 'rough' The rough for some policemen were all the people living 'down the bottom end' plus a number of others. There was an element of ambivalence in police attitudes to these people, for on the one hand policemen said that these were the people who needed a policeman, who had respect for him, and who would turn to him in times of trouble; on the other hand they said: 'The people down here have got no time for the policeman.' They may well have been talking about different groups which were dominant in their perception of the situation, but there is no evidence as to their exact meaning. What is clear is that 'these people' were seen as a separate category. They had to be spoken to 'in their own language' which meant starting a conversation with such remarks as 'look here, mate', swearing and perhaps using physical violence. Two men in labouring clothes were seen leaving Brockborough police station while a sergeant on the steps shouted after them: 'We don't pull bloody policemen off trees. If that's your attitude you can bugger off.' 'You can't go to the book all the time, you've got to treat these people in a way they can understand' or 'It's no good going to these people and talking smoothly to them. I could talk the way they talk'—here are two examples of the dissociation of the policemen from the people with whom they come into contact in the course of their work. Conversely men working on the out-skirts would say, 'You've got to handle things differently round here. If you're not careful there'll be a letter in to the chief constable right away . . .'

There were a limited number of cases which could trigger off understanding with the 'rough' also, or perhaps cause the policeman to redefine them. At Christmas there was a general truce—some aggression maybe, but not arrests for drunkenness except in extreme cases. Again, in the course of one patrol a call was received to an accident. Two Irishmen on a scooter had shot out of a side turning and hit a car. They were the worse for drink. When the men said that they had been to a wedding one PC gave the driver a cigarette and both became sympathetic, remarking that a wedding was something special. The PC did not include in the driver's statement his admission that it was his fault, although it was discussed between the officers as to whether this *should* be done. A wedding, in the policemen's world too, legitimated being drunk.

Criminals Criminals were seen as an out-group, and there was no real sympathy or understanding with them such as was apparent in the county.[9] Again it is difficult to know whether they were labelled 'criminal' because of this lack of understanding—the relationship seemed to go this way round with the respectable—or whether the two were independent. On occasion understanding was feigned in order to get a statement of guilt. An escaped prisoner who had been caught was given a packet of cigarettes and two bottles of beer. 'It's only fair isn't it? There's no sense in being too rough on him', remarked a CID man, but others spoke of how he might be useful. Relationships were fairly specific and contractual

115

and there was no evidence of a more fundamental empathy, beyond an understanding of how the complex system of transactions operates. Of one club owner, it was remarked:

> He's very good to the uniform men [i.e., beer left for night duty men] . . . I mean they know they're going to get done and they just accept it as part of the business. I mean, he's had one club closed down and then he opened up here instead . . .

A CID man said:

> Shall I tell you who my best informant is? A coloured girl who's a prostitute . . . and I'll tell you another thing, she'll never get done, not if I can help it she won't. She's never been to prison and she never will as long as I'm around.

This was a specific contract, but there was no *verstehen* either with her or with the rest of the community . . .

> And I'll tell you this, I've one ambition in life and that's to knock people off. I love it and I'll do it . . . I'd knock off everyone in this room if I could but I can't yet. And most of them will come anyway . . .[10]

Another CID man gave money to a man he had arrested and told him to go and get himself a drink. He did so and later returned voluntarily to the station to be charged:

> He'll be useful to me later you see . . .

Again the relationship involves a specific contract. Next morning the CID officer said in court that he had been in touch with the accused man's employers and that he had a very good work record. The officer had been at court from 9.30 a.m. and the man had not been arrested until late the previous evening. It seems probable that this story was fabricated as part of the contract, as one more bargaining counter in the purchase of information. The securing of bail for the prisoner was another frequently mentioned, though as the researcher was not usually allowed to be present at interrogations no concrete evidence of this could be obtained.[11]

Women Women, too, fall into two categories of the rough and the respectable, perhaps even more clearly demarcated than those for the men. Respectable women were supposed to be both innocent, ignorant, and in need of protection. Swearing in front of a woman caused enormous embarrassment and confusion. Policewomen caused confusion of the two categories and were sometimes resented on these grounds. 'We don't really think of policewomen, you know, as females', one man said at Outpost, and his colleagues on the turn agreed. Several men remarked, 'It's not the right sort of work for women to do, is it?'

Towards the 'rough' women there were again mixed feelings. A number of the men who had been on plain clothes commented how good-hearted prostitutes were and how they would give you money if you were short. But they described these human feelings with some surprise and in the same tone as they described some of the perversions in which the prostitutes indulged. And when it came to the work situation itself there was no real sympathy.

> They were out in droves [the previous Saturday] and they didn't know the car and they didn't know John [a newcomer to the plain clothes department], and I crouched down in the back. It was diabolical the way we did it. There was this girl and she flagged us down and she said to John, 'Can you change a 6d.' So he said, 'Yes.' So she said, 'Two pounds for inside', and I grabbed her and dragged her into the car . . . But three in two hours, that's some going even for a Saturday, it was great it was . . .

Immigrants The other clearly demarcated type in the policeman's community was the immigrants, in particular the coloured immigrants, though the Irish were also subject to stereotyping and abuse. The characteristics attributed to 'niggers' or 'nigs' were that they were 'in the main . . . pimps and layabouts, living off what we pay in taxes'. 'Have you been to a wog house? They stink, they really do smell terrible.'

A number of contacts between the police and immigrants were observed, all but one evidencing lack of any shared meaning. In this exceptional case the man was an African in smart European dress. As a result of a 999 call the area-car crew had been examining a car which was parked by the roadside. The African owner came along while the men were searching it, and explained the situation. The policeman then noticed that the excise licence was outdated. The man explained that he couldn't afford to get it renewed yet. No action was taken. The driver said, 'That's fair enough, that's a good enough excuse, I've been in the same position myself'. The man had been polite and deferential. 'That's why I spoke to him like that', said the driver.

But in other cases statements such as 'the majority of people down here are on forged passports anyway' showed the depths of misunderstanding. When called to a domestic dispute the PC remarked:

> They think nothing of doing that you know. One of them had

117

his head split open and all bleeding, but the women, they just
stand around and watch, they expect it . . .

Another extremely complicated situation involving minor violence
was written off as 'just a bit of landlord trouble with an Indian',
and entered in the 'minor occurrence book'. 'There'll be a wounding
there soon, you just see,' said the inspector off-handedly. This was
common and an exact parallel with the situation recorded by
Banton (1963) in coloured areas in America.

On another occasion:

A van stopped dead ahead of the patrolling sergeant
and inspector, and a figure was seen standing in the road
flagging the police vehicle down. 'Hello, someone in trouble?'
Sergeant: 'Oh Christ, look what's here' It turned out to be two
coloured men, hence the exclamation. The man in the van
remarked that he hadn't realized it was policemen; the police
van carried no sign. The sergeant said, 'Did you hear what he
said? "Just the people I wanted". The cheek of that!' The
coloured man wanted a push to start his car, as he told the
inspector when curtly asked what the trouble was. No help
was given.

Another time

A call came through to the patrol car to a Sikh household
where they had been complaining of people throwing stones.
The son of the family had seen the boy next door do it. The
old man of the house wanted the people next door spoken to
and told that they should pay for the repair. He finally upset
the officer by saying: 'It's your duty to do that.' 'Thank you,
I know what my job is', and later, 'If there's one thing that
makes me angry it's someone telling me what my duty is.'

But in fairness in this case, unlike the landlord/tenant dispute,
action was taken. The policemen did go next door and the woman
neighbour did promise to pay for the window to be repaired. The
officers went back to the Sikhs and reported this.

Lack of consensus with or sympathy for people outside the limited
segment of the population who were 'respectable' was apparent in
the allocation of police officer time as well. Over an hour was spent
trying to find out the address of a party an American Air Force
officer wanted to go to, but a homeless coloured man was turned
away from the station three times in one night without any advice
as to where he could find accommodation.

Again, coloured people were by definition permanently in the area
of suspicion (Wertman and Piliavin, 1967). A woman had her

handbag containing a large sum of money stolen from her in a pub
The researcher was told that there was a 'Jamaican' in the next
bar and that the CID were on to him. (They were right, but they
had no other grounds for suspecting him.) Again:

> When called to a break in a shop the officer asked, 'I believe
> you've got some of our coloured friends living over the
> back?...' The youth in the shop said yes but they were
> all right, they were regular customers. Officer: 'There's a hell
> of a party going on there now. I expect they smoke don't
> they? They'd need 1,200 cigarettes, they could smoke that
> many, smoke coming out of their nose and ears ...'

There was also some evidence of undue harrassment of coloured
people indicative of a lack of sympathy and understanding.

And finally there was the myth of violence. Coloured people,
even more than other 'roughs', were different, separate, incomprehensible. There was, therefore, no good reason for not being
violent if the occasion arose. Since rule by consensus was impossible
and rule by coercion or ignoring the problem were the only alternatives, occasions for violence possibly arose more often. There
was a myth, therefore, about the greater physical strength of the
coloured man, and tales abounded:

> There was this enormous negro and we kept batting him over
> the head with our sticks and he didn't even seem to feel it ... I
> hit him hard where it hurts most and in the stomach and as
> I went past—just happened to knock against him with my foot,
> and he went down like a light ... We had to take him (to
> court) for assault on police or we could never have accounted
> for all those knocks.

Fifty-six persons were prosecuted for an assault on a constable in
the city force in 1962.

Effects of differential interdependence

So far two types of 'evidence' have been brought to bear on the
issue of police interdependence with the community. These are
'objective' data collected during the interviews (e.g., place of birth),
and data from informal conversation with policeman and observation of them, describing the world of relevant others as they see it.
Some 'translation' from my initial formulations of the material has
taken place, but not much. Where in 1969 the discussion was purely
in terms of consensus, implying an agreement on fundamental
values, today concepts such as 'shared reality' or 'shared meaning
system' tend both to replace and to include this. Where the term

E 119

consensus is still used it is with this wider and deeper meaning. But I have left it, especially in the final few pages, because it seemed that to tamper with the language might cause the policemen to speak less clearly through the words. And it is their view which counts. The argument about who has power to define the policeman's role remains the same as when the problem was first formulated in 1961. This thesis is concerned with power. But the influence of phenomenology in sociology has made more complex the understanding of both the scope of this role definition, and the mechanisms whereby a consensus is arrived at.

In this final section a third kind of data is presented. During the interviews six hypothetical situations were presented to the men. About each they were first of all asked the question, 'What do you think you would do?' And then what their superiors, wife, colleagues, and non-policemen living in the area would think they ought to do. The order in which these last four questions about reference groups or role-definers were asked was changed for each successive question. The aim was to locate the *sources* of agreement (support) and disagreement. Although it was recorded, it was not necessary to analyse the specific actions which the men said they would take, only who thought they ought to do the same and who thought they ought to do something different from what they said they would do. (A description of this technique and a discussion of its merits can be found in appendix III, pp. 282–4. The situations themselves are given in appendix I, pp. 252–7.)

The analysis presented in this chapter suggests that, according to the propositions set out in chapter 1, county policemen might be expected to resolve more conflicts than city policemen in the direction of the perceived role definitions of non-policemen. This is so because the analysis has suggested that the interdependence of county policemen with members of the community is greater than that of city policemen. Although there was no single index of interdependence with the community, partly because it was not possible to interview members of the general public, a number of indirect indicators were used. It was seen that the community had power over the county beat man because he needed help with his work, and because his family was dependent on the community for a satisfactory social life. In terms both of his biography and his present contacts county policemen were exposed to their 'parishioners'' definitions of the world. None of this was true of city men. There was also some evidence that *county men accepted a role defined for them by the community, while city men did not accept all the definitions of their job projected even by those they deemed respectable.*

Therefore on the basis of the general proposition of chapter 1, it would be expected that more county than city men would act in the way that members of the general public thought they ought to behave. In the answers to the hypothetical situations this was not the case. Looking at the number of presented situations in which the men said that members of the public would think they ought to take a different action from the one which they said they would take (disagreement)[12] there was no marked difference between the forces, and it was not in the predicted direction. On average men said that this would apply in $2 \cdot 1$ situations in the county and $1 \cdot 8$ situations in the city. These figures (Table 42) apply to situations in which the men said that all or most of the general public would disagree.

TABLE 42 *Number of situations in which action the policeman would take is different from that which all or most of the community would think he ought to take*

	Situations							
	0	1	2	3	4	5	6	*Total*
County	9	16	14	13	9	3	—	64
City	12	8	20	10	2	3	—	55

There were also a number of situations in which the men perceived that there would be lack of consensus on the part of the public. This was usually expressed as a 'fifty-fifty' division between those members of the public thinking the policemen ought to take the same action and those thinking he ought to take a different one. $34 \cdot 5$ per cent of city men compared with $28 \cdot 1$ per cent of county men said that there would be disagreement of this kind in two or more of the situations presented, but the difference was not statistically significant (appendix IV, Table M).

Since the predicted differences between forces on the basis of the apparent differences in interdependence did not emerge, the individual scores of the men within each force were assessed and related to the manner in which hypothetical 'conflict' was solved. No significant differences were found in the city force: men born locally, those who had had a wide previous work experience, those who scored high on the desire for integration with the community scale, and those who had frequent contacts with non-policemen, were no less likely than their opposites to perceive members of the public as disagreeing with the action which they said they would take in the hypothetical situations.

In the county force differences in the expected directions were found on the basis of two variables.

Of those county men who had had only one previous job (including National Service and police cadetship) before joining the police, 83·3 per cent said that the community would disagree with the action which they would take in at least *two* of the six situations; this compares with an equivalent figure of 55·8 per cent for the men who had had more than one previous job. In at least three of the six situations disagreement was anticipated by 58·3 per cent of those who had had only one previous job, and 34·5 per cent of the men who had held more than one job (see Table 43).

TABLE 43 *Number of previous jobs by situations in which community perceived as 'disagreeing'—county*

No. of jobs	Situations							
	0	1	2	3	4	5	6	*Total*
1 only	1	1	3	3	2	2	—	12
2+	8	15	11	10	7	1	—	52
	9	16	14	13	9	3	—	64

Observational data had suggested that even within the county force rural beat men were more highly interdependent with the local community than town or city men. Men operating one-man beats were therefore compared with town men to see if the actions of the country men showed fewer discrepancies with the role definitions of members of the community. A slight difference was apparent on this basis. Of one-man beat men 30·7 per cent felt that the community would think they should take a different course of action in three or more of the six situations presented: the corresponding figure for other uniform men was 53·6 per cent (sig. 0·05 level). The mean number of situations in which the community was perceived as disagreeing (Table 44) was 1·85 for one-man beat men, and 2·5 for other uniform personnel (excluding drivers and administrative staff).

Thus there is some support for the hypothesis that the greater interdependence of rural beat men with the local community means that these men are more likely to act in accordance with the role definitions of the members of the community in specific situations. Although the expected differences were not found in every case, in no case were differences in an opposite direction found, and in the county two of the four variables deemed to be associated with community interdependence were found to be associated also, as

TABLE 44 *Type of post by situations in which community perceived as 'disagreeing'—county*

Type of post	Situations							Total
	0	1	2	3	4	5	6	
One-man beat	6	6	6	3	4	1	—	26
Other uniform	1	6	6	10	3	2	—	28
CID/drivers/ admin.	2	4	2	—	2	—	—	10
	9	16	14	13	9	3	—	64

predicted, with the direction of conflict situation. In particular, one-man beat men, who were deemed on the basis of observational data to be more highly interdependent with the community, were found to act in accordance with community role projections more often than their counterparts in the small towns.

The relative effectiveness of the community as a role-definer, compared with other groups is not discussed here. This point is taken up in chapter 8 when the differences in interdependence between the four groups have all been considered. Thus in the final chapter the complex question of 'who defines the policeman's role' is again tackled on the basis of these four separate analyses. So it is not until chapter 8 when the discussion of interdependence with the role-definers is fully complete that the hypotheses outlined in chapter 1 are finally tested.

Summary

This chapter has argued that county policemen are more likely than city policemen to share a world—a conceptual framework, a set of values—with those they police. Their similar biographies to members of the community suggest that in the past they were exposed to similar definitions from similar power structures. In addition, county policemen had more contacts with those they policed, so were in a better position to learn their norms, standards, expectations, values, and modes of thought.

Not only were they able to learn these things about the community but they were motivated to share them. Members of the community had sufficient power over them to define the world for them. In the terms in which this study was originally couched, their interdependence with the community policed was higher than the interdependence of city men.

The three sources of community power identified were:

(a) that county policemen were more dependent socially on the local people;
(b) that the wives and families of the county policemen were more dependent socially on the local people;
(c) that county policemen were more dependent on local people for help in the work situation.

County policemen, unlike their wives, felt it necessary to maintain social distance from members of the community—to be friendly but not friends. This safeguarded them from stress in *specific* law enforcement situations, yet there was some evidence that in *general* terms the community determined what was important for one-man beat men. This applies less to other county policemen, and not at all in the city (where in any case there was probably not simply a single definition to enforce). The source of the city men's role definitions was not identified in this chapter, but the community policed was ruled out as a role definer.

The perception of the local community by county and city policemen was different. County policemen perceived members of the public 'in the round' and had knowledge of aspects of their lives other than those which brought them into contact with the police. Two 'deviant types' which were exceptions in their thinking were 'yobs' and 'gipsies'. City policemen, on the other hand, had a much more limited knowledge of those members of the public with whom they came into contact. Their responses were therefore more stereotyped. They perceived the community as fragmented and the 'rough' community as consisting of people essentially different from themselves. This made unsympathetic responses possible, but did not necessarily lead to responses of this kind, both on grounds of expediency (cf. Bittner, 1967b) and since it was possible for situations to be redefined in mutually comprehensible terms.

It was also shown that, despite the apparent differences in the nature of interdependence with the community, county men as a whole did not conform to the community's expectations of how they should behave in hypothetical situations presented any more frequently than did city men. As suggested in chapter 1 (p. 10) this tells us as much about different methodologies as about the men studied. It was shown, however, that men on one-man beats were more likely to consider that the community would agree with their actions than were their colleagues in different work situations. Similarly men who had a wider range of work experience before joining the police were more likely to think that the community would agree with them than were men whose previous working experience had been more limited.

5 Interdependence with family—marital integration and domestic life

Here I know everything that goes on and like to take an interest. I'm able to help him. We can both discuss it together as a common interest. I enjoy it a lot more like that. . . . (County wife.)

The thing is, you don't tell your wife everything that happens on this job. You couldn't, could you? You can't tell a woman things like that, they'd get much too hard. You keep it very much to yourself and it's better all round. (City inspector.)

Introduction

These two statements betoken polar attitudes and most of the men and women interviewed in the two forces would not have fallen at either extreme of the scale. But the structure of the two work situations was such that no city wife made a statement of the first kind and no man on a rural one-man beat made the latter. This then is the range within which the policeman's work impinges upon his domestic life in varying degrees.

Marital integration scores

Details of the mode of calculation of the marital integration score are given in chapter 1, p. 9, and appendix I, p. 281. It is a combined measure of agreement between spouses as to roles and goals. Marital integration scores thus measured have been found to be highly correlated with marital satisfaction (Farber, 1957). It is an assumption underlying the use of Farber's scale in this context that marital integration and satisfaction are closely linked with perceived interdependence between spouses, this being the variable here suggested to be the primary determinant of the direction of behaviour in a situation of perceived conflict.

Mean scores on the marital integration index were almost identical in the two forces (see Table 45). Scores were not related to objective

TABLE 45 *Scores on marital integration index* *

	0	1	2	3	4	5	6	Un-known	Not applicable	Total men
County	5	5	9	16	10	7	2	6	4	64
City	2	4	5	7	5	4	2	18	8	55

*The design of the index required that both the woman and her husband be interviewed before a score could be obtained.

data such as rank of husband, length of service, and length of time married, or to specific grievances affecting the marriage such as, for example, lack of privacy and liability to transfer in the county.

However, as in the case discussed in the previous chapter of wives' social contact with the community, the similar overall score marked considerable qualitative differences in the pattern of relationships. This was guessed at because the men on one-man beats moaned about their wives acting as 'unpaid policemen' when they were out. Many could remember a time when a policeman's prospective wife was 'vetted' by the chief constable for suitability. The modern reader may regard this as a joke, but the women (then girls) had found it terrifying. Until the 1950s wives and men were expected to ring in and inform the local headquarters if the beat house was being left unattended. Something of this participation of the wife in the husband's job persisted. I could not observe families at first hand, but the situation seemed sufficiently unusual and interesting to warrant further statistical examination at least. It seemed probable, as in the case of relationships with the community, though for different reasons, that the nature, the quality, of the domestic interdependence might be different in the rural and urban situations.

Accordingly a number of variables were cross-tabulated with marital integration. Positive and interesting relationships were found in the rural area between marital integration and career satisfaction and between marital integration and interdependence with the police. As I was by this time learning to expect, only conversations and often unsystematically collected data made an attempt at understanding this possible.

Effects of career satisfaction

There was no difference in mean career satisfaction scores between city and county men or between city and county wives. Mean career satisfaction (CS) scores are shown in Table 46.

TABLE 46   *Mean career satisfaction scores*

	Men		Wives	
City	County	City	County
31·1	30·4	24·6	24·1

Scales for men and for women contained similar items but were subjected to a separate scaling process so the scales may not be compared. The distribution is given in appendix IV, Table N.

More detailed analysis revealed no correlations between marital integration and career satisfaction within each category, but a distribution appeared in the county scores which pointed to a different *kind* of marital integration. Of the wives scoring above average on career satisfaction, 81·5 per cent scored three or more on the marital integration scale (22 of 27). For wives scoring below average on career satisfaction there was a much wider scatter, only 46·1 per cent of them scoring three or more on marital integration. The difference between these two proportions was significant at the ·01 level. No such relationship was apparent in the city. It would seem from these results that in the county, although high marital integration is not contingent upon high career satisfaction (hence the lack of a linear *r*) it is necessary to have a highly integrated marriage for the wife to be fully satisfied with her husband's career (Table 47). High career satisfaction implies for the county wife that she enjoys sharing her husband's work with him, as in the case of the woman quoted at the beginning of this chapter. She is expected, if not formally required, to take telephone messages and attend to callers in her husband's absence, and the policeman's work is greatly facilitated if he and his wife are accepted *as a team* by the people on the beat. If the wife finds such tasks and the constant intrusions on her privacy irksome, and resents a tie and a requirement for which she is neither paid nor thanked, then her satisfaction with her husband's career will be low. Rural policing therefore seems to require[1] a particular type of joint family relationship (Bott, 1957). A joint marital relationship usually implies, *inter alia*, one in which the husband helps with the cleaning and washing up and care of the children, and in which the two parties have interests and friends in common. Thus in the joint relationships identified by Bott the work

E*   127

TABLE 47 *Wives' career satisfaction by marital integration—country*

	Marital integration							No	
cs *score*	0	1	2	3	4	5	6	*answer*	*n*
Up to 15	—	1	—	—	—	—	—	1	2
16–20	3	2	2	4	1	3	—	—	15
21–3 (mean)	1	1	4	1	2	1	—	—	10
24–5	—	—	1	2	—	1	—	1	5
26–30	1	—	—	7	4	1	2	—	15
31–5	—	1	2	2	2	1	—	1	9
Unknown	—	—	—	—	1	—	—	—	1
	5	5	9	16	10	7	2	3	57

which was shared was domestic woman's work. For the rural police family this is reversed so that the wife participates actively in the husband's work in a way that is not possible in most urban occupations. He may in turn assist with domestic chores, though no systematic observations were made of this. Numbers of the men, however, commented on the advantages of being home for long hours during the day which meant that they saw more of younger children. This would again suggest a joint relationship.

The wife of a PC on a one-man beat had to take over some of the instrumental functions[2] but there was some evidence that, in addition to her duties as clerk and receptionist, she was allocated more expressive functions within the range of the police work tasks. Numbers of anecdotes were told of wives delivering hospital messages; often some verification of these was obtained by hearing the story independently from husband and wife and perhaps an outsider also. One man said that the village people went to his wife rather than himself with their domestic problems. Again, other highly satisfied wives said that they were 'interested in the people' or liked to be in touch with what was going on in the village. On the other hand, considerable amazement was expressed at one wife who took upon herself the task of dealing with an accident single-handed, this being by its nature a more instrumental task requiring a considerable amount of organization of witnesses and public services as well as attention to any injured parties.

Given that this special kind of joint family structure was a prerequisite for high career satisfaction on the part of the county wife it was not surprising that men in the county showed a similar relationship between their MI (marital integration) and the CS scores. The relationship for the men, however, did not show with three as the cutting point on the MI scale. It was necessary to use four or more as the cutting point and this then produced a difference which was significant at the ·01 level. Although there was no difference in the mean CS scores between the county and the city (county, 30·4; city, 31·1), in the county 53·57 per cent of those scoring above the average on the CS scale scored four or more on the MI scale. Of those scoring below average on the CS scale only 15·4 per cent scored four or more on the MI scale. Again no relationship of this kind was revealed in the city (see Table 48). But although the predominant

TABLE 48   *Men's career satisfaction by marital integration—county*

CS score	Marital integration							No. ans./ not applicable	n
	0	1	2	3	4	5	6		
Up to 20	1	—	—	1	—	—	—	—	2
21–5	1	1	2	1	2	—	—	1	8
26–30	—	3	3	9	—	2	—	4	21
31–5	3	1	4	3	5	4	2	5	27
36–40	—	—	—	2	3	1	—	—	6
	5	5	9	16	10	7	2	10	64

pattern in the county for both the men and their wives was for a relationship to exist between level of career satisfaction and level of marital integration there were differences in the nature of the relationship between the two groups. It has been suggested that for the wives marital integration was not a function of career satisfaction or vice versa, but that high marital integration was a pre-requisite for *high* career satisfaction on the part of the wife. For the men the pattern is different. Here, statistically, the scatter is greater for the *above* average scorers on the CS scale. High career satisfaction is possible for the men, as it was not for the women, when marital integration is low. But where career satisfaction is low for the men marital integration is rarely high, suggesting that perhaps the strains which the job imposes on domestic life have served to reduce both, or alternatively that when the required type of joint family structure is lacking the work in itself tends to become less rewarding. The first explanation is favoured since if the latter were the reason differences might have been expected to show up on the job satisfaction scale also. But the strains caused by practical exigencies might be expected to have a more deleterious effect on career satisfaction if the family structure were not the optimal one for the carrying out of the work.

Effects of interdependence with police

Further light is thrown on the problem by the fact that marital integration was found in the county to be correlated with the men's scores on the interdependence with police scale ($r.$ 0·45), as shown in Table 49. A man with high career satisfaction is more highly

TABLE 49   *Men: interdependence with police by marital integration indices—county*

Police inter-dependence	Marital integration							Single men	No answer	No. of res-pondents	n
	0	1	2	3	4	5	6				
0	1	—	1	3	—	1	—	—	—	6	6
1	2	2	4	3	—	—	—	1	2	11	14
2	1	2	1	2	4	2	—	—	—	12	12
3	—	1	1	3	—	1	2	1	3	8	12
4	1	—	2	2	—	1	—	1	—	6	7
5	—	—	—	3	4	1	—	1	1	8	10
6	—	—	—	—	1	1	—	—	—	2	2
Unknown	—	—	—	—	1	—	—	—	—	1	1
	5	5	9	16	10	7	2	4	6	54	64

dependent on the police force for the fulfilment of his needs than a man with low career satisfaction, and to this extent the two measures overlap. But it does not necessarily follow that a man with high career satisfaction will also perceive the police force as being highly dependent on him, which is the other aspect of interdependence (cf. chapter 6). Nevertheless, the relationship between interdependence with the police and MI score was markedly similar to that between CS and MI score, though more akin to the pattern for the female than for the male relationship. The distribution of the scores suggests that while it was possible though less likely for a man to have low interdependence with the police and also a high MI score, a man with high interdependence with police score was almost certain to have a high MI score also. Again this suggests that county police work is at its most satisfactory for the policeman when he and his wife operate as a team, each giving the same degree of priority to the job. Although a policeman's marriage may be satisfactory when this is not the case, his perception of interdependence with the police force will tend to be low.

In the city where families were not directly involved in police work the correlation between MI and police interdependence scores was 0·2. There was no difference in mean police interdependence scores as between married and single me n(appendix IV, Table O).

These results suggest that in the county the following sequence may obtain between the three variables found to be related. Marital integration is largely determined by factors which have not been measured and which seem most likely to be unrelated to police work. Interdependence with the police is a function of a number of structural factors in the work situation (cf. chapters 6–7), but a very high IDP score in the county is more likely when MI is also high. It is suggested that this is because in these cases policing is seen as a shared task and responsibility. Thus the liabilities of a twenty-four-hour job are to some extent turned into a marital asset. There is also the feedback effect that if his wife enjoys the work and the shared responsibility, the man's dependence on the police force will be increased, in that an alternative career would be unlikely to provide either partner with similar gratifications. Conversely, when marital integration is low in the county, not only will this feedback effect be lacking, but the man on a rural beat may well find that the work in itself is less satisfying, and his career satisfaction as well as his interdependence with the police may tend to be lower.

In the county the demands made by the job on domestic life were considerable, so that a high MI was most probable when both partners were prepared to give equal priority to police work. Not all the wives with high initial marital integration would be prepared to do this; nor would all the couples be able to operate the required joint structure. Thus in certain cases marital integration might tend to be reduced.

In the city only a very slight relationship was found between IDP score and MI score, and no relationship was found between career satisfaction and MI score (appendix IV, Tables P and Q). The special type of joint family structure making for most satisfactory policing in the county was neither required nor possible in the city, where the usual urban separation between home and work prevailed. Joint family structures in the more usual sense were doubtless to be found, particularly among a group of people who had a background of high geographical mobility; but family structures in the general sense were not examined in the course of this study.

Practical difficulties in domestic life

Information was collected from the men and their wives with regard to some of the practical difficulties encountered as a result of their work. Not all of this information is systematic and complete, but it serves as a useful illustration of the statistical case made above. All those interviewed were asked questions as to particular sources of inconvenience, and a number of probes were given. Respondents

TABLE 50   *Men: particular causes of inconvenience*

	County		City	
	No.	*%*	*No.*	*%*
None				
Place posted	31	48·4	7	12·7
Timing of transfer	15	23·4	—	—
Other problems about transfers*	17	26·6	—	—
Callers/lack of privacy	7	10·9	—	—
Disruption of family life unspecified	4	6·25	4	7·3
Hours/never normal working day	13	20·3	24	43·6
Delays on duty/unpredictable incidents at inconvenient times. Unable to plan social or domestic life	41	64·1	27	49·1
Lack weekends/bank holidays/annual leave in school holidays	—	—	6	10·9
Shift work—general	—	—	7	12·7
Overtime and long hours	—	—	3	5·4
Night duties	1	1·6	1	1·8
Quick changeovers†	—	—	14	25·5
Training courses	4	6·25	1	1·8
DHQ duties	11	17·2	1	1·8
Lack of car allowance	7	10·9	—	—
Other	5	7·8	—	—
n	64		55	

*Inadequate notice; inability to make long term plans; cost of moves; continual uncertainty; number of moves.
†Shift change with only eight hours off between shifts.

were thus encouraged to complain and replies may not therefore be seen as indices of dissatisfaction. The snags were often seen as inevitable, and the work as offering many compensatory alternatives. Results for the men are given in Table 50. More than one item could be mentioned by each respondent.

The two forces differ widely. Only one cause of inconvenience—unpredictable incidents at inconvenient times—was mentioned to any great extent by men from the two areas. Although the results for 'hours/never normal working day' are both high, the problem with the hours for the county men was their unpredictability, while for the city men it was that the hours prevented them from being like other people and therefore they could not fit in with social or administrative arrangements. This is shown again by their emphasis on lack of weekend leave, holidays during school holidays, and so on.

Hours and factors connected with postings and transfers show up as the main causes of domestic disruption in the county. Reasons for the unpopularity of Hillbridge shifts and section station duties for the beat men have been discussed in chapter 2, and the problem of callers at the house in off-duty hours has been discussed both here and in Cain (1964). The further discussion in the last chapter of the nature of interdependence in rural areas makes the reason for the beat-man's resentment at being taken off his patch even more clear. These last two frustrations reinforced each other, in that callers at the house were particularly a nuisance when a man had just returned home from a fixed tour of duty somewhere else. In these cases he could not build his working days around the demands on him made by his parishioners, and most often he could not formally claim overtime either. Training courses also presented a problem in the county because they could involve leaving a wife alone on an isolated rural beat.

As in the county, city men focused their complaints on things which disrupted their private life. The two areas of complaints identified concerned the uncongenial hours and again unpredictable demands. In the city these latter took the form of calls which made the men late going off duty. This applied mainly to patrol-car crews.

The areas of complaint were in part a result of the structure of the interview, though freedom was given to express complaints on any topic. The fact that difficulties in getting car allowances (cf. Cain, 1964) were mentioned without probe in the county suggests that advantage was taken of this. Most of the results suggest tension between 'home and work'.

Inconvenience to wives

Wives' complaints were similar to those of their husbands though the emphasis was different. A number of them suggested factors connected with their husbands' night work as the major problem. These were being left alone at nights or (in the county) in the late evenings, and anxiety when their husbands were late off duty at night.

Factors concerned with moves are shown separately from factors concerned with the place to which the family was posted, although plainly the two are related. Difficulties concerned with physical isolation, where they occurred, seemed to be greater though not more frequent for the wives than for the men. In the city, under factors concerned with hours, the wives more frequently than the men spoke of problems arising from lack of weekend and bank holiday leaves, and inconvenient dates of annual leaves. In the county uncertainty was the cause of 'disruption of social life' rather than hours *per se* as in the city. In the county the men who did not work discretionary duties had hours which varied from week to week and sometimes from day to day in an entirely unpredictable way. They were known a week in advance, but even then were subject to last-minute alteration (see also chapter 2, pp. 40–2, 164–5).

Wives' responses in Table 51 have been grouped under the

TABLE 51   *Major cause of inconveniences—wives*

	County		City	
	No.	%	No.	%
Concerned with transfers	19	33·3	1	3·3
Place posted	10	17·5	1	3·3
Concerned with night duties, etc.	7	12·3	2	6·6
Concerned with home being police station and disruption of domestic life	6	10·5	1	3·3
Disruption of social life	7	12·3	3	10·0
Concerned with hours, etc.	—	—	14	46·7
DHQ duties	2	3·5	—	—
Leaves and holidays at different times from children and other people	—	—	6	20·0
Accommodation when retired	3	5·3	—	—
None	3	5·3	2	6·7
	57	100·0	30	100·0

heading of the *major* inconvenience experienced, and therefore total 100 per cent.[3]

Despite this long list of specific complaints a commonly expressed attitude on the part of the women was:

> It's part of the job—you get used to it after a time, don't you, and I don't expect anything else . . . but it can be disappointing. (County sergeant's wife.)

Or:

> You just get into a routine and can't bother about it; I fit my things in with whatever shift he's on. (City man's wife.)

The inconveniences were recognized but accepted like a rainy Sunday. But not all the women could manage this:

> I married him when he'd just come out of college. This isn't what I expected at all. I'm very dissatisfied . . . I must say the hours on this job are really appalling. (City wife.)

This woman's husband left the job after the end of the research period, although he had claimed that he liked the work itself.

One or two of the points on the above list need further illumination. Transfers and accommodation will be dealt with in the following chapter, since these concern important aspects of the power of senior officers. The inconvenience of the place of posting was mainly concerned with geographical isolation. Monthly payment by cheque or into a bank account presented a problem for people who lived at some miles from a bank. Rural primary schools were not always considered satisfactory. Shopping could be difficult, requiring a joint expedition to a town if village general stores carrying expensive and not always fresh stock were to be avoided. The 1962 and subsequent pay increases helped, in that thereafter most men could afford to run cars or vans, but wives who could not drive were still dependent on their husbands, with their uncertain duties, for help in this respect:

> There's one bus into the town but that leaves early in the morning and the return bus leaves [town] at 11.30 a.m. so that means you've only got three-quarters of an hour for shopping anyway.

Visiting relatives required a major expedition, yet was more necessary because of the loneliness of living in a village where even the most friendly maintained social distance because of status isolation.[4] The effect of the policeman's peculiar hours and duties on his domestic life is touched upon in various places in this book. But since this remains, despite all the changes, a crying problem for those involved, some of the points must briefly be reiterated.

On one-man beats the problem was the constant intrusions. On duty, off duty, leave day, no matter, licences were sought, thefts were reported, the telephone rang, some boys were being a nuisance, a passer-by stopped to ask the way, all the public-initiated activity went on, from sudden deaths through road accidents to an outbreak of swine fever or an obscured road sign. Policemen were called in from the garden, from their meals, from decorating, from games with the children, usually only for ten minutes, though often enough family outings had to be postponed or abandoned. Men felt obliged to go out for the day on their day off—the only way to be really off duty. But like most of us they wanted just to sit around and enjoy the comfort of their home in peace from time to time. This they could never be sure of doing.

For the wives the lack of predictability imposed the main strain. They could never bank on keeping an appointment or getting away on time; something might crop up. And in the cultural environment in which they moved, expeditions without the husband and father were 'not the same'. The other major problem for the beat wives was that callers continued even when their husbands were out, and they had at least to drop what they were doing and answer the door or phone, because 'it might be something serious and you'd never forgive yourself'. They conceived the police role at least as much in terms of the protection of life as of the detection of crime (which could wait).

In the country towns the problems arose from unpredictable shifts, split shifts, and the many late evening duties. I heard the same complaints in small towns on other divisions in the county force. Where only relatively few, say eight to a dozen, men were posted yet there was also need to keep the station open until 1.00 a.m. or 2.00 a.m. if not all night, this invariably happened. Complaints were mainly about the irregularity and unpredictability, even from day to day (though some sergeants managed to let their men know a week in advance, barring accidents), which ruled out any planned social or domestic activity. Because there was no routinized rota of duties, police families could not even plan their lives around the shifts. A particular day off could usually be arranged for a special reason by request, but this meant that the sergeant working out the duties had to regard the reason as legitimate, and he had to be informed—an intrusion on privacy.

In the city shifts *per se* were seen as detrimental to family life. Where county wives felt that just to know what one would be doing the week after next would be bliss, city wives found that second watch, first watch, nights, fortnight about, year in and year out, carried its own problems. It was fine when the children were little. The husband was at home in the day when they were up and about, could baby-mind while the wife went out, could take the family out on weekdays when roads were clear. But once the children started school they rarely saw their father, who was home only one weekend in seven, able to breakfast with them only two weeks in every six, and as often as not had his annual leaves during their school terms. City wives saw other families doing things together, complete units, and felt cheated of the companionship which they as married women were entitled to, and on behalf of their children who were similarly entitled to a father like the others. They also felt that for the children outings without father were not so much fun.

Some of the rural wives were bitter about being 'used' by the police force, in particular about messages which were not urgent being phoned through when it was known that the PC was out.

I don't see why we should be penalized just because with the children we can't get out.

In one case duties were phoned through to the section station and recorded there but messages were sent through from the sub-divisional station, so that there was no co-ordination with actual hours of duty. Some women could make a joke of callers coming while they were feeding the baby or baking, but many found the cumulative effect of these interruptions a considerable strain.

Children

Another cause of stress in the rural situation was the effect of the job on the children, and this again could have had a negative effect on marital integration. Half the county wives who answered this question (21 of 42) felt that transfers had had a deleterious effect on their children, either emotionally or academically. The percentage distribution of replies to the question about the effect of the job on the children (excluding those who did not answer) is shown in Table 52.

Some difference of opinion between the men and their wives in the

TABLE 52 *Effect of job on children (wives' opinions)*

	Positive No. %		Negative No. %		Neutral No. %		Total %	No answer/ not appli- cable
County	6	14·3	19	45·2	17	40·5	100·0 (n42)	15
City	10	35·7	5	17·9	13	46·4	100·0 (n28)	2

county is shown by the fact that only 15 per cent of the sixty married men said that the job had a negative effect on their children. The city figure was six of the forty-seven married men, or 12·8 per cent—more closely akin to the perceptions of their wives.

TABLE 53   *Men: opinion of the effect of job on children*

	Positive		Negative		None		Total married		Single men	Sample
	No.	%	No.	%	No.	%	No.	%		
County	9	15·0	15	25·0	36	60·0	60	100·0	4	64
City	11	23·4	6	12·8	30	63·8	47	100·0	8	55

More detailed analyses of these perceptions of the effect of the job on the children than that made in Table 53 are given in appendix IV, Tables S and T.

Marital integration and conflict solution

To what extent do policemen's wives and families influence their actions *qua* policemen? To what extent do police wives define their husband's roles for them, tell them what they are about? Their power compared with other role-definers will be examined in the final chapter. Here differences between men with high and men with low marital integration are examined. The particular marital integration scale used incorporated agreement as to roles but the behavioural aspects included did not relate closely to the husband's work. It thus just escapes being tautological to ask whether, in the hypothetical situations, men felt their wives would think they ought to take a *different* action from that which they chose, more frequently when marital integration was *low*, and vice versa. On the basis of the original propositions one would expect more men with high marital integration to resolve conflicts in the direction of the expectations projected by their wives.

Just as there were no differences between the forces in levels of marital integration, so there were no differences in responses to the conflict questions (Table 54). Eighty per cent of county men compared with 74·5 per cent of city men said that their wives would disagree with the action which they would take in at least one of the situations but the difference was not statistically significant.

When differences within forces between men with high and men with low marital integration are compared a more interesting picture emerges. No differences were found within the county force

TABLE 54   *Number of situations in which wife would disagree with action*

	0	1	2	3	4	Single men	Total
County	12	28	10	5	5	4	64
City	12	21	10	3	1	8	55

when the actions of men with high MI scores were compared with those for men with low MI scores. In the city, as was predicted, men with low marital integration said that their wives would disagree with their action more frequently than men with high marital integration. The differences are set out in Table 55.

TABLE 55   *Marital integration by situations in which wife would disagree with action taken—City Force*

MI index	0	%	1	%	2	%	3	%	4	%	Total married men
0–3	—	—	9	50·0	6	33·3	2	11·1	1	5·6	18 100·0%
4–6	5	45·4	4	36·4	1	9·1	1	9·1	—	—	11 100·0%
No infor-mation	7	38·9	8	44·4	3	16·7	—	—	—	—	18 100·0%

$\chi^2 = 10·2$

Summary

Conjugal relationships in the rural areas were found to be different from in the city. In the county marital integration (agreement as to roles and goals) was related to the career satisfaction of both husbands and wives, and to police interdependence for the men. It seemed that a special type of 'joint' relationship, in which the wife participated in the husband's work, was required in the county. In the city no such relationships were found.

Causes of domestic inconvenience in the county were predominantly transfers, unpredictability of hours, and, for the beat wives, constant intrusions. In the city the hours of work were the major problem; shift work and weekday leaves meant that activities as a family were almost ruled out, and annual leaves which fell during school terms did not help. More so than in the county, the women compared themselves with other families.

County wives felt that the job was damaging for their children, especially the frequent moves. County husbands did not regard this quite so seriously, but even so a quarter of them thought the job had predominantly negative effects. In the city far fewer of either men or women thought this.

In the city men with low marital integration felt that wives would disagree with their actions in significantly more situations than men with high marital integration. No such relationship was found in the county.

6 Interdependence with senior officers

I'm a very religious man myself. I pray every night before I go to bed: 'I love my chief superintendent and I hope he loves me'. (City constable.)

Introduction

Referring to a rigidly hierarchical organization it is scarcely necessary to point out that the lower levels are dependent on the higher levels, the latter having formal authority and a more or less equivalent degree of actual power. But the extent of this authority and power can vary between different hierarchies, even of the same broad type. Real power, as distinct from formal powers, is modified by the countervailing powers of the lower echelons. Any organization, therefore, constitutes an *interdependent* system. Both the degree of actual interdependence and the extent to which a state of inter-dependence is perceived by the participants can be subject to analysis and, perhaps, measurement.[1]

Duties of superiors

Senior officers (superintendents and chief superintendents)

The hierarchy of authority as it affected the men in the county was chief constable ⟶ deputy chief constable ⟶ divisional superintendent ⟶ two sub-divisional inspectors ⟶ five section sergeants ⟶ uniform constables. (For specialists it was more complex.) In the larger city force the hierarchy was longer. A chief superintendent was in charge of the division, under the deputy chief constable. Formally subordinate to the chief superintendent was the superintendent, and subordinate to him were three sub-divisional chief inspectors. On each sub-division there were four watch inspectors and subordinate to them were the sergeants and the constables.

In the county the superintendent was responsible for administration, discipline, the collection of statistics, and the manner of dealing with the input of work reports relating mainly to offences. He would also be expected to attend the scene of major crimes and other events. Similar responsibilities were shared by the chief superintendent and the superintendent in the city, though the definition of what constituted a major incident varied. The county superintendent was observed to attend a fatal road accident, the scene of a mysterious fire, and a serious breaking offence; the chief superintendent in the city was only seen by the researcher to attend a murder. 'Breaks', for example, were so commonplace in the city that his personal attention was neither possible nor regarded as necessary. The county superintendent also visited each beat station approximately once a year and section stations more frequently; the city chief superintendent was seen on only one occasion to visit a section station, following the re-capture of an escaped prisoner: in general it was easier for him to summon his senior officers to see him when necessary, though he did make visits to sub-divisional stations.

Intermediate ranks (inspectors and chief inspectors)

The duties of the chief inspectors in the city were similar on a smaller scale to those of the superintendents. Like the more senior officers they did not work fixed hours but had overall responsibility throughout the day. They were also expected to live in at the sub-divisional station (though one CI did not). The men were in more frequent contact with the chief inspector and could approach him or be approached by him without undue formality. One CI made regular use of the same canteen as the men.

Sub-divisional *inspectors* in the county had similar overall responsibilities to the *chief* inspectors in the city. They were expected to know their personnel since they had authority over the same body of men continuously. But they saw the men less often than city chief inspectors because of the distances to be covered. This applied to the inspector from the DHQ sub-division more than to the Hillbridge inspector, since the latter saw all the constables from his area when they came to do fixed duties in Hillbridge station. Inspectors attended the [scenes of most incidents above the merely trifling, though some section sergeants resented this. But county inspectors were accountable for whatever was done in their area and therefore felt it wiser to be present. On roughly one occasion in three an inspector or more senior officer would attend the monthly meeting of constables called by the sergeant on each section.

Inspectors in the city worked to a rota of four shifts, the three normal 'watches' for two weeks each plus a fortnight on relief. They 'paraded' the men before each shift, met them in the canteen and station office, advised them about their work as occasion arose, and were responsible for the allocation of the personnel on their 'turn'; they would usually turn up at more serious incidents and they also patrolled themselves. In the course of each shift the section station(s) on the sub-division would usually be visited. City inspectors also had responsibility for the monthly visit to licensed premises, made by constables in the county.

Thus city men saw far more of their inspector than county men, whereas for more senior officers the reverse had been the case. But the county inspector, because of his continuous and undivided responsibility, had greater power over the men.

Immediate superiors (sergeants)

The division of duties for sergeants as between city and county was similar. County sergeants worked a permanent geographical section and thus had continuous responsibility for the same body of men; city sergeants worked the same rota of four two-week shifts as the city inspectors. A county sergeant, therefore, had more sanctions at his disposal both in his direct influence on the working conditions of the men and in his position as intermediary with senior officers. County sergeants saw their men when they came to do section duties, at monthly section meetings or 'assemblies', at 'points' which were arranged on two sections, and when they attended special events or major incidents on the beat. Each beat man, however, contacted his sergeant daily by phone to inform him of his hours of duty, and other information could be exchanged at the same time. Sergeants also visited the beat stations to check and sign the various record books kept. They thus knew the families of the men as well as the constables themselves.

City sergeants saw more of their men while at work. They met them in the station before and after the shift, at refreshment breaks, when the men came in to write up reports, and outside when keeping points and dealing with incidents on the beat. But the sergeants' authority was limited by their regular shift changes and by the fact that when they were on duty the inspector, and possibly also the chief inspector, had greater responsibility for the same men and the same geographical area. In the city these more senior officers were on the spot to be consulted, whereas in the county they were distant and only the sergeant was readily accessible. City sergeants had to patrol as did constables in the course of their supervisory duties, and this, together with the overall responsibility of the watch inspector, tended

143

to place them in a similar work situation to the men under them. They tended, therefore, to operate as senior constables or supervisors, guiding and advising the recruits, but indulging in a number of the same forms of easing behaviour as the men under them.

Communication Patterns

Formal communication

In both forces each item of administration, whether related to such personal matters as, for example, uniform, housing, and leave or, on the other hand, reports concerning crimes or other offences, had to be passed from the constable up through the entire hierarchy, each rank appending a signature. There were a number of consequences of this formalized system of upwards communication.

In the first place, the inability to by-pass any rank except in very special circumstances was regarded in the city as something of a joke. This was so particularly for the intermediate ranks who were sometimes in the position of having to sign reports twice, in their own rank and in a higher 'acting' rank. Taking over each other's tasks in this way reduced the social distance between the ranks, in particular by removing the mystery surrounding the tasks and the incumbent of the rank above.

A second consequence of the same procedure was an increased awareness that power and authority attached to the office rather than the officer.

Neither of these two effects was apparent in the county where the responsibilities of a rank above were sometimes taken over but not the rank itself.

Most of the vertical communication passed upwards in this formalized way. This provided some shelter from possible negative sanctions for the men. If it were desired to keep some item of information from senior or even intermediate officers, it was relatively easy to avoid setting the formal process in motion.

Communication 'down' the hierarchy

Communication in the other direction, from senior officers to constables, was less frequent. Most 'informations' concerning the work were circulated centrally and entered in the 'message book' at each station. Communications from senior officers were, therefore, either instructions peculiar to the division—and here the communication would be written rather than verbal—or concerning matters peculiar to an individual officer or group of officers. On one occasion during the research period the chief superintendent held a divisional 'crime conference' attended by all CID men and uniform men of the rank of sergeant and above. In theory the purpose of this was an information interchange, but in fact information was issued by the chief superintendent and the chief inspector CID (chief DI) with only a few comments from the floor. The men subsequently claimed that little of the information was new to them. The fact that senior officers did not know that the information they were putting forward was common knowledge among the men in itself shows the inadequacies of the system of communication which existed. The senior officers' lack of direct control in the working situation was such that they were dependent on information fed up to them by the men or the intermediate ranks, not only about the on-going work but also about the actions which might have rendered the men liable to either reward or punishment.

The structural forces promoting illicit activities in the work situation and the necessity for keeping these secret from senior officers, coupled with the relative ease of doing so, meant that upwards communication was incomplete and often unreliable. It was often insufficient for adequate supervision or control. Downwards communication on the other hand was transmitted accurately and completely through the formal system but senior officers had little direct control over its application. Nor were they always in a position effectively to assess its relevance.

Informal communication

Less formal upwards communication in the main took place with intermediate superiors in the course of work contacts. Men were afforded 'protection' here by the physical distance of the sergeant in the county and by the relative invisibility of the constable in his work situation. In the city the intershift mobility of intermediate ranks helped to prevent the close contact between the ranks which might have led to verbal indiscretions on the part of a constable.

Informal communication with senior officers was possible at either sporting and social functions (gimmicks) or, for officers working at DHQ, by repeated occasional contact. For administrative and other specialist staff such contacts in the course of work were frequent. Constables not directly involved in these informal communication patterns saw them as a risk. The trouble with being at DHQ, they said, was that you couldn't trust anyone and you were 'too close to the gaffers'. Frequent informal contacts increased the risk that the PC might, even inadvertently, bring to the notice of senior officers such illicit behaviours as easing or infringements in dealing with offenders. An administrative officer or 'gaffer's driver' might be present at some informal canteen or snooker-room discussion and

145

subsequently 'drop' information from a beat man to a senior officer, probably in the course of ordinary conversation and without intending to. For the same reasons a man in the team for a sport particularly favoured by senior officers (the bowls team in the city and the rifle shooting team in the county) might be distrusted.

Perceived interdependence

A single 'interdependence with police force' index was used rather than twin indices for colleagues and senior officers. Unfortunately, the importance of this distinction *within* the force was not apparent at the pilot stage. However, one item in the 'dependence on force' scale concerned senior officers specifically (see pp. 303, note 2; 258; 281–2), and after being subjected to the Guttman scaling procedure this item was found to have the lowest cutting point. One could interpret this as meaning that dependence on senior officers was axiomatic for the men, and that if it were denied then dependence on the police force as a whole was negligible.

The relationship of interdependence scores with other variables will be examined in detail in the next chapter concerning relationships with colleagues. However, it is relevant here to point out that mean interdependence scores (Table 56) were higher in the city, 3·7 as against 2·6 in the county (sig. 0·01). City men in fact scored higher

TABLE 56   *Interdependence with police scores by force*

	0	1	2	3	4	5	6	No answer	Total
County	6	14	12	12	7	10	2	1	64
City	1	6	8	8	10	14	8	—	55

on both of the component scales on which the index scores were based (Table 57). For the 'dependence on the force' scale 38·2 per cent of city men scored twenty or more compared with 18·75 per cent of county men. For the perceived dependence of the force on ego (respondent) scale 90·9 per cent of city men scored twenty or more compared with 75 per cent of county men. Scores on the two scales cannot, of course, be compared. Total dependence on the force in the county was not determined by the objective power of senior officers, against which invisibility in the work situation was a strong defence. The county men tended to function independently and regarded themselves as less dependent on both colleagues and senior officers than their city colleagues.

TABLE 57 *Scores on constituent scales of IDP index*

	County				City		
	10–19	20+	NA	n	10–19	20+	n
Dependence of man on the force	51	12	1	64	34	21	55
Dependence of the force on the man	16	48	—	64	5	50	55

Dependence of men on senior officers

Discipline

When comparing two police organizations as in the present case the differences in formal authority are few. The chief constables had slightly differing powers,[2] in that in the city the watch committee had nominal control over matters of recruitment, promotion and discipline (cf. Critchley, 1967, p. 290). But, the force being too large for the committee to scrutinize each detail closely, effective control of matters relating to personnel remained firmly in the hands of the chief constable. Right of appeal to the watch committee against a disciplinary decision existed in the city, though the right to be defended at a hearing by a Police Federation spokesman seemed to be considered of greater importance.

Formal disciplinary powers were considerable, ranging from dismissal (involving loss of pension rights and home) through fines and stoppages of pay to a simple reprimand or caution. In most cases the penalty of dismissal was reserved for offenders who had been convicted of a criminal offence—though criminal traffic offences were not usually deemed of sufficient gravity to warrant this. The areas of behaviour circumscribed by formal police regulations were also many, off-duty behaviour being affected as well as behaviour at work (see appendix V, Discipline Code).

In the year of the research there was only one substantiated discipline charge in the county, the offence being 'living at an address without the approval of the Chief Constable'. Charges in the city between 1962 and 1966 were for offences as varied as 'idly gossiping' in a service station (neglect of duty), being late on duty or on other occasions such as court, making false statements in official documents, making false statements to colleagues concerning the 'moral character' of another officer, permitting a prisoner to escape, entering licensed premises while on duty, insubordination, and being convicted of criminal or other offences.

147

In other less formal ways the sanctions at the disposal of senior officers in the county were greater than those of their counterparts in the city. County men claimed that these informal sanctions were used in preference to the formal disciplinary procedure to avoid the necessity of recording charges in the annual report. Direct evidence on such an issue could not be obtained. However, the ratio of formal charges to men serving was considerably lower in the county area. In 1962 there was one discipline charge among 256 constables; none of the forty male sergeants then serving was found guilty on a discipline charge. There were no discipline charges in the force in the previous year. An examination of the records for the years 1962–6 inclusive in the city revealed an annual average of one discipline charge for every 57·1 constables and one for every 25 sergeants. The sergeants' figure was boosted by one man who was found guilty on five charges. As against this there was in the city one compliment or commendation per annum for every 1·8 constables serving, suggesting a more formalized system of rewards as well as punishments. These last figures are for the three years ending December 1962.

Promotion

The greater semi-formal powers in the county were in the two areas of promotions and transfers. In the county there were far more qualified men than could ever hope for promotion. Of the 260 constables in the force when my count was made in 1962, 112 had completed all the requirements for promotion, namely, they had served for the then minimum of four years, and had passed the two formal examinations (Table 58). Sixty-two men had passed in addition as much as they were allowed of the qualifying examination to inspector.[3]

On the research division, of the forty-five constables with four years' service or more, nineteen (42·2 per cent) were fully qualified for promotion, and of the twenty-four men with nine years' service sixteen (66·7 per cent) were fully qualified. Yet from 1950 to 1959, before the Royal Commission influenced retirement as it did temporarily while the research was going on,[4] there were in the whole force only three and a half vacancies for sergeants per year on average. This with 112 ambitious and qualified men waiting, and a constant replenishment of the pool as further men qualified.[5] The mean length of time since qualifying for promotion was 7·7 years. Thus in selecting from a large pool of equally well qualified men, senior officers had of necessity to fall back on particularistic and subjective variables as a basis for their choice. Inevitably in this situation there were allegations of unfairness and favouritism; more important, senior officers had the very real power of 'passing over' for promotion a man who had met with disfavour—and regardless of the use to which this power was put the men believed that a single relatively trivial mistake could ruin one's career prospects.

Senior officers in the city had a similar power of recommending for promotion, and there were indeed a few qualified men who were deemed unsuitable for personality reasons, but in general the relative shortage of qualified personnel meant that the onus of proof was reversed and that reasons for *not* promoting a man had to be very strong indeed. In the city only 18·0 per cent of the 194 constables serving on the research division (27·6 per cent of those with four years service or more) were qualified for promotion to sergeant, though the average number of years since qualifying, 9·4, was slightly greater than in the county (Table 58). Only eight (22·9 per

TABLE 58   *Constable—length of time since qualified for promotion to sergeant*

	Years						
	0 *and* under 5	5 *and* under 10	10 *and* under 15	15 *and* under 20	20 *and* under 25	25+	*Total* qualified*
County	27	60	16	6	1	2	112
City	7	16	6	3	2	1	35

*County: whole force   City: research division.

cent) of these qualified men had less than ten years' service. This suggests that the large bulk of them had been deliberately excluded from promotion because they were deemed unsuitable. In the city this required a conscious decision; in the county it was possible simply to promote someone else who was equally well qualified in objective terms.

In the city the same kind of feelings of dissatisfaction were apparent at the level of promotion from sergeant to inspector. But this had less effect on the overall attitude to senior officers because only those already promoted to the rank of sergeant were in a position to be subject to this need for approval based on particularistic criteria; and of those only twelve of thirty-four were qualified for promotion to inspector. This represents over a third (34·5 per cent) of sergeants, but the absolute figure was insufficient to influence the general perception of dependence on senior officers. In the county eighteen of the forty sergeants (45 per cent) were fully qualified for promotion to inspector.

As well as the chance of *ever* getting promoted, there are important sanctions attached to the speed of promotion. First, there is the negative effect that the longer a qualified man remains unpromoted the longer the sanctioning power of senior officers continues. This could be called the state of *dependent uncertainty*. This is a state in which a man has no direct control over some important aspect of his environment, this control being vested in visible power figures,[6] but at the same time the man perceives his contemporary actions to influence the prospects of changes in his environment by virtue of the visibility of these actions to those with power and authority over him: but the manner, direction and extent of this influence is unknown.[7]

The second possible effect of too long delayed promotion is that a man may 'lose heart', and allow interests outside the police force to predominate in his life. To avoid this effect—to perpetuate the state of uncertainty and therefore the power of senior officers—a number of 'late promotions' are regularly made, alternating with the promotion of short service men consequent upon increasing rationalization of the career structure. But scores on the police interdependence (IDP) index in the county (Table 59) indicate that despite this policy a stage is reached for men not promoted whether or not they are qualified at which disillusion, or at least a lessening of interdependence, with the police force sets in. I have here taken nine years service as the cutting point, since this is when maximum salary is reached.

The difference between long service men and others is signi-

TABLE 59   *Mean police interdependence scores by rank, qualification and length of service—county force only**

	No. of men	Mean IDP score
PCS under 4 years	9	2·7
PCS 4–9 years, not qualified	17	2·8
PCS 4–9 years, qualified	3	2·0
PCS 9 years and over, not qualified	7	2·2
PCS 9 years and over, qualified	16	2·3
Sergeants and above	10	3·0
Total	62†	

*For distributions see appendix IV, Table U.
†In one case qualification was not recorded, and in one case IDP score was unknown.

ficant at the 0·05 level. The mean length of service of sergeants and higher ranks was twenty-seven years so that, were length of service the relevant variable, their scores should have been more nearly akin to those of the long-service constables.

The third set of sanctions associated with the speed of promotion are the positive ones of a higher income and job status sooner, rather than later—and the earlier the promotion the bigger will be the income differential—and the increased probability in either force of a subsequent promotion if the first is relatively early.

Among men who had been promoted at least once, those in the county were kept in a state of 'dependent uncertainty' for longer than were their city colleagues. In the county

the average length of service of a constable when 'made up' was 15·8 years and no man . . . serving as a sergeant had been promoted with less than nine years service . . . [For inspectors the] average length of service on promotion was 22·8 years. On average, eight of these twenty-three years had been spent as a sergeant, the mean length of service when first promoted being 14·9 years . . . it is a significantly shorter period than for those who were not subsequently made inspector [0·05 level]. (Cain 1964.)

In the city the average length of service of sergeants on promotion was 12·0 years, eleven (31·4 per cent) of the men having been promoted with less than nine years service. Inspectors and higher ranks had been first promoted with an average of 11 years service, and further promoted to inspector with an average of 16·9 years.

Tables 60 and 61 both emphasize the much later promotion—and longer period of dependent uncertainty—in the county force.

As in the discussion of interdependence with the community, the point must be emphasized that although it is of interest and importance to examine the differences between the two forces—

TABLE 60 *Sergeants—length of service on promotion*

			Years			
	5 *and* under 7	7 *and* under 10	10 *and* under 15	15 *and* under 20	20+	*n*
County*	—	4	15	12	9	40
City†	2	13	11	8	1	35

*Based on data for whole force.
†Based on data for research division only.

TABLE 61 *Inspectors and higher ranks—length of service on promotion*

		Years					
		5 *and* under 7	7 *and* under 10	10 *and* under 15	15 *and* under 20	20+	*n*
County*	Promoted Sergeant	—	—	7	7	—	14
	Promoted Inspector	—	—	—	2	12	14
City†	Promoted sergeant	—	7	7	3	—	17
	Promoted inspector	—	1	4	9	3	17

*Based on data for whole force.
†Based on data for research division only.

particularly if behaviour is to be understood in terms of these differences—yet the similarities between the two forces are greater than the differences. Table 61, for example, shows that although there were differences in the period of dependent uncertainty, yet even in the city force the length of this period was by no means negligible. The power of senior officers in this respect was, therefore, considerable in both areas, though greater in the county.

Transfers

The difference in dependence between the city and the county was greatest in respect of transfers. In the city a man would usually be transferred to another sub-division only *after* formal disciplinary proceedings had been taken. That men who displeased senior officers were subjected to 'punishment moves' without such an official hearing was widespread belief in the county. There was no means of testing its validity, though it would seem not altogether unreasonable that a man should be moved from the area of jurisdiction of a senior officer with whom he did not see eye to eye. But for the men any move had one important element of punishment: it was usually considered unpleasant. And from the fact of its unpleasantness the men extrapolated the fact that it was also intended as a punishment if no credible alternative reason were presented to them. Transfers will be examined from the three points of view of frequency, punitiveness, and communications, and the discussion will concentrate on the county force where the problem was most extreme.

Frequency of transfers　　Table 62 shows number of transfers by rank and length of service. The mean number of in-service transfers was 3·1, excluding the two probationary constables still in their first post.

TABLE 62　*Number of in-service transfers—county force*

Transfers	Constables under 10 years' service	Constables 10 years' service and over	Sergeants	Inspectors	Superintendent	Total
1	14	1	—	—	—	15
2	9	4	—	—	—	13
3	5	8	2	—	—	15
4	1	6	1	—	—	8
5	—	2	—	2	—	4
6	—	1	3	—	—	4
7–10	—	—	1	—	1	2
11–15	—	1	—	—	—	1
	29*	23	7	2	1	62*

*Excludes two men in first post.

For all officers the average length of stay in any post was 3·4 years (Table 63). This figure is an underestimate since it includes the duration of the present posting. For men with upwards of ten years' service the mean number of transfers (one less than the number of posts held) was 3·7; for officers of the rank of sergeant and above the figure is 5·5 transfers per man, but these officers in general pointed out that moves on promotion were to their own advantage. A move for any other reason *could* be interpreted by the men as a 'punishment move'. However, if moves 'on promotion' are subtracted from the total moves of each ranking officer the mean number of moves for other reasons is 3·7 per man.[8] This would suggest that, so far from being detrimental to a man, a move is likely to be to his advantage in career terms. Officers who were subsequently promoted experienced no fewer moves than officers who retained the rank of constable. This is not the result one would expect if a move were usually a sign of disfavour.

TABLE 63 *Length of stay in post*

Years	Under 1	1, under 2	2, under 3	3, under 4	4, under 5	5, under 6	6, under 7	7, under 8	8, under 9	n
County	2	15	13	15	8	4	4	2	1	64

Punitiveness of transfers But the fact that a transfer is not a disadvantage in career terms does not mean that it is not punitive. Punitive as used in this section does not imply a conscious 'punishment' by senior officers; it refers to the unpleasant aspects of a transfer which are perceived by the men. Because of these, a transfer can be experienced as a punishment, even if this was not the reason for it. To appreciate the strength of the sanction involved it is necessary to bear in mind the evidence of chapter 4 showing the dependence of the country policeman and his family on the local community. The work itself will have less intrinsic satisfactions for a man immediately following upon a transfer. In his new beat he will have to create new bonds of trust with the local people, new opportunities for easing behaviour, and build up a new store of knowledge about the locality. It will be some time before local people in turn will come to him either to offer or to ask for assistance. In addition it will be necessary to build up a new social life in the community. But the man has a pre-established position in the new community to go to, even if his performance in that position will be subject to close scrutiny and appraisal. His wife has to start from scratch unless she wishes at all times to act in her role as 'the policeman's wife'. Even then she has to work for an acceptance which for the policeman is partially given. As indicated in the previous chapter, if her interdependence with the police is high she may well be able to cope with many of the disadvantages involved. But in either case she will have to leave behind an established friendship grouping and seek to create a new one in the new environment. For the children the situation is even more difficult. (A table showing number of children is in appendix IV, Table V.) They too will have to leave behind them friends and familiar surroundings; their education may also be disrupted (See Table 64). Eldest children aged eleven or more in the county had experience on average of 4·1 schools: the equivalent figure for city children was 3·3. But school changes in the city resulted from the children's or their parents' choice, and in any case did not involve leaving at the same time friendship groups based on the area of residence. In the county these children had on average had 2·2 school changes each *as a result of transfer* (Table 65). The picture becomes clearer if one looks at the extremes: 34·0 per cent

TABLE 64   *Number of schools of eldest children aged 11 years or more at the time of the study**

	No. of schools							Unknown	Not applicable	No. of respondents
	1	2	3	4	5	6	7			
County	1	1	3	10	5	3	1	1	32	57
City	—	3	2	2	—	—	1	—	22	30

*Information only from interviews with wives.

TABLE 65   *Number of school changes of eldest children aged eleven or more caused by transfer**

	No. of changes					Not applicable	Total respondents
	0	1	2	3	4		
County	1	5	8	8	3	32	57
City	5	3	—	—	—	22	30

*Information from wives.

of all first children in the county had attended five or more schools; this applied to only 12·0 per cent of city children (0·01 level); see Tables 66 and 67.

Another punitive aspect of a transfer is the expense and effort involved. An allowance of £30 was paid by the police authority on receipt of bills as evidence that that amount had in fact been spent, and the authority also paid the cost of removal. But a move usually involves re-decoration of the new house to suit the taste of the new incumbents. This may be done over a period, and the man will not, in this case, receive compensation. Apart from this, curtains, carpets and other fittings will have to be altered, and garden produce will

TABLE 66   *Number of schools of first child**

	0	No. of schools							Unknown	Not applicable	Total respondents
		1	2	3	4	5	6	7			
County	19†	7	5	3	10	5	3	1	1	3	57
City	7	2	12	1	2	—	—	1	—	5	30

*Information from wives.
†Under 5s plus one handicapped.

155

TABLE 67 *Age of eldest child**

	No children	Age: Under 5	5 and under 11	11 and under 15	15 and under 18	18 +	Total respond- ents
County	3	18	11	10	3	12	57
City	5	8	9	4	2	2	30

*Information from wives.

have to be left behind. New school uniforms will have to bought. Lack of standardization in design of police houses exacerbates the problem; at the time of the research there were eight police houses in a cluster in the county DHQ town, with five different designs.

It will be apparent from this that a single move is unpleasant in its effects. The degree of punitiveness is also influenced, however, by the frequency with which moves have been experienced in the past. In particular this will apply to emotional problems associated with a move. Stress experienced by wives or children as a result of frequent moves was reported by a number of men, but figures on this were not systematically collected. Again, the expense of one or even two moves in the course of a career of twenty-five years or so could readily be absorbed; it is when a man reports five moves in a period of eighteen months (exceptional but known to happen) that these more practical aspects too begin to present serious difficulties. Wives in the county reported an average of 3·6 houses each since marriage or their husband joining the force. In the city the wives had lived in 1·9 houses on average (Table 68).

TABLE 68 *Wives—number of houses since married or husband joined police force*

	No. of houses									
	0	1	2	3	4	5	6	7	Unknown	Total
County	—	3	14	14	6	9	4	4	3	57
City	1	7	9	3	1	—	—	—	9	30

Communications in relation to transfers If the communication system were better a number of the practical disadvantages of a transfer could have been ameliorated. To a large extent the men lived in a Kafkaesque nightmare in which decisions about them were made on the basis of criteria which they did not know; they felt that those decisions which were ultimately communicated to them, such as that they were to transfer, represented only the tip of an iceberg—that an irreversible assessment about each had probably been made at 'headquarters'. That senior officers paid this much attention to the personality and potential of each of their subordinates is unlikely: the important point is, however, that belief in the existence of such as assessment was strong. And the behaviour of the authorities in relation to transfers did little to dispel belief in a set of criteria which were either completely arbitrary or, even if rational and consistent, completely secret from the men.

The first uncertainty in relation to transfer concerned the duration of the stay in any posting or in any house. This was impossible to predict, and particularly after a period of two or three years a man would begin to wonder as to the wisdom, for example, of indulging in any new expenditure on improving the house; it might remain his home for a further ten years after this; alternatively, he might be moved within a month. Examples were cited in which senior officers had given 'guarantees' to men that they would not be moved—in one case a man bought his own accommodation as a result—only to be followed within a few months by an order to transfer against which there was no appeal save to leave the force, or at best to get oneself 'labelled' as a 'trouble-maker'. County men (if married) had been on average 3·1 years in their present house, compared with 5·3 years for the city men (Table 69). One-quarter of men in the

TABLE 69   *Wives—length of time in present house*

	Years											Un- known	No. of respond- ents
	0+	0·5+	1+	2+	3+	4+	5+	6+	7+	10+	15+		
County	11	3	11	9	10	4	3	1	2	3	0	—	57
City	1	2	2	2	7	1	0	1	1	3	1	9	30

county had lived in their present house for less than one year compared with one-seventh of city men. *As in the case of promotions, county men were kept in a position of dependent uncertainty.*

The second failure in communications in relation to transfers was in the manner in which the men were told of these moves. This has two aspects. A gross lack of cencern was shown by the shortness of the notice given. Again systematic information was not collected on this point, but the amount of notice of transfer given varied in those cases cited from two months, which seems reasonable, to two days, which clearly is unreasonable. A transfer could be postponed for a matter of weeks in extenuating circumstances, though the only cases which fell into this category appeared to be the terminal stages of pregnancy on the part of a wife, or having a newly born child.

Single men were moved with even greater despatch. One man had less than twenty-four hours' notice before his move to the research division. Duty at the old post ended at 2 a.m.; duty at the new post (thirty miles away) began at 3 p.m.; packing up and changing digs was an incidental necessity.

Even more important than inadequate notice, the men were not given reasons for their moves. An interview with the divisional superintendent or even the chief constable could be requested to ask for an *explanation* (the actual *cancellation* of a move was unheard of at this stage). But there was a widespread belief that at such an interview one was fobbed off with spurious 'reasons', the real reason being either punishment, malice, or inefficiency. Men who had undergone specialist training courses, sometimes with exceptional success, pointed out that their skills were wasted if they were moved to a post which carried no specialist responsibilities. In the four and a half months of intensive observation two such transfers of specialists from the division took place; no doubt there were sound administrative reasons for these, but neither the researcher nor the men involved ever learned what these were. In one case a man had been posted because he was told that his specialist skill was required in his reception area. This information was elicited at an interview with the chief constable which the man had requested. He had already experienced a series of four moves in relatively quick succession. After a few months in his new area he was moved out of the specialist department on to normal beat work. Not surprisingly, he confronted his divisional superintendent with the remark, 'What's the excuse this time then, sir?'

Accommodation

In both the city and the county areas the police force, through its senior officers, could have power over the fate of a man's whole family through the allocation of police housing. In the city this tended to end a few years after a man's marriage, when he was finally allocated a permanent family home. In the county the two issues of accommodation and transfers were inextricably linked, and the power therefore persisted throughout a man's service. Only 1·9 of the men whose wives were interviewed in the county owned their own homes; 16·7 per cent of them did so in the city. Half of the wives in the city and 42·3 per cent of them in the county expressed themselves satisfied with the structure of the house (Table 70). Excluding those who had their own homes and those who expressed no opinion, as well as those who expressed general satisfaction, 48·1 per cent of county wives expressed dissatisfaction with their present house or with its condition, as compared with only 13·3 per

TABLE 70   *Wives—opinion of present accommodation (structure)*

	County	City
Own house	1	5
No opinion/don't know	9	5
Like it, satisfied	22	15
Structural defects:		
age/damp	6	2
size	4	1
design	8	—
Bad condition on arrival	6	—
Noise from other flats	1	1
Enjoy garden	—	1
Total	57	30

TABLE 71   *Wives—opinion of present accommodation (situation)*

	County	City
Own house/no opinion expressed	28	8
Physically isolated	9	2
Satisfactory compared with others or previous experience	6	5
Unsatisfactory compared with previous experience	—	1
Lack of privacy/gossip	4	3
Dislike living near men from other departments	2	1
Dislike area, type of people	2	10
Like it, get on well	2	—
Don't know	4	—
Total	57	30

cent of city wives. On the other hand, only one-third of county wives complained about the situation of their house (15·8 per cent of them complained of physical isolation) compared with 56·7 per cent of city wives (Table 71). One-third of the city wives were anxious for a fairly immediate move, and of course dependent on the senior officers to provide this. As one city PC said: 'So long as you're in

F*

one of their houses you've lost that bit of independence and they've always got that over you.' In the city, home ownership was seen as an ultimate way out, with the rent allowance helping to pay off the mortgage. Transfers over long distances precluded this for county men.

The work situation

Power of senior officers in the actual work situation was limited in both areas by the low visibility of the men while at work. In the county senior officers were responsible for the allocation of duties which took the beat men away from their 'patch'; this affected their relationships with the local community and, therefore, indirectly affected all their work on the beat. In the city allocation of tasks was delegated to the watch inspectors (intermediate superiors).

Rewards

A positive sanction at the disposal of senior officers concerned the disposition of places on training courses. Subsequently, favoured postings, such as to the cars instead of the beat, were made by the inspectors. Again, in the city more senior officers in consultation with specialist personnel were responsible for the allocation of attachments and particularly favoured postings such as a twelve-month period with the plain clothes section. As already indicated (chapter 3, pp. 72–5) specialist postings of this type not only had intrinsic job interest but also constituted one type of official easing in so far as one of their main effects, was to reduce the monotony of the work. Senior officers' powers of reward as well as punishment were therefore of considerable importance.

Dependence on immediate and intermediate superiors

Because of the wide range and strength of the sanctions, both positive and negative, at the disposal of senior officers, men 'on the ground' were in an extremely vulnerable situation. There were a number of situations in which they were dependent on their immediate and intermediate superiors to insulate them from punishment or to ensure that they received appropriate rewards. Sergeants and inspectors could also affect their work by the allocation of duties.

The three main defences against the negative powers of senior officers were secrecy and invisibility, the support of the colleague group, and the support of intermediate and immediate superiors. The last defence was particularly apparent in the city where easing behaviour was more necessary in order to make the job tolerable and where the perception of the community as segmented made legal infringements against various out-groups more common.

Support in extra-legal situations

Men were dependent on their superiors to protect them from sanctions when allegations were made against them by members of the public either in private or in the court room, and this maintained whether or not the allegations were true. It was recognized that a policeman acts on his own authority and must accept full responsibility for his actions—but it was also recognized that a word in support from an intermediate or senior officer could prevent the matter going any further. If an inspector says, for example, that the use of physical violence in a particular situation was both justifiable and necessary—either to effect an arrest or because the constable was defending himself—then it is unlikely that his word coupled with that of the officer concerned will be called into question. The alternative would have been for the inspector to accept the complaint and arrange for an investigation. Men pointed out (and the truth or falsehood of this assertion will not be argued here) that it was impossible to do their job 'to the book'.[9] This applied particularly in the questioning of suspects, where the goals were in part organizationally set. The importance of improving the clear-up rate by persuading an offender to have an offence 'taken into consideration', for example, has already been emphasized (pp. 52–3 and Lambert 1969, 1970). The assertion also applied where the goals were set by the men. To bring in a few prisoners for drunkenness made the job interesting and was a form of easing behaviour. That quarter of offenders arrested for drunkenness who had no fixed abode, for example (see p. 67), would be particularly vulnerable here. If the man resisted arrest on the grounds, for example, that he was not being disorderly, force would have to be used and this would be initiated by the constable. Another member of an out-group came to grief in the following encounter:

> I was in trouble because I hit a Jamaican with my stick in his
> house, and I charged him with assaulting the police and I got
> witnesses to prove the assault and I got them to sign the
> charge sheet. They were civvie witnesses and they charged him
> with me. And the inspector said he was drunk and wanted me
> to charge him with drunk and disorderly but I stuck to my
> guns and it turned out I was right because he cross-served
> assault charges on myself and the sergeant and if we'd only
> done him for drunk we'd have been in trouble over that. (PC.)

This shows dependence on the inspector in two ways. First, for advice—a less experienced policeman might have done what the inspector said and 'come unstuck'; second, to receive the charge and support the man in putting the report through to senior officers. If an office constable, sergeant or inspector refused to accept a charge, on some occasions the constable might be in trouble for making an unlawful arrest.

Intermediate and immediate superiors were in a position to know most of what went on in the stations if not elsewhere. The men were, therefore, also dependent on them not to notice certain infringements, such as when a prisoner who was methodically breaking the glass in the cell windows was quietened by a group of men—by means unknown. Or again, as an inspector said of a PC who had in fact been hit by a coloured man:

> But then, from the charge-room to the cells he had a chance to get his own back and I don't blame him . . . I'd do the same. These people have got to be taught, you see.

Another set of infringements of which the immediate superiors often shared knowledge with the men and to which they gave their support concerned the recording of offences. In order to retain a high clear-up rate, it was necessary that as many offences as possible should be written off as 'no crime' or, failing this, recorded as relatively trivial offences. In the latter group would be offences of housebreaking at which nothing was stolen; one such attended by the researcher was 'written off' as damage to the front door—a non-indictable offence. Gas and electricity meter breaks were not recorded at all if nothing was stolen, and otherwise recorded as simple larcenies rather than breaks even if the premises had been entered.

But from recording discrepancies of this kind there was little danger of 'comeback' from either senior officers, members of the public or insurance companies. In the case of assaults, the situation was different. Again, the PC dealing with the case was partially dependent on the inspector for advice as to the charge. In the following example a man had hit his wife with a poker during a domestic fracas, and the wife had been taken to hospital. An area-car crew had dealt with the incident, but since it was potentially serious the watch inspector, quoted below, had also attended.

> Like tonight, this is a wounding, but it won't be a wounding,
> I don't think it's bad enough. And you'd be cluttered up; you
> haven't got the time . . . but then suppose that something goes
> wrong and there's compression of blood on the brain and she
> dies or something, I've got to carry the can then. I'm on my
> own. But they'd soon shout if I made everything that came into

wounding. But they'd want to know why I hadn't crimed it, and I'd have to get out of that one, see.

This also shows that the inspector, in insulating his subordinates, is placing *himself* in a vulnerable position. Another incident of a similar kind was observed. In this second case the wounded person was found next day to have a fractured skull, and again no crime had been recorded. The inspector later said that he had 'squared it', though how was never made exactly clear.

Progress reports

Dependence on immediate superiors in this respect is greatest for probationary constables. A report on each probationer is submitted monthly by a sergeant, and a succession of bad reports could lead to dismissal. Dependence here is greater too in the county where a man is responsible only to one section sergeant over a long period. In the city, where the sergeant changes every six weeks, a bad relationship with one sergeant can speedily be compensated for by a later good one. Reports were made annually on men of all other ranks.

The reward system

Formal rewards of compliments, commendations and merit stripes—often accompanied by a small financial reward—were highly prized by the men, though in the city there were complaints that these were now given for first-aid prowess and other activities which did not constitute, in the opinion of the men, 'real police work'. Another complaint made was that the number of these awards was not taken into account in decisions concerning promotion. These questions were less often raised in the county; they were less relevant as the reward system was less formalized and a commendation was a rare occurrence. For the three years ending December 1962 there was an average of $109 \cdot 3$ compliments or commendations each year in the city division. This is an average of one such formal reward for every $1 \cdot 8$ constables. In the county force no such formal rewards were recorded for this period. The importance of formal rewards in the city comes through in the following extract in which a PC speaks. A merit stripe is the highest award in the force.

I was thrilled when I got mine like. I mean, everyone who joins as a pro-con. thinks . . . well . . . I mean, when I was a pro-con. I never thought I'd get a merit stripe, but everyone who joins would like to, you know. But I never thought I would. Only I was lucky really; I mean, well, I'd had quite a run of felons like. I mean, mine was for police work. But

I'll never forget. When I walked on to parade that day they all started clapping and I thought, well, I might have got an award or something. I mean, I never dreamed I would, you know. When they told me yes, I was thrilled, yes.

In both forces it was necessary that a man be 'put forward' by his immediate superior in order for him to be considered for such an award. Senior officers could not themselves initiate the proceedings, though they could encourage a sergeant to put in a recommendation. But in general only the immediate superiors would know the full extent and value of a man's work, and if they failed to make a recommendation there would be no formal recognition or reward.

Immediate superiors could also reward by putting favourable comments on a report so that this would come to the attention of senior officers. Here the actual rewarding ability is in fact indirect, rather similar to the insulating function with regard to negative sanctions, since the ultimate power to reward rested with the senior officers.

Working conditions

The section sergeant in the county had considerable control over the working conditions of his men. This resulted largely from the regular need of men on one-man beats to incur overtime. A section sergeant could instruct a man as to when he should take hours off in lieu of overtime, or he could accept or reject a man's own proposals as to the most convenient time for him to do this.

In the small towns senior officers had direct control over the hours the men worked and were also responsible for the allocation of specific tasks.

Table 72 shows how the authority to allocate duties could be used. The power attached to it was considerable, since a high proportion of late duties could mess up completely a man's domestic life.

From these figures it would seem that allegations made against R and T that they received favoured treatment were justified. T was in part excused for this by the men since he was on call each night by telephone. R had no such excuse, so although his hours of duty approximated more nearly to those of the other men, he remained unpopular. In a similar way S was singled out for particularly *un*favourable treatment.

In the city the regular rota of three main shifts reduced this power, though duties of single men in particular were sometimes changed if there were a shortage of manpower on a particular shift. Inspectors in the city had the power of agreeing to a man taking 'time off in lieu of overtime', but since these requests were almost invariably

TABLE 72 *Proportionate distribution of hours of duty worked by the men*

	Days (up to 8 p.m.)	Evenings (after 8 p.m. up to midnight)	Time of ending shift Short nights (after midnight up to 3 a.m.)	Nights (up to 6 a.m. or 7 a.m.)	No. of shifts
	%	%	%	%	
P	31·5	12·9	27·8	27·8	54
Q	32·7	13·8	25·9	27·6	58
R	48·7	5·4	21·6	24·3	37
S	29·5	19·7	8·2	42·6	61
T	46·5	37·9	13·8	1·7	58
U	30·5	5·1	33·9	30·5	59
W	33·4	1·6	28·6	36·5	63
Totals	37·4	12·3	24·6	25·7	390

acceded to, the power was not experienced as oppressive. Watch inspectors were also responsible for the allocation of personnel to a particular station on the sub-division, those needing closer supervision tending to be posted to the sub-divisional headquarters. But again custom played a large part in this distribution of manpower, so that senior officers exercised these powers only if forced to do so by circumstances such as a particular shortage of manpower at one station or after the behaviour of a particular constable had been brought to their attention. Following a formal discipline charge, however, a man would customarily be posted to a different subdivision.

Inspectors controlled the work situation of men working from sub-divisional headquarters directly in some cases—a man could be posted to 'the straight' (a particularly boring beat) as a kind of informal punishment; again, as one man at DHQ pointed out, 'We have nine-to-fives (days) in turns after first watch; it's a thoughtful inspector.' Officers of sergeant and inspector level varied in the extent to which they were prepared to turn a blind eye to informal easing behaviours or to create opportunities for semi-formal easing such as the 7 a.m. 'tea warmer' in the back of the station. Provision of formal easing opportunities was at the discretion of the intermediate officers; but again the negative power had largely fallen into abeyance since these were usually granted.

Welfare

It was frequently stated in both areas that the police force are 'very good about real welfare'. By this the men meant that duties would be changed to allow for such things as hospital visiting when a member of the family was ill or in some other domestic crisis, and, as has been noted, transfers could be delayed for reasons of this kind. On the other hand, it was noted in the city especially that senior officers were closely and paternalistically involved in the private lives of the men. Privacy was exchanged for these welfare considerations. A man with 'domestic trouble' (quarrelling seriously with his wife) was given a week's leave; the wife of another man was visited by a chief inspector in his absence for similar reasons, and the CI subsequently 'had a word' with the man about the state of his domestic affairs. In another case a man was asked by an inspector whether he thought it wise to spend so much of his *off-duty* time drinking, and in both forces cases were quoted where a man had been advised to do his leisure time drinking in a particular public house or in the police club. One man, whose wife's ill health prevented him from moving, was a little perturbed that the inspector found it necessary to go and see *her doctor* in person. Responses of the men to this paternalism varied, but however it was received it was apparent that the intermediate officers were *assuming* powers and responsibilities over a wide area of the men's lives.

Miscellaneous 'backing'

The number of situations in which intermediate and immediate superiors could assist their men, or prevent them from getting into trouble with either senior officers or members of the public, was myriad and their variety endless. Two examples may serve to indicate this range of possibilities. In the county there was considerable difficulty about getting a mileage allowance when a PC used his private car for police purposes. A sergeant could facilitate this process if he told the superintendent that he had instructed the man to use his car, or by saying that he felt the use of the vehicle had been necessary. In the city a sergeant could 'cover' a man if he, for example, failed to keep a point for any reason; alternatively, if the reason were not a valid one he could, though he probably would not, report the man.

Dependence of superiors on the constables

Information

Senior officers were dependent on the men serving under them first because they were themselves accountable for what was done on the division and they therefore required both that the men should do what was necessary and that they should tell them through the formal communications system that it had been done. If the chief constable wanted parking offences reported rather than cautioned on the spot the senior officers could communicate this to the men but *they could not enforce the practice.*[10] A man who appeared not to comply might be denied favourable treatment, but he could not be formally disciplined. *For these reasons such a request carried most force in the county where the informal sanctions were more important than the formal ones.* But in both areas the men were protected by their low visibility, by the fact that essentially they worked as individuals and it was virtually impossible to *prove* that they had overlooked anything.

In the second place senior officers were dependent on the men and the intermediate officers to feed them with the information necessary to carry out much of their work, especially the supervision. Again they were not in a position to observe for themselves.

Restraint and discretion

Intermediate superiors were partially dependent on the men in this way, too, but there was also an informal bargaining process. Intermediate superiors indulged in similar forms of easing behaviour to the men. These were known to the men, though they were not often directly observed by them. Similarly intermediate superiors did not spy on the men, though they usually felt obliged to report easing behaviour should a man be caught in the act. Sergeants in this respect were most closely dependent on the men since they might often, for example, call in at a public house in the company of one or more constables.

Sergeants, and particularly inspectors, were also dependent on the men in relation to legal infringements. They would usually support their men otherwise they might find that little work was done on their shift and they might themselves be questioned as to why this was so—*but they depended heavily on the men not to leave them in too vulnerable a position.*[11] If support was expected, then the demands could not be too great since the inspectors were themselves subject to disciplinary procedures. A tale was told (indicative though possibly apocryphal) of an inspector who lost his rank and was disciplined for covering his men for drinking on duty when knowledge of this was brought to the attention of senior officers from another source. Another inspector, who helped some men on a discipline charge by keeping them informed of what was going on in relation to the charge within the CID and at the top of the hierarchy, was reported to have been transferred to a 'backwoods' sub-division from whence any further promotion was unlikely. Finally, when a charge was accepted the intermediate superiors were largely dependent on the judgment of the men on the ground if it was decided not to record an offence. In return for this restraint backing would be given where it was mutually deemed to be necessary.

Efficiency

The formal accountability of intermediate officers, coupled with the impossibility of constant direct control and the expectation from below that intermediate superiors should 'carry the can' and 'cover' the men when necessary, meant that intermediate superiors were also dependent on the men to perform their normal duties with reasonable efficiency. The risks for an inspector attendant on non-performance of a routine task by an office constable are shown by the following extract. The inspector said that he was in the cart over the accident. A complaint had come in that a lorry was standing by the road, left there with no lights, but they had done nothing about it.

> We hadn't got the men as they were all tied up. If anyone was
> at fault it was (the office constable) at Maypole. He didn't tell
> the PC who was going out on that area . . . Then later on in
> the evening there was a bad accident there. A Ford Consul
> hit it and two people were seriously hurt.

Senior officers quite reasonably wanted to know why no action had been taken to move the lorry earlier in the evening, which would have prevented the accident. The inspector was not allowed by the informal rules governing his relationship with the men to give the real reason, namely, that the office constable had forgotten to mention it. He had either to accept responsibility himself and render himself liable to reprimand or, as in this case, to seek to evade the issue, using here the shortage of men as an excuse.

Processes of bureaucratization

Both police forces were undergoing rapid change in the direction of increasing rationality in organizational structure. This helps to explain a number of the overtly expressed attitudes of men to senior officers and vice versa. For older constables in particular, normative expectations as to the behaviour of senior officers were based on a system which now no longer existed. In the city re-organization had been such that even the formal outlines of the structure had been changed. In 1952 sergeants and inspectors ceased to have individual responsibility for sections and sub-divisions and began to work shifts. Actual and perceived interdependence between ranks were influenced by these changes.

(i) One of the consequences of increasing scale and rationalization has already been indicated in this chapter, namely, the vesting of power and its legitimation in the office rather than the officer. Factors influencing this process in the city were identified as:

(a) the relative remoteness of senior officers so that their unique personal characteristics were not directly apparent to the men;
(b) the interchangeability of personnel between adjacent ranks, shown by the practice of 'acting' a rank above one's own to cover manpower shortages;
(c) the interchangeability of intermediate and immediate superiors as a result of working shifts.

(ii) Another aspect of bureaucratization already mentioned and associated with this was the *de-sacralization* of senior officers, and consequent reduction of social distance.

(iii) A third aspect already dealt with is the more rational and formalized system of rewards and punishments in the city. These followed publicly and more or less automatically upon information concerning a good or bad action being fed into the formal upward communication system.

(iv) There was rationalization of the promotion procedures. Again this had progressed farther in the city than in the county where particularistic criteria still played a large part in selection for promotion and the passing of the official examination was simply a pre-requisite for consideration. However, both forces were affected by the newly introduced rapid promotion schemes,[12] though the anxieties consequent upon their introduction were greater in the county where it was feared that the limited vacancies would be expropriated by these young men, and that because of their youth the promotion ladder for others would be blocked for years to come. A second feared consequence of the new system was that those promoted would have no understanding of the rigorous demands and informal codes of behaviour of ordinary beat work. They would want to work 'to the book', since they would not realize the 'impossibility' (from the constable's standpoint) of this. Men would thus no longer be able to expect 'backing'. In the city resentment was mostly directed at rapid promotion to inspector.

(v) The change in the career experiences of those promoted is linked with the next characteristic of bureaucracy to be identified. This is an increase in 'rules orientation', which implies what was known to the men as 'working to the book' and the invocation of sanctions on those who did not. Loss of knowledge of and opportunity to identify with beat norms and practices is one factor in this; loss of personal authority is another; the existence of similar processes in the external environment and consequent demand for accurate statistical records is another. The increasing divorce of those 'on the ground' from those at the top was self-perpetuating, as the beat men closed their ranks in self-defence against the threats to their mode of operation produced by the rules-orientated system. They therefore fed even less relevant information into the upwards communication system, with the result that the gulf continued to widen.[13]

(vi)   Related again to this point is the increasing desire of senior officers for a more rational control system (cf. Meyers, 1962). Their loss of *rapport* with the men on the ground, coupled with the loss of their personal authority, plus the environmental pressure for records (experienced as a demand from the top of the police hierarchy on which they themselves were dependent), led them to seek for a *quantifiable* means of assessing the merits of their men and their relative efficiency. The one they chose corresponded with the most favoured police self-image of a body of men devoted to catching dangerous criminals. Numbers of criminals caught can readily be counted. With the proliferation of Road Traffic Acts a further set of measurable end products in the form of offence reports was readily available and added to the quantifiable material. In the county especially the men complained of an increasing emphasis on the reporting of offences. They saw this as an encroachment on their valued autonomy and as potentially damaging to their relationship with the local people, since it removed one of their bargaining counters. Although the sentiment was often echoed in the city, the remark of a county sergeant perhaps best sums up this section:

> Those chaps who go putting reports in all the time, that's not police work at all. You could send a child down to stand on the corner and make a note of all the people who went past without rear lights, couldn't you . . . ?

(vii)   Specialization is perhaps the most obvious sign of increasing bureaucratization in the police force. This complexity had serious disadvantages. One was the bad horizontal communication between departments, sometimes consciously induced, as when relations between CID and uniform personnel became strained. Another was the ambiguity of allegiance. It led to inefficiencies caused by hesitancy and uncertainty in the carrying out of instructions. This was experienced mainly by men in the smaller specialist departments which did not have their own hierarchy to parallel that of the main body of the force. Mobile patrol men in the county complained of their dual allegiance to senior divisional officers and to the traffic and communications department at headquarters. In the city the most complex organizational structure was that of the dog section (Figure 1), and the problems were accentuated by the fact that dog men carried out normal patrols from police stations in company with other uniform men, though they had what appeared to be certain privileges. The 'dog sergeant' on the division occupied a bridge position, and was described by the dog inspector as a liaison officer between the division and the specialist department.

FIGURE 1   *Chain of command of dog section—city force*

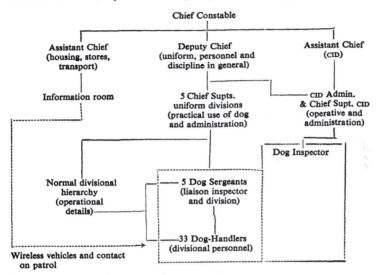

(viii) The development of a formal representative organization (the Police Federation) as a necessary defence against increasing bureaucratization (Lockwood, 1958) had proceeded further in the city. In the county it was still regarded as rather 'dangerous' to speak one's mind too publicly—though there was not much evidence that this was so—and as a result of this the federation was considerably emasculated. At a meeting of the joint branch board it was decided in the case of every matter raised that the best means of achieving the desired objective would be an informal verbal approach to the chief. In the city, by contrast, it was announced that a total of eighty formal letters had been sent to the chief in the course of the year. Eight of them were sent from the meetings[1] attended. The city federation played an important part in defending men on discipline charges, and at the time of the study was awaiting the outcome of a series of recommendations concerning improvements in efficiency which had been submitted to the chief. The county federation was not held in very high esteem by the men, but there was considerable interest in its activities which were felt to be directly related to real problems; in the city federation officials spoke of the customary problem of apathy among the vast membership.

Attitudes of sergeants to men

Contacts between senior officers and men were not sufficiently frequently observed for generalizations to be based upon them, and only three senior officers (two inspectors and the superintendent in the county) were interviewed. Sergeants, however, were interviewed in both forces, and a number of informal discussions were held with city inspectors. It is therefore possible to make some suggestions about their views of interdependence.

Overtly expressed attitudes of sergeants could be classified under the headings of paternalistic, instructional, autocratic and protective. The categories are not discrete in themselves; also each of the attitudes but the autocratic was seen in all the sergeants. Snatches of conversation or incidents typifying each of these attitudes are presented from a total of 408 items in my field diary indexed as 'attitude of superiors to men' or 'relationship with superiors'.

Paternal

County P.C.:

> 'I don't suppose I have time to eat, sarge?' 'Oh yes, boy, you go home and get your dinner, then.' 'Thanks, sarge, I'll be back about quarter past one.' 'That's all right, boy . . .'

Paternalism was less apparent in the city except with the very young constables. One sergeant, for example, gently chided a young man for not going to bed earlier while on first watch. But older constables and most of the younger ones mixed with the sergeants as equals, and older ones did not always give the formal greeting of 'all correct, sarge' or 'sir' which was invariably given to inspectors. The involvement of senior officers in constables' marital problems, already discussed, also indicates paternalism.

Instructional

County Sergeant:

> His trouble is he's too boyish, and what I'm doing now, I'm treating him like a cadet and starting him right from scratch. I shall get him right down and then I can build him up slowly . . . I'll show him how to do something and let him watch a couple of times and then the next day I'll come in and say, 'Why isn't so and so done?' . . . And then that teaches him to do things for himself, don't it?

City Force:

> There had been an accident in which a stolen car had been

involved which had had three minor bumps. A PC from the area car which had dealt with the accident suggested a way of phoning up and finding out the name of one of the drivers involved. Inspector: 'Do you want to know then?' PC: 'Yes, of course, that's going to make the whole thing more complicated, isn't it?' Inspector: 'You're far better not knowing.' 'Well, I'd like to know for the sake of my own curiosity.' Inspector: 'If you're going to phone up about that you do so from outside as an interested member of the public, not from the station.'

Here an inspector is instructing a PC in the informal rules. Less experienced constables also had to be instructed in the safest or most discreet way of handling senior officers.

County Force:

Questions had been raised from headquarters as to why a relatively new section motor-bike had a burst tyre, and the riders of it had been asked to put in a report giving an explanation. Sergeant: 'I told him what to put: "With regard to the burst tyre on the motor-bike number so and so, I have no explanation to offer", because as soon as you start making an explanation you're admitting there's something to explain aren't you? And that's what he done, except I think he did add another bit saying he'd only ridden it a few miles . . .'

Autocratic

Only one of the five county sergeants was seen to behave in this way, and none of the city sergeants, though such behaviour was reported of certain inspectors in the city. The example from the county is cited.

There was a carnival in a small country town with narrow streets. One PC had already told a motorist that he would not 'book' him for obstruction if he moved, which he did. On the sergeant's instruction another PC [X] had taken the man's particulars. Afterwards he said to the sergeant: 'You know it's going to be a little difficult to book that man, sergeant.' 'Why ever not, was he causing an obstruction or wasn't he?' PC: 'Yes, but he moved the car.' 'That's not the point. Did you or did you not have to go into the road and control the traffic? Well, that means he was causing an obstruction. How many cars did he hold up? A hundred?' 'No, not as many as that, sir, only about forty at most.' 'What do you mean forty?

173

There were more than that when I saw him. You book him
for obstruction. You had to step into the road and control
the traffic didn't you?' . . . Later he said to the researcher:
'You see, he was trying to wriggle out of that one. He's no
good. If the man was causing an obstruction you've got to book
him for it. You've got to be firm, it's no good messing about'.
On previous occasions he had indicated to the researcher that
he had little time for PC X. On other occasions the same day
he himself was observed to overlook offences so as not to
make extra trouble on carnival day.

Protective

This is perhaps the most important attitude of the sergeant towards
his men. His position is equivalent to the marginal position of the
foreman, but all those sergeants who discussed the issue suggested
that their main responsibility was to the men under them—with
whom, of course, they had more frequent contacts than with senior
officers. In the city a sergeant after 'sticking up' a situation to test
the trustworthiness of the researcher remarked: 'That's all I've got
to do really, isn't it? Look after these men.'

A county sergeant, not on the research division (and subsequently
promoted), gave as good an account of the situation as any sociologist could wish.

I had a choice to make. There were twelve men under me there
and the inspector and I was the bridge between. Well, I
thought about it and I decided that the twelve were more
important than the one, so I didn't play it the inspector's way.

Qualities admired in senior officers

A total of 140 free comments recorded in the field diary were
classified under this heading. The qualities required in superiors in
both forces stem directly from the nature of the dependence. It
seemed, too, that the men had been made more acutely aware of
these requirements for senior officers by the processes of bureaucratization already outlined; they became aware that they valued
these characteristics only when they were faced with a 'new type' of
superior who lacked them.

Legal knowledge

One of these valued characteristics was legal knowledge and good
judgment in police matters. This is surprising only in that 'book

men'—those who had been promoted without much practical beat experience—were generally deplored. But that a senior officer must be able to give sound advice as well as possessing other qualities was readily acknowledged.

Fairness

Second, the men required in their senior officers that they should be fair in their distribution of favours and less popular tasks as between the men. This was mentioned more frequently in the county where particularistic criteria of distribution generally had more importance. The requirement stems from the wide range of positive and negative sanctions at the disposal of senior officers coupled with the need to maintain the unity of the working group both in order to function effectively and as a defence against these sanctions. Favouritism in any form would be disruptive of this. This was shown by the powerlessness of the divided and unhappy group at Hillbridge.

Personal interest

Third, senior officers were admired for taking a personal interest in the men and treating them with respect. In the city there was resentment that the chief superintendent had not visited the hospital to which two of his men who had been injured in a fracas had been taken, but rather had gone home to bed having ascertained that the matter was being perfectly adequately dealt with. His predecessor, it was alleged, 'would have been there. He'd have wanted to see what they were doing to his men. We haven't had much time for this one since.' Or take this remark from a county man about the ex-superintendent there:

> You know, he'd do anything. He was a man you could really admire. He'd go round to the men on a check point and take them fish and chips . . .

The men welcomed the fairer and more rapid promotion procedures, the reduction in the amount of 'bull' (formal acknowledgment of status) required, the slightly increased amount of give and take between ranks, but they still hankered for the old type of personal authority, for a man in charge whom they could respect as a person and who personally embodied authority and gave expression to core values, rather than a bureaucratic incumbent of an office.

Decisiveness

This showed, too, in the next requirement, that the senior officer

175

should be decisive. What the men wanted was a large and clearly defined area of personal responsibility, but a clear instruction when they needed it. In the county the men felt that they had neither of these things. This requirement was mentioned less frequently in the city.

Willingness to give 'backing'

Another requirement was that the senior officer should be a 'good practical policeman'. By this the men meant that they wanted senior officers who understood the need for certain legal infringements and were not rules-orientated. They felt that this did not hold true of men who had been rapidly promoted or who for other reasons lacked beat experience. Senior officers of the latter type left the men vulnerable and with the feeling that they were being judged by false standards or by criteria which they did not hold legitimate. Associated with this was the requirement that senior officers should give them backing. Wilson (1963) has also argued that the authority of a senior officer depends on the extent to which he exemplifies the fundamental norms of the police 'code'.

Requirements for a good senior officer and for a good intermediate officer were similar, though the need for intermediate officers to back their men *vis-à-vis* senior officers was seen as increasing in view of the change in the nature of the authority.

Interview evidence

Opinions expressed by sergeants

All respondents were asked a question as to whether their colleagues, subordinates, immediate superiors and senior officers were aware of and appreciated the work which they did, pre-coded responses being a permutation of awareness and appreciation (Table 73). In practice the most meaningful breakdown of the responses was between those who described the group concerned as both aware and appreciative, i.e., 'perfect', and the others who felt that there was a shortcoming in respect of one or other or both variables. Sergeants in the county, it will be remembered, worked in a situation of isolation from senior officers and from most of the men under them. In this way their bridge position was emphasized, and possibly also as a consequence of this their feelings that both superiors and subordinates did not know of the work they did and did not appreciate it were stronger than the equivalent feelings of city sergeants. Over two-thirds of the county uniform sergeants felt that their senior officers were 'less than perfect' in this respect compared with only 30 per cent of city sergeants. Half of the county sergeants felt that subordinates were not fully aware or appreciative, compared with only 20 per cent of city sergeants. By contrast in the county the three senior officers on the division all expressed total satisfaction with their seniors though only one expressed such satisfaction with subordinates.

TABLE 73 *Proportion of sergeants perceiving constables and senior officers as being both aware of and appreciative of their work*

| | Proportion | | | No. of respondents |
| | Constables | | Senior officers | |
	No.	%	No.	%	
County	3	50	1	16·7	6*
City	8	80	7	70	10

*Excludes CID sergeant.

Opinions expressed about sergeants

There was no significant difference between sub-divisions in the city in expressed opinions of sergeants; 42·3 per cent of the men felt that these were 'less than perfect' in one respect or another. In the county the overall figure was 45·7 per cent not totally satisfied, but there were marked differences by section. Differences between sections can perhaps best be explained by differences in the personalities and approaches of the sergeants concerned; proportions of men in the section stating that their section sergeant was neither aware nor appreciative or both ranged between 75·0 per cent in one section to 14·3 per cent in another. The fact that these differences were so great is an indirect indication of the personal importance of the individual sergeant in the county.

Even more striking is the difference between the proportion of men perceiving their sergeant as aware and appreciative compared with the far lower proportion who felt that their senior officers had these characteristics (Table 74). This again emphasizes the crucial importance of the sergeants' bridge position. Hillbridge, understandably, was an exception here.

Opinions expressed about senior and intermediate officers

Satisfaction with more senior officers was less great in both forces

TABLE 74 *Proportion of constables* perceiving section sergeant and senior officers as both aware and appreciative (county)*

| Section | Sergeants | | | Senior officers | | | No. of beat patrol constables in section |
	% saying both	No.	No answer	% saying both	No.	No answer	
DHQ	60·0	6	—	10·0	1	—	10
Hillbridge	25·0	3	—	33·3	4	—	12
A	25·0	6	—	57·1	4	—	7
B	55·5	5	1	22·2	2	1	9
C	62·5	5	—	37·5	3	—	8
	54·3	25	1	30·4	14	1	46

*Excluding mobile, CID, admin.

(Table 75). Of city men, 73·8 per cent felt that senior and intermediate officers were either unaware of what they did or unappreciative or both. Here there were significant differences between subdivisions in the numbers of men who attributed ignorance of their activities to senior officers. The proportion was greatest (81·2 per cent) at Central subdivision. This is perhaps a reflection of the real situation in that Central constituted the 'roughest' area where the number of reported infringements was greatest with the result that many aspects of the work were deliberately kept from senior officers. On the other hand Central had the lowest proportion of officers saying that senior officers were unappreciative, or would be even if they knew of the activities (18·7 per cent).

In the county differences between sections were less marked in

TABLE 75 *Proportion of constables perceiving senior officers as ignorant or unappreciative of work by their sub-division—city*

| | Ignorant | | | Unappreciative | | | Total sample |
	No.	%	No answer	No.	%	No answer	
Rushbridge	8	50·0	1	5	31·2	2	16
Brockbrorough	3	25·0	2	4	33·3	3	12
Central	13	81·2	—	3	18·7	—	16
Other	1	100·0	—	—	—	—	1
							45

respect of opinions of more senior officers than they had been in respect of sergeants, though the numbers expressing the opinion that senior officers were 'less than perfect' was generally higher. Seventy-two per cent of one-man beat men said this compared with 65 per cent of small town or Hillbridge men. But although the difference between towns and country beats remained, the rank ordering of the sections in this respect was different from the rank ordering in respect of opinions about sergeants. The smaller discrepancy between sections can best be explained by the fact that senior officers were the same for large numbers of men. The informally expressed opinions by the sergeant in some cases seem to be related to the opinions of the men, but not in respect of every section. The variation may well be accounted for by differences in the ability of the sergeant to act as a filter or buffer between the ranks.

Effectiveness of senior officers as role-definers

Perhaps the most important deduction in respect of both forces concerns the tremendous divorce which is shown to exist between men on the ground and senior (as distinct from intermediate) officers, bearing out comments already made about the inadequacies of the communication system, and that senior officers are seen as possessing considerable power but as being impermeable to influence from below. This discussion of the evidence suggests that *dependence* was apparently greater in the county. But *inter*dependence, involving mutuality and the perception of higher ranks as being also dependent on the men, was greater in the city.

Since interdependence with the police (IDP) scores were higher in the city (3·7) than in the county (2·6), on the basis of the general hypothesis it would be argued that more city than county men would act in accordance with the role definitions of senior officers. (To do this it is necessary to assume that the intervening variables of low visibility and the support of the colleague group in county and city respectively to some extent cancel out.)

This prediction was supported by the evidence. The mean number of situations in which the men claimed that senior officers would disagree with the action which they would take was 1·4 in the county and 0·9 in the city. Of county men, 73·4 per cent, and 54·5 per cent of city men, said that senior officers would disagree with the action which they would take in at least one of the six situations.

In the county, the mean number of situations in which superiors were perceived as disagreeing was 1·2 for above average scorers on the interdependence with police index, and 1·6 for below average scorers.

In the city force, for men scoring above average on the inter-dependence with the police index the mean number of situations in which senior officers were perceived as disagreeing was 0·8; for below average scorers the mean was 1·2. (See Table 76 for a summary.)

TABLE 76 *Situations in which superiors would 'disagree' with action by police interdependence score*

			IDP score				
Disagreement—		County				City	
no. of situations	Above mean	Below mean	Unknown	Total	Above mean	Below mean	Total
0	10	7	—	17	16	9	25
1	8	8	—	16	9	6	15
2	9	10	1	20	6	4	10
3	3	6	—	9	1	3	4
4	1	1	—	2	—	1	1
5	—	—	—	—	—	—	—
6	—	—	—	—	—	—	—
Total	31	32	1	64	32	23	55

Thus the differences were in the expected direction when high and low scorers *within* forces were compared, as well as when broad comparisons between the two forces were made.

As before, the *relative* effectiveness of senior officers as role-definers compared with other role-defining groups is taken up in the more general discussion of the propositions in chapter 8.

Summary

Officers on the divisions above the rank of constable were grouped into senior, intermediate and immediate superiors, and their duties were examined. County sergeants and inspectors were shown to have greater authority than men in the equivalent ranks in the city.

The vertical communication patterns in the two forces were examined and found to be similar. Upwards communication was mainly formal, and higher ranking officers were shown to be dependent on junior ranks to feed in relevant information. Direct supervision, even by immediate superiors, was not possible. It was thus relatively easy for information to be kept from senior officers. Informal communication was not an effective substitute for the inadequate formal system, since men in a position to interact informally with senior ranks were known and were not trusted by their colleagues.

Downwards communication was accurately transmitted, but senior officers were not able to ensure that their instructions were put into effect. Perceived interdependence with the police (IDP) scores were higher in the city than in the county.

Constables were shown to be dependent on senior officers in respect of the following variables:

(a) formal discipline procedures (dependence greater in the city);
(b) promotion (dependence greater in the county);
(c) transfers (dependence greater in the county);
(d) accommodation;
(e) welfare;
(f) formal and informal rewards.

Constables were shown to be dependent on immediate and intermediate superiors because of their needs for:

(a) support in extra-legal situations;
(b) good progress reports;
(c) recommendations for formal rewards;
(d) congenial working conditions;
(e) miscellaneous backing in relation to senior officers.

In the county the ability of senior officers to affect the lives of the men was much greater. This power was also exercised informally, so that to the men it appeared either arbitrary, malicious or sinister. The concept developed to describe the on-going situation and experience of most county men was that of *dependent uncertainty*.

All superiors were shown to be dependent on the men for:

(a) information;
(b) restraint and discretion in engaging in easing behaviour and legal infringements;
(c) efficiency in their work.

In the last two respects immediate and intermediate superiors were more dependent on the men than senior officers. An informal bargaining process between the men and immediate and intermediate superiors was observed.

Evidence of increasing bureaucratization was found in both forces, though the process had developed further in the city. These changes gave rise to discrepancies between the normative expectations of the men about the way their officers and senior officers should behave and their actual behaviour.

Observed attitudes of sergeants to constables were classified under four headings, namely:

  (a) paternal (mainly found in the county);
  (b) instructional (found in both forces);
  (c) autocratic (only found in the county);
  (d) protective (found in both forces).

Characteristics thought by the men to be necessary in superiors were:

  (a) sound legal knowledge;
  (b) fairness;
  (c) the willingness to take a personal interest in their subordinates;
  (d) decisiveness;
  (e) the willingness to support their men *vis-à-vis* higher ranks, the general public, and the courts.

Evidence from the interviews with the men confirmed that inspectors were rightly classified with senior officers in the county, and that county sergeants were in an isolated 'bridge' position between senior officers and constables. In both forces a divorce between senior officers and constables was apparent from the responses, although there was variation between sub-divisions and sections in respect of this.

As predicted, senior officers proved more effective as role-definers in the city force than in the county force. Within the two forces high scorers on the interdependence with the police index were more likely to conform to the role definitions of senior officers than were low scorers.

7 Interdependence with colleagues

> The trouble is that a cadet does six weeks on the beat with
> a PC, and you don't know if you're sent round with one of
> them whether he'll back you or run away if you get into
> trouble. Of course, it's the same with some policemen . . .
>
> (City constable.)

The index of interdependence with police

Mean interdependence with the force scores (IDP) were higher for
city than for county men. The problem in interpreting the IDP
index or the two scales of which it is composed[1] is how far these
are reflections or measures of interrelationships with senior officers,
with colleagues or with some more general notion of 'the police'.

The scales were designed to tap the latter before the necessary
distinction between colleagues and senior officers as role-definers
was fully elaborated.[2] In the previous chapter it was pointed out
that the item in the dependence on the force scale which specifically
mentioned senior officers had the lowest cutting point when the items
were subjected to a Guttman type scaling procedure. On the other
hand, the next lowest cutting point was that of item I (cf. appendix I,
p. 258), the only item specifically mentioning colleagues. Of the
four items ultimately included which had higher cutting points
(i.e., with which a higher proportion of the men failed to agree or
strongly agree) two referred to support from a rather generalized
and amorphous 'force' and two were concerned with the respondent's
personal identification as a policeman and his need to remain in the
job. The men found it easier to recognize or to admit to their
dependence on more readily recognizable units; slightly more of
them felt that they were highly dependent on the support of senior

G

officers than felt that they were highly dependent on the support of colleagues; none of those who did not admit to high dependence on colleagues admitted to dependence on the force in any more generalized sense; none of those who refused to admit to a high dependence on superiors admitted to a high dependence on colleagues. But the item concerning dependence on colleagues was perhaps the best discriminator since there were only 8 per cent of errors following the scaling procedure.

The other scale which is a component of the police interdependence (IDP) index measures perceived dependence of the force on ego (respondent). Neither colleagues nor senior officers were specifically mentioned in the items; six of the seven items referred to 'the force' in some form, and one to 'those who come after them', i.e., successors on the beat or the next generation of policemen. The item with the highest cutting point on this scale (i.e., that with which the greatest number of men felt free to express less than total agreement) was 'all policemen are constantly aware that what they do now will influence the attitude of the public to those who come after them'; the item with the lowest cutting point (i.e., that with which the greatest number of men expressed strong agreement) was 'if I were to make a serious mistake all the rest of the force would have to suffer for it as a result of the report in the press'.

The IDP index, therefore, indicates mainly perceived interdependence with the police force as such—both the body as a whole and the individuals who compose it. However, those with an IDP score of 0 include all the men who failed to admit to being highly dependent on either colleagues or senior officers. It would seem, from the very fact that the items scale, as well as from free comments made by the men, that there is some conception of 'the force' or 'the job' about which the men have a fairly coherent set of attitudes.

Given that IDP scores are not necessarily a more accurate reflection of interdependence with colleagues than they are of interdependence with senior officers, but are in fact a combination of the two plus a third variable which is perhaps a synthesis, it is none the less useful to examine the relationship of IDP scores with other structural factors. These relationships may well indicate which men are most likely to behave, in a situation of perceived conflict, in the direction of what they perceive to be generalized police norms. In this chapter these relationships will therefore be examined first. An examination of relationships and interdependence with the specific colleague group will follow.

Variables associated with IDP scores

Numbers of social contacts, both formal and informal, with other members of the force were found to be unrelated to IDP in both the county and the city areas, and so also was the number of friends a man had in the police force. Similarly, contact with the community, desire for integration with the community, and perceived relative numbers of civilian friends were found to be unrelated to IDP. The fall in interdependence with the police with increasing length of service for non-promoted men in the county has already been noted (chapter 6, p. 150); no such relationship was apparent in the city, nor was IDP in any way associated with rank in the city force. Other

TABLE 77 *Interdependence with the police by career satisfaction— city*

CS score	0	1	2	3	4	5	6	No. of respondents
			IDP	score				
13	—	1	—	—	—	—	—	1
19	—	1	2	—	—	1	—	4
20	—	—	—	—	—	—	—	—
21	—	—	—	—	—	1	1	2
22	—	—	—	—	1	—	—	1
23	1	—	1	—	—	—	—	2
24	—	—	—	—	—	—	—	—
25	—	—	—	—	—	—	—	—
26	—	1	1	1	—	—	1	4
27	—	—	1	1	—	—	—	2
28	—	—	1	1	1	1	—	4
29	—	—	—	—	1	—	—	1
30	—	—	—	—	2	2	—	4
31	—	1	1	1	1	1	—	5
32	—	2	—	—	1	—	—	3
33	—	—	—	2	—	—	—	2
34	—	—	—	—	1	2	—	3
35	—	—	—	2	—	1	—	3
36	—	—	—	—	—	3	—	3
37	—	—	—	—	1	—	—	1
38	—	—	1	—	—	1	1	3
39	—	—	—	—	1	—	3	4
40	—	—	—	—	—	1	2	3
	1	6	8	8	10	14	8	55

variables which proved to be unrelated to police interdependence were job satisfaction and willingness for one's son to become a policeman.

Three positive relationships with IDP were found, in addition to that with marital integration for county men, which has already been examined in detail in chapter 6. A linear correlation (*r*) of 0·43 was found between police interdependence and career satisfaction for city men (Table 77).

Such a relationship, it will be remembered, was not found in the county although for county men both variables, career satisfaction and IDP, were found to be independently related to marital integration (chapter 5, pp. 127–31). It first appeared that, in the city, a man who was highly satisfied with his chosen career might be more heavily dependent on the sources of that satisfaction (the police force); he might be less likely to put himself at risk of being removed from these. But a further examination of the data suggested that the correlation between CS and IDP in the city was not in fact a direct relationship but the misleading result of an independent relationship between IDP and type of post (Table 78).

TABLE 78 *Interdependence with police by type of post*

| | IDP score | | | | | | | No | No. of |
	0	1	2	3	4	5	6	answer	respondents
County:									
Town patrol (6–20 men)	3	3	3	3	3	1	1	—	17
Country beat (1 man)	1	9	6	2	2	4	1	1	26
Other	2	2	3	7	2	5	—	—	21
Total	6	14	12	12	7	10	2	1	64
City:									
City beat only	—	6	7	5	3	6	5		32
Other	1	—	1	3	7	8	3		23
Total	1	6	8	8	10	14	8		55

Interdependence with the police was found in the city to be lowest for men engaged solely on beat work, without the official easing or relief from boredom provided by occasional stints on the cars or in other specialized branches. Career satisfaction was also found to be lowest among these men. When posts at the time of interview were taken as the basis for the analysis (rather than posts ever held) men engaged solely on beat work were found to have a mean scaled career satisfaction score of 29·7 compared with a mean score of 33·9 for men engaged in all other tasks (sig. 0·05) (see Table 79).

TABLE 79   *Career satisfaction by type of post—city*

| | CS score | | | | | | |
	19–20	21–5	26–30	31–5	36–40	Unknown	Total
Beat only	3	1	9	11	2	1	27
All other	1	1	1	5	9	1	18
Total constables	4	2	10	16	11	2	45
Sergeants	—	3	4	—	3	—	10
Total	4	5	14	16	14	2	55

The second variable found to be statistically related to IDP in the city was a total 'awareness and appreciation' score (Table 80). This 'score' was calculated from the permutation of items concerned with the broad issues of communication and integration, described in the previous chapter (pp. 176–9). The response 'both aware and appreciates' was scored 3, 'not really aware but would appreciate if they knew' was scored 2, 'aware but does not appreciate' was scored 1, and 'neither aware nor likely to appreciate' was scored 0. The scores were added for responses in relation to the three groups about whom the question was asked, namely (for constables), colleagues, sergeants and more senior officers. Thus total scores for the item could range from 0 to 9. The method both raises and begs a lot of statistical questions, such as the equidistance of the items, the rank ordering of the centre two, and the giving of equal weight to responses in relation to each of the three groups. But in view of the fact that the separate responses proved analytically useful (pp. 176–9) and that the responses could indicate a man's perceived position in a network of communications and relationships it was felt desirable to reduce the information to a unified 'score' in order that it could be related to other variables. No relationship with IDP was found for county men, but there was a slight positive correlation in the city ($r = 0·42$). In other words, men who felt that both colleagues and higher ranks (or in the case of senior and intermediate officers, the men under them and their immediate superiors) were both aware of what they did and appreciative of it, were more likely to be highly interdependent with the police force as such—to

TABLE 80   IDP *score by 'awareness and appreciation' score —city*

Awareness and appreciation score	IDP score							No. of respondents
	0	1	2	3	4	5	6	
0	—	—	—	—	—	—	—	—
1	—	—	—	—	—	—	—	—
2	—	—	—	—	—	—	—	—
3	—	3	2	—	1	—	1	7
4	—	—	1	—	—	1	—	2
5	—	—	2	2	1	1	1	7
6	1	2	1	2	2	1	1	10
7	—	—	1	2	—	6	1	10
8	—	—	—	2	4	3	—	9
9	—	—	1	—	2	2	4	9
No answer	—	1	—	—	—	—	—	1
Total	1	6	8	8	10	14	8	55

perceive themselves as dependent on the force and the other members of the force as being dependent on them. It seems likely that this relationship did not hold in the county because there the additional factor of physical distance and isolation affected the communication pattern, in particular the extent to which men of all ranks were aware of each other's work.

The third variable found to be related to IDP was the *type* of post held by the men. This has already been discussed for city men in relation to the links between type of post and career satisfaction (pp. 186–7). (In the county differences on the basis of type of work were not significant.)

Fourth, interdependence with police was found to be linked to the *place* to which the man was posted. In the county significant differences were found between sections (Table 81) and in the city between sub-divisions (Table 82). In the county first, one rural section was higher in mean IDP score than the others. No structural factor could be isolated to explain this, and one therefore has to fall back on the idea that the personality of the sergeant and his skill in filtering and organizing communications in both directions were the major reasons. The importance of the personality of the individual sergeant in the county, both in this and other respects, has already been shown.

TABLE 81   *Interdependence with police by section—county force (all ranks)*

Section	0	1	2	IDP score 3	4	5	6	Unknown	Total	Mean score
DHQ	2	5	2	—	2	—	2	—	13	2·2
Hillbridge	1	2	3	4	2	2	—	—	14	2·7
A	2	3	—	1	1	2	—	—	9	2·2
B	—	2	3	2	—	1	—	—	8	2·4
C	—	1	3	—	1	4	—	1	10	3·1
CID/Admin./ Mobile	1	1	1	5	1	1	—	—	10	2·7
Total	6	14	12	12	7	10	2	1	64	

In the city IDP was lowest in Central sub-division (mean score 3·2 as compared with 3·7 and 4·2 elsewhere). Here again a possible explanation has been suggested by the foregoing analysis. It has been pointed out that in Central sub-division there was more unadulterated beat patrolling and as a consequence more need for easing behaviour, both social and in terms of a search for activity leading to legal infringements. Partly as a result of this, a strong

TABLE 82   *Interdependence with the police by sub-division—city*

	0	1	2	IDP score 3	4	5	6	No. of respondents	Mean score
Rushbridge	—	1	3	2	4	6	4	20	4·2
Brockborough	—	2	1	3	2	3	2	13	3·7
Central	1	3	4	3	4	4	2	21	3·2
Other	—	—	—	—	—	1	—	1	
Total	1	6	8	8	10	14	8	55	

colleague group had formed as a defence against senior officers becoming aware of these activities. In Central sub-division, therefore, the loyalty to the face-to-face primary work group is of relatively greater importance than loyalty to rather more nebulous collectivities such as 'the force as a whole'.

Interdependence at work—city force

Some bases of interdependence with colleagues in the work situation in the city have already been indicated (see also Westley, 1951, 1953,

1956). These are the need for mutual trust and secrecy within the colleague group as an insulating factor against negative sanctions which might result were intermediate or senior officers to become aware of specific easing behaviours or legal infringements. The 'necessity' for each of these types of behaviour has also been shown— in the case of easing as a means of making the job tolerable or simply more pleasant; in the case of infringements as a result of the need for 'action' and excitement in the work and for high status, consensually supported activities to legitimate the occupation, resulting, for example, in an over-anxiety to 'knock off' drunks. Infringements also resulted from the desire for results in the form of statements admitting guilt (see also La Fave, 1965; Lambert, 1970). Infringements were made possible and sometimes occasioned by an 'us and them' view of the police in relation to the criminal sub-culture and other 'rough' groups.

The third reason for mutual support within the colleague group, and that most frequently cited by the men, was the necessity for assistance in the event of a physical fight with members of the public. Finally there is a fourth miscellaneous category which is mainly concerned with the need for mutual assistance in order to achieve organizationally set goals.

Easing behaviour When men use the same pub or café as a night or late evening 'put-up' it is in the best interests of all concerned that inspectors and senior officers should be kept unaware of this. All involved are in a vulnerable position and if one man leaked the information the tables could easily be turned on him on a future occasion. Indeed, he would have to explain his own reason for visiting the put-up on the occasion when he saw the other men there. Easing is more congenial when it is communal; also the number of establishments available to be visited in the early hours of the morning is limited, which means that it is often necessary for a number of men to use the same one. Other types of easing, such as a sleep in a parked car found unlocked, for example, are individual activities, so that in outlying areas where other types of easing facilities are less available there is less incentive for strong in-group bonds of trust involving secrecy in relation to outsiders to develop. Strong feelings between members of a 'turn'—those regularly working the same shift—appeared to be most highly developed in Central sub-division where there were a number of late night establishments, and at Outpost where easing was communal in that men would con-gregate together around the canteen fire. But there is an overlap between individual and group easing. Even where a man is in the habit of using a property regularly left insecure as his night-time haunt he is dependent on his colleagues, who may patrol that beat on another night while he is on leave or on a different shift, not to report the building as insecure so frequently that its owners lock it up and a valuable easing facility is lost (cf. chapter 3, p. 64).

The need to preserve a good easing facility in such a case necessitated shared knowledge of an individual action. Sometimes, however, total secrecy was wiser in order to achieve the same result.

A lot of the places we call for tea and so on are communal. But some of the really good ones where you get your tea laced with whisky or something, you keep those to yourself or else you'd spoil it if too many went. (City PC).

Secrecy was the other side of the coin from mutual trust. Usually the men did not talk to each other in specific terms about their easing behaviour. This would place the PC at unnecessary risk, making him too much indebted to his colleague, and place on the colleague an unnecessarily great burden of responsibility to keep quiet. On one occasion the researcher was with two regular 'mates' in a patrol car on second watch. On a previous occasion with one of the men (A) and another partner beer had been bought at an outdoor (off licence) to drink in the car.

A started making remarks to B such as 'I wish we had someone with us we could trust, Tom', and B replied in the same vein. This continued until the researcher enquired what all the fuss was about as 'we've done it before'. There was a silence for a few seconds, then A remarked, 'Ah, but Tom wasn't with us that night, was he, ducks?' After this reprimand for being indiscreet the researcher was sent to the outdoor to buy beer as on the previous occasion.

Another time a PC was in an outdoor having a beer when a man on duty came in officially to make some enquiries. He pretended not to recognize the other PC, and during the time that the second man was there the PC did not recognize the researcher. The two men met subsequently in Walker Street station where it was made plain that they did in fact know each other.

Other forms of easing behaviour are perhaps not the cause of group solidarity but they are made possible by it and serve further to increase interdependence with colleagues. Examples of this are 'covering' for each other by men in plain clothes when one man wants time off, and 'booking off' for each other. One young PC came unstuck over this when he told the sergeant he was going off half an hour early, and relied on the sergeant to book him off. But he had not asked the sergeant specifically to do this and the sergeant did not do so. Instead he went home and left the inspector waiting for the apparently missing PC. The inspector guessed what had happened and finally went home himself. But he was angry, for he could have been in trouble himself if in fact the reason for the PC's failure to book off had been that he was injured in some way and unable to get back to the station.

Infringements The second main source of dependence on colleagues has been identified as the need for mutual support in preventing senior and sometimes intermediate officers from becoming aware of specific cases of legal, recording, procedural and other infringements against the formal rules. Sometimes these infringements would be individual actions, but most often at least two men would be involved. Numbers of examples of infringements have already been cited; that below shows the degree of despatch with which an incident could be handled when the policemen concerned had a high degree of mutual trust and understanding.

> The area car received a call to 'what might be a wounding'.
> It turned out to be a 'Mick' with a kicked face. The full story
> appeared to be that he was very drunk, had upset a girl in
> some way, and had subsequently been attacked by two other
> Irishmen. 'OK then, he fell over and hurt himself right?' said
> one officer. The other agreed, also remarking with some
> disappointment, 'I thought that was going to be good.'
> Information room were told that there was 'nothing in it',
> and that in any case the local sergeant was there.

On another occasion two cars had had a minor collision while coming off a pub car park. They were on the road but the policemen agreed to say that they were on private property so that the matter could be written off. After all, the drivers were 'only Micks and coloureds'.

Other instances of infringements also occurred in the search for legitimating, high status activities—in pursuance of activities analogous to thief-taking, such as arresting 'drunks' (see pp. 65–70 for the major discussion of this).

Physical attack The men spoke frequently about the risks which they ran of physical attack and of the importance of the support of colleagues at such times. But it is necessary here to separate the fact from the mythology. Only one such attack was observed during the field period of twenty weeks. In this case an obviously disturbed man, who had had an encounter with the police earlier in the evening, came to the police station demanding to be 'taken in'. This was refused and after heated talk the man finally took a swing at the office constable, whereupon one of the other constables leapt over the counter and restrained him. The man was detained in the cells, about which detention he now vociferously complained.

Some concrete evidence of the extent of such risks is provided by figures for men 'hurt on duty'. This is an underestimate since it is unlikely that any serious injury would be sustained in the large majority of encounters. Constables and sergeants serving at the time of the research averaged 0·5 injuries on duty per man. Their combined mean length of service was nine years five months. But only 37·0 per cent of the men had ever sustained an injury, and of these less than a third, or 11·7 per cent of the total, had been injured two or more times. Six of these men who had been injured on more than one occasion had less than five years' service. These figures would seem to suggest that some men are more at risk of receiving an injury on duty than others. An analysis of figures for injuries on duty by sub-division showed 30·0 per cent of the men serving on Central sub-division as ever having been injured, 31·2 per cent of those in Brockborough, and 34·2 per cent of those in Rushbridge (DHQ) (Table 83). The latter slightly higher figure could perhaps be explained by the fact that it was to Rushbridge sub-division that policemen who got into trouble in any form were generally transferred. But concrete evidence was not available to support this suggestion.

TABLE 83   *Injuries on duty of sergeants and constables by sub-division—city*

	Number of injuries					
	0	*1*	*2*	*3*	*4*	*n*
Rushbridge	50	15	8	2	1	76
Brockborough	42	14	3	1	1	61
Central	63	20	6	1	—	90
Total	155	49	17	4	2	228*

*One sergeant was on secondment to the Police College at the time of the research.

Given that there was at least some element of truth in the idea that beat men in the city were particularly vulnerable to physical attack,[3] the emphasis on colleague support is less surprising. Numbers of men referred to the area-car system in terms such as these, spoken by a young constable:

It helps in the city. Here you know you can get help within five minutes any time. If you're in trouble they'll just drop everything else and turn out.

Only one radio call to a 'policeman in trouble' was witnessed. The patrol car drivers did indeed dash to the scene with far greater haste than was customary. Similar haste was witnessed on only two other occasions: once, when the crew were asked to inform a beat PC on patrol that his father-in-law was ill; the second time was when a call was received to a house fire at which a baby had been burned. Colleagues and children were given top priority in deed as well as in word. The two extracts below sum up the situation.

> The trouble is you see, when you're out on the patch you've got to have someone with you you can rely on. Size isn't the main thing at all. I've been out with some right big fellows who've just walked off . . . at the first sign of anything blowing up. And I've known sergeants who've done that too. They just walk away and don't want to know. And then there's others who should never have been policemen at all. They're game enough and they'll have a go and stick by you but they just haven't got it.

> If there's an accident or someone in trouble it's the easiest thing in the world just to turn up the street and not see anything, isn't it? But a good policeman won't. He'll go straight there

The last quotation shows perhaps more clearly than the other that loyalty to colleagues, to be effective, must be an internalized value, not dependent for its translation into action on sanctions in the immediate situation.

Organizational goals This is a residual category, though most of the items in it could be seen as a means of achieving goals set by senior officers or of making the work task easier. The distinction between this and easing behaviour is a fine one, and items such as the one below could be placed in either category.

> We always hand the book [accident report] in at a station over the [divisional] border in a case like this, so if there's any further enquiries someone else has to do them.

This remark was made by an area-car driver whose concern was to take work off the shoulders of his beat colleagues.

Constables are dependent on each other to improve or maintain a favourable work situation. The job of 'clearing a patch' could not be tackled too diligently. A neighbouring division were reputed to have tackled a section which was handed over to them in just this way. Such enthusiasm, it was claimed, results in the patch being 'killed'—rendered vice and crime free—and therefore boring to work. The aim at this level is to keep a constant flow of prisoners, enough to make the work interesting and the records look good, but not so many as to drive petty criminals and others away from the area.

Finally in this category there is an example which is more the result of an existing colleague relationship rather than a cause. An office sergeant said that it had been an especially busy night; his counterpart on the previous shift had done his 'duty states' for him because he too had been busy and had guessed that the next turn would be 'really pushed'.

Evidence of solidarity between colleagues

If these are the prime causes of a strong colleague relationship in the city, what then are its results? The first is an attempt to 'cover up' for other men, to prevent senior officers from becoming aware of others' mistakes even when the PC doing the 'covering' is not himself at risk. Thus on one early morning patrol a call was received to a reported shopbreak, and it turned out that there had been a delay of some two hours and a half between the reporting of the break and the message being received over the radio from control room. There had been a slip up in control and they had thought that the car had been notified at once when in fact it had not. After dealing with the matter the car drivers put a false time on their report so as to 'cover' the information room staff. On another occasion a traffic car spent the better part of a night shift trying to sort out the rightful ownership of a car which they had stopped but which was reported stolen. The driver, who turned out to be the rightful owner who had recently purchased the vehicle, had been detained in the station for several hours, and could have made a complaint of wrongful arrest. It was discovered that the car had indeed been stolen and then recovered before being sold, but the recovery had not been notified. A CID sergeant had known of the recovery, and it was his responsibility to have notified information room, but he had failed to do so. The drivers who had tracked the problem down related the details to the watch inspector, but left out the fact that the CID sergeant had known of the recovery so as not to get him into trouble.

Solidarity was also shown in the matter of welfare and private life. Men without children said that they would offer to work Christmas Day so that family men could have the time off. A man whose wife was in hospital was assisted by his colleagues on the turn to go and visit her each evening.

A trusted 'mate' was valued. One attempt to prise open such a partnership was witnessed, A suggesting to B that they should swop vehicles from their postings so as to be together again. B at

195

first thought that A was arranging for him to pair with his regular mate and was agreeable, then became acutely embarrassed when it became apparent that A wanted to pair with him himself. A became annoyed and said angrily, 'Oh, if that's the way you want it . . .', while B mumbled in embarrassment, 'I thought you meant for me to go with Bill'. B's position was a difficult one since he did not want to quarrel with his current partner, but he could not be disloyal to his 'mate'.

A sergeant verified that in his experience all the men felt that their 'turn' was the best. The men would vie with one another in telling hair-raising anecdotes of their individual or joint exploits. Then, of course, as in all professions, there were the specifically police jokes which supported the men in their feeling of belonging to a distinctive body.

> I met this man one night carrying a parcel, a big parcel all wrapped up in brown paper and I said to him, 'What've you got under your arm?' and he said, "Airs, mate, what've you got, feathers?'

Qualities admired in colleagues

As in the case of senior officers, the qualities admired in colleagues stemmed directly from the structure of the work situation and the nature of the interdependent relationship. One obvious characteristic required was to be reliable in a fight, and those who could not be relied on were despised.

> He's weak. He got flattened once by a Mick that I'd scared just by shouting at him when I was on plain clothes.

And related to this was the importance of being physically tough.
Again, for obvious reasons, men were admired for being discreet:

> There's some things you can tell the gaffers and some things you can't, like drinking on duty . . . His trouble is he talks too much [said by one PC about another].

Finally, men were admired for being 'good practical policemen', which was in a sense a summing up of all the other admired characteristics. A 'good practical policeman' would know all about easing behaviour and be familiar with all the best put-ups; he would be willing to 'have a go' either in a physical fight or in the sense of being prepared to charge a man or bring him to the station for questioning with insufficient evidence; he would know all about acceptable infringements and the extent to which one could reasonably expect support from intermediate officers; he would take a chance but he would 'cover' himself and less experienced men involved with him, and not be unduly rash; he would know his value as a leader and a teacher of recruits and thus be able to 'handle' intermediate officers when necessary, and they in turn would rely on his judgment; he would bring in prisoners.

Interview evidence   In the responses to the question about the extent to which colleagues were aware of and appreciated one's work, only 37 per cent of beat men said that their colleagues would know of what they did. This suggests that despite the strong bonds of mutual dependence suggested by the observational data, in fact men regarded discretion as the prime quality. They were unprepared to place either their colleagues or themselves at risk by making their activities too public. Help was there when needed, but even in the city the policeman's work was essentially individual and invisible, and in the main the men preferred that it should stay that way.

Socialization

Socialization and social controls are dealt with together here because the former implies that the colleague group are in a position to impress their patterns of thought and behaviour upon recruits. But social controls continue to be exerted throughout a man's service when there are signs of deviant tendencies, and this aspect of the problem will be dealt with secondly.

A recruit is in a peculiarly difficult situation in that he is highly dependent on immediate, intermediate and senior officers. He is dependent on the former two categories for good reports, and on senior officers because they may terminate his service if they find his work unsatisfactory. Yet at the same time he is highly dependent on serving constables. These can show him how to make his work interesting, introduce him to easing facilities, and provide the necessary 'backing' and 'cover' for him in his relationships with both members of the public and senior officers. In some ways these two sets of demands are incompatible. Senior officers might want to see the probationer frequently submitting reports, whereas longer serving constables might not approve of this. However, the conflict is partially resolved in the sergeant role. Sergeants are in many senses members of the colleague group and will judge the probationer by the standards of the group and report favourably to senior officers if they find him satisfactory. Thus conforming to the norms of the colleague group may indirectly stand a probationer in good stead with senior officers as well.

One sergeant regularly took three recruits on after-hours drinking expeditions with him (the researcher accompanied them on three occasions), taught them how to work their beats and instructed them in the operation of the entire informal code. But one other young officer at the same station, who 'went round booking people all the time' and admitted that he felt that this was his job, was excluded from all the social gatherings. On the other hand, when this isolated officer 'got a breaker' the sergeant concerned was among the first to congratulate him. The probationer was being shown that 'real police work' was rewarded though 'overdoing' the reporting for road traffic offences was censured.[4]

Another 'over-diligent' young officer was defensive:

> Some of these chaps here, they laugh at you if you go in with, say, ten or eleven reports for, say, no lights, even if you've been told to go out and do it. I don't mean that anyone has ever actually told me that I'm doing too much, but they laugh, you know. But the way I look at it that's your job isn't it . . .?

When a young officer was posted as observer to an area car it was possible to observe the socialization process at first hand. On these occasions young officers were usually left sitting outside 'put-ups' to listen to the radio. One pro-con. observing on a night patrol kept asking the driver, 'Shall we do him?' when he saw a vehicle speeding or having no lights. The driver took no notice, but later when they passed a car without an illuminated number plate he remarked bleakly to the pro-con., 'There's an offence for you', at which the young man looked embarrassed. However, when a 'worthwhile' offender was found—the driver of an overloaded, not fully insured van, who was mildly drunk (though 'not quite good enough') and speeding—the driver 'gave' the offence report to the pro-con., not so much to save himself work as because he knew that the probationer needed to put reports in to gain approval from senior officers. Again, the recruit was being shown the informal definition of what constituted 'real' police work as distinct from pettiness.

On another occasion there was an accident. A stranger to the city had driven across a 'halt' sign, thinking, he said, that it applied to the next junction.

> His wife was hurt. The car crew took the husband and wife to hospital but forgot their belongings so had to return again with them . . . After leaving the hospital . . . [the experienced driver] told . . . [the pro-con.] how to do the report. 'Shan't I do him for careless then?' asked the pro-con. 'You do what you like. You asked my advice and I'm telling you. I should do him for failing to stop at a halt sign. That's enough; he's been punished enough already.' He told the pro-con. how to word the report bringing in that the man was a stranger to the

town and had thought the sign applied to another road. Later the pro-con. asked the same question of another PC, who didn't know the circumstances and who therefore suggested [a charge of] careless or without due care and attention . . . The driver remarked of the pro-con., 'You get some of these bumptious youngsters, but they've never proved themselves.'

There were myriad items of the informal code which a recruit had to learn. Most important, he had to learn to hold his tongue.

These youngsters, they think they know it all some of them, and they try so hard to be one of the boys, but they can't, not till they've learned. His trouble is he's all yap, yap, yap.

Or again, from another experienced PC:

The thing is on this job you must never let on how much you know.

The rule was to know which of your colleagues were trustworthy in any kind of a tight corner, and to this end to find out as much about them as possible. But there was also a rule to keep your knowledge to yourself. Recruits were told this, as the researcher was, and were frozen out of the conversation if they spoke out of turn; their introduction to easing facilities and infringements was gradual, and after each step they were carefully watched to see if there was any 'come back'—the whole procedure closely paralleling that to which the researcher was subjected.

In the researcher's case there were first of all isolated incidents of 'easing' on patrol cars—news of which did not spread very quickly; then there was an arranged visit with a non-uniform officer to a well known put-up on another sub-division, at which time uniform officers were seen drinking on duty; after passing this test I was invited to a gathering in a locked cupboard at one of the stations—the whole shift being present—at which a crate of beer and a bottle of whisky were consumed on duty. Conversation and humour were muffled since a senior officer was in the station at the time. After this I was allowed to see easing behaviour, though full acceptance in the sense of being allowed to witness legal infringements was never attained since it was impossible for me to share the associated risks. 'Blooding' was impossible as far as infringements were concerned, since to be fully accepted it was necessary for either researcher or probationary constable to have done the deed himself.

But the youngsters, they prove themselves by this sort of thing. Like in court they have to get up and say they never touched him. In this case I was telling you about there were four

witnesses and I had them all up to my office and warned them:
'You know what you're doing; if this is proved you could be
guilty of perjury.' But when a youngster does that he's blooded,
you see, and then you know you can trust him. There's some
you can't trust and some on my watch who haven't yet proved
themselves. But there's one who proved himself last night as
far as I'm concerned. He got into a bit of trouble with four
yobs and he got knocked about but he brought them in and
I got him here and said to him, 'Do you want to charge them
with assault?' and he said, 'No sir, I gave as good as I got
and that's it.' And he proved himself by that in my eyes.
(Inspector)

Social controls

Social controls were brought to bear against more experienced
officers if they talked too much, proved unreliable in a physical fight,
or took actions likely to disrupt the unity of the group.

You can trust most people on this job, and there's ways of
telling those you can't trust. What we do, you see, we start
a story and see where it goes. There was one time when we
wanted to know who shopped us for being in a pub. We didn't
know who it was though we had an idea it was one particular
bloke so what we did—and we told the landlord what we were
going to do—we spread this story that the landlord's wife
was supposed to be having an affair with this young policeman
who was just married not very long. And we told him about it
too of course. And the only [other] person we told about it
was this bloke we suspected, and it got back. And from then
on he was always in trouble. We made his life a misery for
him and eventually of course he was moved to another division.

One of the discipline charges for a year after the close of the field
period was of willingly making a false statement—to five officers,
therefore five charges—that an officer had had an improper relationship with a single woman. There is no evidence, but it seems possible
that this may have been a similar 'stick up' as a form of reprisal.

Memories were long, and tales from years back were told of men
who had 'chickened out' of a fight. On one sub-division there was a
standing joke about a PC who had seen a fight and walked to a call
box—'Excuse me, there's a policeman in trouble'—rather than
himself joining in the fight. The story was spiced by the fact that the
offending PC had a BBC voice, though for other men who had
proved themselves successfully such an accent was regarded as a
foible to be admired.

Another tale was told of a sergeant who had similarly walked away from trouble. As he left, the PC involved had said to him: 'If you're going, Sarge, will you take my mac? I don't want to have to carry that as well.'

After a man had failed in this way he became isolated from the work group and thus cut off from a supply of useful information about both the work and his colleagues, from many easing facilities, and from support in the event of his needing 'covering' himself.

Finally there were the men who showed signs of breaking up the colleague group. Most of these deviant tendencies were not major threats to the group, and were accordingly dealt with lightly. One man who had had an office job for over ten years, and was therefore in a suspect position, made frequent self-deprecating jokes about it. Similarly well known 'gimmick men' would find it necessary to excuse or explain their behaviour or make cracks at their own expense. (A gimmick, as distinct from easing, was suspect because if often brought the gimmick man into too frequent informal contact with the gaffers and thus turned him into a security risk.) One man who was acting sergeant was asked jokingly by a PC before he went out, 'What I want to know tonight, Harry, is are you with us or against us?' He was being warned not to be too diligent in his temporary role; a few shifts later he would be a PC himself again and would need to be part of the group. Usually such a warning was not necessary, but the man concerned was known to have 'a touch of promotionitis'—another disruptive symptom.

> You have to trust your mates on the cars, otherwise you don't get anywhere. There's a few here with promotionitis we call it, but not many . . . You can tell them because they are all edgy when there's wind of the new promotions coming through. We tease them about it. There's one bloke who's really upset about not being made, and every time we kid him on that he's going to be made this time, and he believes it, you know, and gets all excited, and then when it falls flat you can tell by his face. (City PC.)

Interdependence at work—county force

Before examining colleague relationships across departmental boundaries and social contacts between colleagues, it is useful to look at the comparative picture of the relationships between colleagues in the work situation of county men. Here, it will be recalled, easing behaviour was an individual matter; the men did not need to use their easing facilities simultaneously, nor, except in the towns, did they need to share the same place over a period of time. The term 'put-up' was unknown. It was understood between the men that they all behaved in this way, but colleagues did not need to know—in a concrete sense—of each other's actions. They did not, therefore, need each other's support in order to keep their easing behaviour safe and secret; low visibility was their main defence against possible sanctions from senior or intermediate officers.

Similarly, colleague support was less necessary as a result of infringements or risk of physical attack. Infringements were fewer because there were fewer crimes, fewer drunks, contacts with the 'at risk' members of the public were fewer. Members of the public most frequently encountered were members of the local community and for this reason less vulnerable (cf. chapter 4). Cases of physical aggression against police were less than in the city, and in any case it was not to colleagues who were several miles distant but to members of the local community that the beat man had to look for support if such an attack were made.

In respect of the final source of interdependence—co-operation in the achievement of work tasks and organizationally set goals—there were occasions when a similar co-operation developed in the county among the one-man beat men. But though this co-operation facilitated the achievement of the work goals and also made the task more congenial, it was not a pre-requisite of the achievement of these goals. Thus though men might meet to keep a point and 'get offences' together, one constable alone could achieve the same result.

In Hillbridge co-operation and interdependence could have developed as in the city. The nature of the work was similar in many respects, as were its drawbacks. The differences between the town and the big city were matters of degree rather than kind. But there was one difference which prevented colleague co-operation from developing to the same extent, and this was in the structure of the authority hierarchy. Whereas in the city there had been a large number of sergeants and watch inspectors who changed at six-weekly intervals, and a large number of men, so that perhaps even the sub-divisional chief inspector could not know all of them very well, in Hillbridge there were one sergeant and one inspector and usually only seven constables and a detective constable working in the town itself. Thus the inspector had absolute and continuous authority and, as was pointed out in the previous chapter, a considerable number of sanctions at his disposal. He was also in a position to know each of his men very well and to favour some rather than others (cf. chapter 6, p. 165). The position was worsened by the fact that the sergeant at the time of the research did not get on with the inspector and was not respected by the men, which was partly cause and partly the result of his inability to play a key 'buffer' role. Thus men who were thought to be favoured by the inspector were distrusted by the others. The result was fairly general suspicion, with pairs of men at most trusting each other and working together. Only 38·4 per cent of the Hillbridge men felt that their colleagues were both aware of and appreciated what they did compared with proportions ranging from 58·5 per cent to 75·0 per cent in other county sections (Table 84).

Relationships between beat men—town versus country

One-man beat men were independent of their colleagues in the work situation. Their points of contact with each other were special duties, 'points', duties in section or sub-divisional headquarters and monthly assemblies. These meetings provided sufficient contacts for a common viewpoint to be thrashed out. Sometimes a particular opinion would be limited to men on a section. Main communication lines between sections seemed to operate in some cases by meetings of the sergeants—two in particular got on very well—and in others by men from adjoining beats in different sections keeping points. Both information and norms were diffused in this way. The very invisibility of their colleagues made men the more anxious not to be the odd one out, and to be sure that they had the same methods of working and opinions as the others.

Again, low visibility led to more rather than less trust. The norm of secrecy which was so prevalent and pervasive in the city was rarely apparent except in Hillbridge. This was partly because there was less easing behaviour and infringements to hide; partly, too, it was because the men did not witness each other's behaviour and were therefore not so threatened by their colleagues. They could, without anxiety, pool information as to how they worked their beats.

A considerable feeling of comradeship thus developed between clusters of one-man beat men, and they were prepared on occasion to support each other as a defence against senior officers in the same way as city men. One man failed to attend court, having had verbal permission to stay away, but was unexpectedly required by the magistrates. He was asked for an explanation of his non-attendance. He would have been 'in trouble' had not one of his colleagues verified that he had heard the verbal permission given.

On another occasion the personnel carrier was late arriving for a special duty. The reason was that one of the officers had arrived at the rendezvous without his helmet, which had had to be brought from his station by another constable. The entire party had had to wait until the helmet arrived. But none of the men complained. And when the driver was subsequently asked to submit a report explaining the late arrival he first telephoned the PC responsible and told him what had happened, and then contrived to phrase a report which did not incriminate the other man although it eased the responsibility off his own shoulders somewhat. The driver was none the less held responsible; nor was it ever suggested by the other men that he had any alternative but to carry the can himself. On the next occasion when personnel had to be transported by the same driver it was explicitly stated in the instruction that he would be 'responsible for personnel during the trip'.

But even given a willingness to 'cover' each other, it was not really possible for county men to do this because of the isolation in which they worked. A man usually had to 'cover' himself if he were to forestall in any way possible negative sanctions from senior officers. The promotion battle made this the more necessary, since one public mistake was thought to be sufficient to ruin a man's chances; it also made colleagues more reluctant to support each other lest they too be involved in a public mistake. The fact that almost half of the men were qualified for promotion not only gave senior officers greater powers of selection (cf. chapter 6, pp. 148–51) but also placed colleagues in a position of direct competition with each other. Thus 'covering' was individual, and often to be equated with caution. Some men noted down the time of each visit in their pocket books; most were anxious to 'work to the book' where possible in a way that would have been incomprehensible to city men whose repeated claim was that this could not and should not be done.[5]

> On a night crime patrol . . . the observer suggested a route to follow. There was by custom a considerable extent of discretion given to the men on these patrols. The driver said, 'No, if we do what they say we can't go wrong, can we?' The patrol therefore took what seemed on the face of it a far less satisfactory course, where the property to be checked was unfamiliar to both the driver and the observer.

But despite this anxiety to be 'covered' there was one major respect in which beat men sought to hold out against the wishes of senior officers. This was in the matter of reporting. The sentiment of the PC quoted below was echoed by many other beat men. It was never heard from a Hillbridge man, and was voiced only once by a man who served briefly at DHQ. The man speaking averaged two non-indictable offence reports a month (the mean for one-man beats was 15·9 per annum).

> The amount of reports he sends in aren't the way to judge a good policeman. You may get a man with a file as thick as anything, but when you sort through it most of it is only chaff, isn't it? He's just one of those who reports every little thing. Well, I don't believe in that way of going to work.

For the men on one-man beats it would seem that the ties with the local community remained primary. They believed that too much reporting would damage this relationship. Town men did not have the same intimate local ties, and could therefore conform to the wishes of senior officers in this respect. Men with this latter attitude thus threatened the one-man beat men. The dichotomy was reflected in the monthly assemblies at DHQ. Three of these were attended, and it was observed on each occasion that the beat men sat along one side of the table while the town men—four at most—sat along the other. The sergeant and any senior officer attending would sit at the end. Conversation across the table was unusual, though beat men or town men would engage in conversation with each other, or directly with the sergeant or senior officers. No outward display of antagonism was ever observed between beat men and the others, though beat men made several jokes about the zeal of one or two of the young town men. The following examples of town men's attitude to 'booking' people point up the contrast with the mutually dependent exchange system (cf. chapter 4) within which the one-man beat man and his 'parishioners' operated.

Damage had been reported at the women's institute hall and a young PC had interviewed four boys thought to be responsible. 'It wasn't a malicious damage but I got a larceny out of it . . . larceny of twenty-four playing cards. Still, that's only a little thing but that's a larceny. We didn't know they were missing until we went and saw them though; they didn't report it.'

A PC recently transferred to the town spoke about a case he had got when out on the van. He had seen two airmen riding together on a lady's bike. He said it was good to start off on the right foot and get a case the first day, and it was good to give that impression in the town too. On another occasion this man remarked: 'If a chap gets told off by his superiors for not putting enough reports in he's just not screwing his nut, is he?'

Socialization

Socialization processes similar to those in the city were not observed The colleague group in general had less to offer and less sanctions at its disposal. But it was noticeable that one-man beat men with only three or four years' service echoed the sentiments of older beat men concerning reporting. At assemblies and points they were taught this approach. They also recognized the dichotomy.

This is my first country beat, and you've got to work it different in the country from in the town. You've got to concentrate on getting to know the people and winning their confidence.

Country policemen did not say that the town men were wrong. They simply felt that they would not understand the one-man beat situation. In the same way they felt that senior officers who had never had a country beat could not appreciate the situation. With regard to a stray dog:

> If that were on your own beat you wouldn't do anything about it, would you, but here that'll mean a report. That's an offence you see, letting a dog on the road without a name and address on its collar.

This feeling of mutual understanding, which was not shared with any other group within the police force, drew rural beat men together in spite of those centrifugal forces in the system such as isolation and competition for promotion. Thus, 61·5 per cent of one-man beat men claimed that their colleagues were both aware of and appreciative of the work they did. Contrast this with the equivalent 40·0 per cent of town patrol men in Hillbridge and the city force figure of only 37·8 per cent of the men claiming that their colleagues would know of what they did, let alone appreciate it (Table 84).

TABLE 84 *Constables' perceptions of colleagues*

	Aware and appreciative of work	Ignorant but would appreciate if knew	Know but don't appreciate	Don't know and unlikely to appreciate	No answer	Total
County: one-man beat	15	5	1	4	2	27*
County: Hillbridge	4	2	4	—	—	10
County: other non-specialists	6	3	—	—	—	9
County: CID/admin. mobile	6	1	1	—	—	8
City: all constables	12	22	5	5	1	45

*Includes one constable who operated a section station beat, where the sergeant was also posted but no other constable.

The understanding in the rural areas did not usually involve concrete knowledge of particular events. Since behaviour was invisible, no effort to keep things from colleagues was needed. In the city the opposite paradox held: behaviour was often visible therefore secrets were valued, not least because they were indicators of a measure of autonomy—a characteristic which has been (deliberately) under-emphasized in this chapter.

Although the rewards at their disposal were not tangible, it was important for the man on his first rural beat to gain acceptance by the group of rural policemen, particularly in his own section. They could give him advice about his job and about people living on his beat, and they could alleviate for him the loneliness involved in his job as a result of being 'friendly but not friends' with the local people. Moreover, the PC could no longer belong to the town group with whom he rarely worked and had little in common. Acceptance by the remaining one-man beat men was the only form of group affiliation and support open to him.

Town men were not socialized by senior colleagues in the same way. They came into contact with older one-man beat men on duty in the section stations, but they did not need to conform to their standards.

Because they were constantly visible to the senior officers, and because in the main they had only a short period of service and were anxious to map out a career, senior officers' expectations carried far greater weight. So long as they remained in the towns they were not subject to any counter-socialization.

Qualities admired in colleagues

These qualities differed from those which were deemed important in the city, though there were some similarities. In particular, physical strength and discretion were rarely mentioned as important in the county, though no doubt these characteristics would have been approved where they were found. Men were not so much admired for conforming to the prevailing norms about reporting as derided if they failed to do so. They were admired for knowing how to cover themselves and keep out of trouble with senior officers while at the same time working their beats in such a way as to keep in favour with the local people. They were also respected if their knowledge of their area was particularly intimate. All these characteristics were implied by the appellation of 'real old-time policeman'. Another characteristic much admired was 'being straight', or standing up for one's principles rather than following the lead of senior officers. This characteristic was attributed to only two or three men on the division, all of whom had more than ten years' service. These people were regarded as something of a bulwark against the rising tide of bureaucratization, and the consequent eating away of the beat man's status and powers of independent action. The touch of self-immolation, in terms of promotion prospects at least, which such actions were perceived as containing added glamour to those who were noted for them, but ensured that the bulk of the men were reluctant to follow the admired example.

Relationships between departments

City force

> Like CID now . . . they don't tell you anything of what they're
> doing . . . and I suppose if I got on it I'd be the same . . . I've
> known beat men get a bit of information and pass it on to the
> CID and then we get cut right out of it. Maybe he doesn't hear
> any more about it until they bring the prisoners into the office
> and he may be there . . . Here they won't tell you the time
> and the way I look at it is this, we're all in the same job and
> it could be done a lot better and made more interesting if they'd
> show you a photograph, say, of someone who was wanted, or
> tell you something. Because I know for a fact there's people
> they suspect of breaks around here but they won't tell me
> about it, oh no. There was one good CID sergeant here . . .
> and he used to parade with the men and tell them about the
> crime . . . and of course you don't mind doing things for a
> man like that. But in the main none of the others will; even
> the attached man once he's done about two months of his six
> months' attachment. I'll give any attached man two months
> and he's just the same as they are and won't tell you the time.
> And when he comes off he's just one of the boys again
> grumbling about the CID . . . I suppose he's sort of on trial
> and he wouldn't be very popular if he went bandying all their
> information about.

This is an extreme case of dissatisfaction. Most of the men in the
city force appeared to accept the division of functions between
departments as a necessity, albeit possibly an unfortunate one.
Thus one of the first things a recruit had to learn was to leave other
departments' work alone. One young man told of how he had gone
to 'knock someone off' one day and had been politely told that
this person was a sarbut for the plain clothes.

> Since then I've left prostitutes and that type of person alone.
> That's their job and we don't quite know what they're doing.
> Same with crime. You never know but what you could be
> treading on their toes in some way, so crime or anything like
> that, I always leave it to them.

Men of all ranks up to inspector repeated this. There were
occasions when an inspector was heard specifically to tell a man to
leave things alone 'in case the plain clothes are concerned'. The
plain clothes, on the other hand, were anxious not to be 'lumbered'
with investigating a lot of non-indictable offences which did not
really interest them. A plain clothes man on Central sub-division

208

was presented by a recruit with a piece of paper giving details of some anonymous phone calls—officially a plain clothes matter. But the response of the PC was to screw the paper up and ostentatiously to throw it into the waste bin with the remark, 'You ought to know better than to give me that stuff, boy.' Similarly, the uniform men were schooled by the CID into not 'criming' the more trivial larcenies and other offences which they encountered.

There was thus a moderately conflict-free working relationship resulting from clear definition of tasks. But even so communications between departments were bad, and this enhanced suspicions that the man in the other department had an easier time. Horsemen and dog-handlers were frequently taxed about the value to police work of their particular branches, though where the particular specialist concerned was well accepted as an individual these remarks were given a humorous front. Dog-handlers in any case worked more or less the same shifts as ordinary beat men (though they did not do nights on foot) and wore the same uniform, so there were fewer barriers to communication in this case. Plain clothes men were drafted for twelve months, but knew that they would ultimately revert to uniform and usually had considerable beat experience before being posted to the specialist branch. They were therefore able to maintain reasonable communications, and met with little direct antagonism. Office men and the mounted branch were baited more frequently. The contacts of these men with the gaffers made them suspect, and their permanent postings meant that their interests were no longer necessarily those of the uniform branch as a whole. Moreover, meetings with these people were relatively few, limited to the canteen, and mainly at DHQ. Communications were thus inadequate.

Communications between the CID and the uniform branch were somewhat facilitated by the system of six-month 'attachments'.

> I'd say I like the CID best though I refused to go on
> permanently because of the hours involved. It's a prestige job,
> that's the thing. But the family life must come first.

This man had no occasion to be bitter about the CID. His rejection of it was a conscious and rational choice. Another man found his understanding broadened as a result of his attachment.

> There's a hell of a lot of paper work on this job that I hadn't
> realized. Because when you're in uniform you just put your
> hand down a bloke's collar and that's it, isn't it? You hand it
> all over to the CID and don't think any more about it.

But there remained some resentment of CID as of all specialist branches. This stemmed largely from the low status of the beat man, his feeling of being part of a residual category to the importance of which everyone paid lip service, though more tangible evidence of this importance was lacking. Uniform men disliked the practice of having the night CID man aboard one of the night shift area cars. This meant that they were largely at his beck and call, chauffeuring him hither and thither, and therefore getting few interesting calls with which they could deal themselves. 'That's the only time I've ever known a CID man be useful on nights,' muttered one driver when the night CID man wandered off to view a suspect vehicle while the patrol car waited round the corner.

Some misunderstanding stemmed from the CID side too. The Chief DI on the division remarked on the relatively poor promotion opportunities in the CID compared with the uniform branch. In the CID there were at the time ninety-five detective constables and sixty-one detective sergeants, compared with divisional figures for the uniform men of 194 constables and thirty-seven sergeants. The myth that there was an opposite ratio remained prevalent among CID personnel.

In general, then, the picture from the city was of a reasonably viable system of co-operation based on clear demarcation of function, with some residual resentment of specialists on the part of beat men, and the efficiency of the whole system being impaired by poor interdepartmental communication.

County force

In the county force feelings on this issue ran much stronger. The only specialists serving on the research division were the CID sergeant and two detective constables, and four 'mobile' men (five mobile men were interviewed as one man was transferred in the course of the research). In addition there was some feeling of antagonism with and alienation from headquarters administration.

Hostility towards CID was greater in the county for two identifiable reasons. One was the promotion battle and the widespread feeling that CID men were favoured in this respect. The other was the less clear demarcation of responsibility as between the branches.

Evidence of the career background of those promoted, apart from those officers on the research division, was not collected, so it is impossible to say whether or not there was truth in the assertion and belief that CID men had an above average chance of being 'made up'. But one or two points can be made in this connection. In the first place, given the particularistic criteria upon which it was necessary to base selection for promotion with the large number of equally well qualified candidates, CID men would be well placed in that by the very nature of their work they would be more likely to excite individual attention; working in a relatively small department meant that they would rapidly become known to their own senior officers and probably also to those in other departments and areas. Next, the structure of the CID was such that personnel were more likely to be put forward for promotion by their senior officers: as a result of working in a small closely-knit group, strong feelings of responsibility to each other tended to develop between the ranks. Again, at the time of the research there was a plan to put into practice a new policy of having only qualified men within the CID Then, too, there was the established practice of giving men already singled out as likely candidates for promotion a wide range of interdepartmental experience, which would mean that they would serve a stint on CID and enhance the figures for promotions out of the department. Finally, there was the point most frequently made by the men, that the large majority of the most senior officers in the force had been CID men and therefore favoured people from their own ex-branch. It seems likely that this played a much smaller part in the process than the other structural features outlined above, but it may have had a marginal impact. After all, as a rural sergeant a man would be responsible for crime on his section, and it was understandable in view of this that the authorities should regard CID experience as a useful additional qualification. But be all this as it may, the important point was that the uniform men *believed* that CID men were unfairly favoured in the distribution of promotions. They attributed this to either favouritism or downright maliciousness, and as a result tended to express some resentment of CID officers, though this was observed to be translated into overt action on only one occasion.

It was accepted that CID men should deal with 'serious' crime, which broadly meant break-ins, larcenies of goods to a high value, and offences against the person where there was considerable injury. They also dealt with offences where there were indications that professional criminals were involved or where there was a series of similar offences, or indeed with anything unusual, which left the beat men to deal mainly with larcenies and less serious assaults and non-indictable offences. As has already been shown (chapter 2, pp. 29–31), CID personnel assisted with 32·2 per cent of the crimes on one-man beats, excluding the two beats in the Hillbridge section where the resident CID man at Hillbridge dealt with most of the crime. But the demarcation of responsibility was vague. In Hillbridge, for example, the DC complained that he was left to deal with too much of the local crime, including many lesser offences for which he felt the section sergeant should have taken responsibility.

The men expressed discontent about other related issues. Beat men had a strong possessive feeling about their 'patch', and resented the intrusion of CID or indeed any other officers when the resident beat man had not been notified. In one case of a homosexual assault at a school, the local beat man was not even present when the matter was dealt with. In another case:

> Two CID men went round to question one of my old farmers without my knowing about some job or other. Of course, he wouldn't tell them a thing. Then, being a loyal old boy to his local copper, as soon as they'd gone he rang me up and told me. I went round, of course, and he told me all about it but he wouldn't tell them, you see, because he'd never seen them before. That makes you mad though, when people do things like that behind your back.

Another aspect of the situation which the beat men resented was that they felt they were not given due credit for any assistance which they did give to the CID in the solution of a crime. This, they felt, was the direct result of the promotion block which meant, as one probationary constable put it, that 'they like to take all the glory, if you see what I mean'. Two examples of this were directly observed, and other verifiable cases recounted.

Finally, communications were bad. This had several consequences: it impaired efficiency in that neither branch could make use of the information pool of the other; it was bad from the point of view of the morale of the beat men, and their resentment of being kept in ignorance of facts which concerned their beats and which they therefore felt entitled to know had the negative feedback effect of further impairing communications; it meant that there was little encouragement for younger officers in towns to assist the CID. In one case a young officer spotted and stopped a car which was wanted in connection with an offence, and the driver was questioned, but to no avail. Later the driver was incriminated from another source, and he finally admitted the offence. The young PC was ignorant of what had happened, believed that the arrest was as a direct result of his work, and was disappointed (though resigned) because no one gave him a word of congratulation. In this case the feeling was unfounded, since his 'lead' had not been the conclusive factor in the solution of the crime. Better communications could have avoided the misunderstanding and left one officer more willing to help again in future.

The position of the beat man is summed up by the following extract:

> Things are getting worse. They won't tell you what they're doing nowadays and there's nothing annoys a beat man more than not being in the picture . . . And they don't even tell you they're coming [to interview people on the beat], you know,

not even out of courtesy . . . At one time I used to manage all
that on my own.

There was another indicator of the position. There had reputedly
been one 'first-class' CID man on the division at one time. And the
qualities attributed to this legendary figure, the antithesis of the
contemporary staff, suggested the sources of dissatisfaction in the
current position. First, he had not stood on rank, he had been 'one
of the boys' when off duty; second, he had kept the beat and mobile
men 'in the picture' as to the crime situation and developments so
that in fact the men worked for and with him; third, he had always
notified men when he was coming on to their beats, and often taken
them on enquiries with him, or alternatively phoned up afterwards
and informed them of his actions; fourth, he had been a 'family
man' 'the same as the rest' and had taken his rest days and got his
work done within reasonable hours; fifth, though this was less often
mentioned, he had been very successful at his work.

If the local CID were 'the brains', senior CID and uniform officers
when they attended a crime were referred to as 'the circus'. Reasons
for resentment here were similar: a reduced opportunity for the
beat man to shine and a reduction in his status because other people
were 'making free' with his beat. Headquarters staff in general were
resented for similar reasons. They were felt to be favoured men in
the promotion race; they were felt to have little understanding of
what beat work was actually like and therefore both to expect too
much on some occasions and to give insufficient credit for good work
on others. It was thought that they wanted the beat man to make his
work calculable and thereby, in his view, to destroy his relationship
with the local community. They were felt to be 'on to a good thing'
in that they suffered none of the inconveniences of the policeman's
life but none the less had the advantages of a house or rent allowance
and early retirement on a good pension which were supposed to be
compensation for these hardships. Men on the division were fighting
a strong rearguard action to preserve their independence and their
own traditional ways of operating.

There seemed to be no antagonism to mobile men, though it was
recognized by beat men that, like the town men, they were anxious
to 'get reports', mainly because this was expected of them. But their
work was so different from that of the beat men that they did not
constitute a threat. Apart from the men posted to DHQ, beat men
tended to meet mobile men only when they were posted as observers
on the night patrol car or when they attended special functions.
The mobile men themselves were anxious to emphasize their distinct-
ness from the men of DHQ section, and therefore did not attend
assemblies, did not assist on the switchboard even when requested,

and made a point of emphasizing that they were responsible to the chief inspector in control room rather than to the local inspector. On the other hand, when the divisional van broke down one night when it was due to go out on patrol, one of the mobile men turned out, when requested by the inspector, to repair it, although he had been in bed when the call came. On another occasion when the divisional van broke down a mobile man came to repair it on his rest day, saying that he didn't really mind as he was only digging his garden. Thus there was working co-operation so long as the mobile men were accorded their due status and asked rather than ordered.

Social relationships between the men

The relative interdependence of county and city men on the social level shows a complex pattern of differences (Table 85). City men claimed to have significantly more friends in the police force, an average of 5·1 per man (n49) compared with 3·6 per man (n62) in the county. Those giving vague answers have been omitted. Twenty-nine per cent of country men compared with 16·3 per cent of city men claimed to have no friends in the police force. But city men

TABLE 85 *Estimated number of friends in the police*

	No. of friends									No. of respondents	Numerous/ several	No answer
	0	1	2	3	4	5	6	7–10	Over 10			
County	18	6	9	7	7	2	4	1	8	62	2	—
City	8	3	7	6	3	3	8	2	9	49	4	2

had also claimed to have more non-police friends (chapter 4, p. 85) so that it could not be said on this basis that they were more dependent for friendship upon other policemen than were county men. The most reasonable explanation of the difference seems to be that city men had more opportunity to get to know their colleagues well than did county men, the latter often claiming that the only friends they had were those with whom they joined. However, it might be argued that since county men had fewer civilian friends, particularly in their immediate area of residence, they were in fact more dependent on those friends within the force which they had, although these might be fewer in number. The figures are open to a choice of interpretation.

What is definite is that there were considerable differences in the natures of the contacts which county and city men had with each other in off-duty hours. There was no significant difference between the forces in the mean scores on the index for contact with other policemen in the preceding fortnight, figures being 2·3 in the county and 2·1 in the city (Table 86). When the index is broken down into

TABLE 86   *Index of social contact with police*

			Score					
	0	2	3	4	5	6	No answer	n
County	26	9	4	11	8	5	1	64
City	27	4	5	4	11	3	1	55

its component parts of number of occasions on which meetings took place and numbers of people present at each meeting (Tables 87 and 88), there is no significant difference in the number of meetings, but a slight difference in the number of people involved. County men on average met 3·2 other policemen on each occasion, compared with 2·5 in the city. Some light is thrown on this difference by the related finding that 40·6 per cent of county men engaged in some police 'activity or hobby'—usually a sport—compared with only 36·4 per cent of city men (Table 89). More of the meetings between county men, therefore, tended to be formal social occasions such as

TABLE 87   *Number of occasions on which other policemen were seen socially in the last two weeks*

				Occasions						No. of	No
	0	1	2	3	4	5	6	7–10	11+	respondents	answer
County	26	18	7	2	4	2	2	0	2	63	1
City	27	6	6	4	3	3	2	2	1	54	1

TABLE 88   *Number of police seen in last two weeks*

				No. of people							No. of	No
	0	1	2	3	4	5	6	7–10	11–15	16+	respondents	answer
County	26	15	2	2	2	0	0	11	1	3	62	2
City	27	7	3	3	0	0	8	3	3	0	54	1

an organized sporting activity, whereas a higher proportion of social, as well as work, contacts between city men were informal.

H

215

TABLE 89   *Number of men engaging in any* social activity or hobby involving other policemen*

	Any police	Activity None	No answer	Total
County	26	37	1	64
City	20	35	—	55

*Includes 'main' activity as indicated in Table 22 and occasional activities mentioned, e.g., attendance at divisional dances.

Social contacts, in that they cut across formal boundaries of the work units, played an important part in the communication structure of both forces. But this function of breaking formal barriers to communication was less important perhaps than the counter-function which many of the meetings had of reinforcing certain other group boundaries. Thus in the city, CID men were not observed at any of the gatherings, either formal, such as a dance or football match, or informal gatherings in pubs or the men's houses, which were attended by uniform men. (The exceptions here were two gatherings partly initiated by the researcher—exceptions perhaps which prove the rule.) At one Christmas gathering only men from divisional headquarters, and then not the uniform beat men, were present—though other men serving in the same station were in the police club at the time and could have joined in.

In the county the divisive function of formal social gatherings was even more marked. True, men from different sections met together in, for example, the cricket team. The imbalance towards one sub-division here was a result of the fact that the organizer naturally knew the men in his own sub-division better and was in a better position to round them up for the game than other men whom he saw less often. But the team did field men from both sub-divisions. Those who were noticeably absent were members of specialist branches. Certain of the sports in both forces were favoured by the senior officers, and regarded as 'gimmicks' as a result. One such was the rifle shooting team in the county. At the interdivisional and force versus special constables match—the major event of the police rifle shooting year—the team from the research division contained only one man from a one-man rural beat, the remainder being mobile or town men. This beat man had only been transferred to the division a few weeks previously. Yet more than half of the divisional personnel were one-man beat men. Thus formal social activities reinforced in the county the solidarity of one-man beat men as opposed to the others who had a somewhat different approach to the work.

216

Relationships between wives

The dependence of the men on the force could be presumed to be enhanced if the lives of their wives were closely bound up socially with other police families, in the same way as the involvement of the wives in the work itself was shown (chapter 5) to be related to interdependence with the police. Wives with such high police interdependence would be those in the county who organized the refreshments for the rifle shoot or the divisional flower show, who prepared the show ground, manned the stalls, and remained behind to clear up; highly interdependent city wives had fewer opportunities of this kind to assist actively, though on one sub-division there was a social at which the wives provided refreshments. But in the city many of the social functions at which the men met each other were dances and gatherings which the wives could also attend. There was in fact a dance at the police club every week, though men might not wish to attend one organized by another division or specialist branch. But county wives had only some three or four opportunities per year to meet each other, and most of these were far more formal than the city gatherings.

Comments offered by the men and their wives in the city suggested that in general they did not like living in too close proximity to large numbers of other police families; county wives who lived in clusters of police houses expressed all shades of opinion on the subject, differences seeming to be a result of personality and past experience rather than the structure of the existing situation.

More concrete evidence is provided by the responses of the wives interviewed to questions concerning their numbers of contacts with other policemen or police families in the two weeks preceding the interview (Tables 90 and 91). The mean number of occasions on which a member of another police family was met was 2·2 in the county and 4·1 in the city. 51·8 per cent of county wives had had no such meeting in the period compared with 26·7 per cent of city wives. Not only did city wives meet with representatives of other police

TABLE 90 *Wives: number of occasions on which a member of a police family was 'seen' socially during the previous fortnight*

					Occasions						*Don't*	
	0	*1*	*2*	*3*	*4*	*5*	*6*	*7–10*	*11–15*	*16+*	*know*	*n*
County	29	9	8	2	2	1	—	—	4	1	1	57
City	8	6	3	3	1	1	1	3	2	2	—	30

families more often, but they also saw more people on each occasion. Mean numbers of people seen (for those who had had at least one meeting) were 3·6 in the city compared with 2·1 in the county. And difficulties of physical isolation and transport were not the sole reason for these discrepancies. County wives actually claimed to

TABLE 91   *Wives: contact with police families—number of 'people'* *
seen during previous fortnight

				Number seen						Don't	
	0	1	2	3	4	5	6	7–10	11–15	know	n
County	29	16	8	1	—	—	—	1	1	1	57
City	8	7	4	5	1	2	—	1	2	—	30

*See appendix III, p. 282 for definition.

have fewer friends in the police force than did city wives, means being 1·8 and 2·6 respectively (Table 92). 34·5 per cent of county wives and 29·6 per cent of city wives said that they had no friends connected with the police force.

TABLE 92   *Wives: number of friends in police*

			No. of friends					'Several'	Don't	
	0	1	2	3	4	5	6–10	etc.	know	n
County	19	8	13	6	5	—	4	—	2	57
City	8	4	2	3	6	1	3	2	1	30

Thus while the wives of county men were more closely bound up with their husbands' work, the wives of city men were bound up with the police force indirectly through the associated social life. But city wives had a choice of whether or not they wished to participate thus fully in their husband's occupation; county wives were forced willy-nilly to participate in the work, however much they might resent having so to do.

Effectiveness of colleagues as role-definers

Since interdependence with colleagues was higher in the city the prediction was that more city men than county men would act in the way in which their colleagues thought they ought to act. Again the prediction was borne out (Table 93). The mean number of situations in which city men said that their colleagues would disagree with the action which they would take was only $0 \cdot 2$; for county men the average was $0 \cdot 5$. Of city men, $11 \cdot 6$ per cent, compared with $37 \cdot 5$ per cent of county men said that their colleagues would disagree with them in at least one situation. The differences within the two forces

TABLE 93 *Number of situations in which colleagues would disgree with action*

| | Situations | | | | | | | |
	0	1	2	3	4	5	6	Total
County	40	15	9	—	—	—	—	64
City	46	8	1	—	—	—	—	55

between high and low scorers were slight, but in the expected direction in both cases. In the county the mean number of situations with which colleagues were perceived as disagreeing was $0 \cdot 6$ for those with below average scores on the police interdependence index, and $0 \cdot 4$ for those with high police interdependence. The means in the city were $0 \cdot 3$ for low scorers and $0 \cdot 1$ for high scorers. Thus there is

TABLE 94 *Number of situations in which colleagues would disagree by police interdependence*

| IDP | Situations | | | | | | | |
	0	1	2	3	4	5	6	Total
County:								
Below mean	18	8	6	—	—	—	—	32
Above mean	21	7	3	—	—	—	—	31
No answer	1	—	—	—	—	—	—	1
Total	40	15	9	—	—	—	—	64
City:								
Below mean	16	6	1	—	—	—	—	23
Above mean	30	2	—	—	—	—	—	32
Total	46	8	1	—	—	—	—	55

further evidence to support the hypothesis that behaviour is in the direction of the role projections of the group with which inter-dependence is highest (Table 94). Low scorers in the county perceived lack of consensus among their colleagues more frequently than high scorers. Details are given in Table 95.

TABLE 95 *Number of situations in which colleagues' opinion would be divided, by police interdependence*

| | | | | Situations | | | | | |
IDP	0	1	2	3	4	5	6	Total	Mean
County:									
Below mean	13	8	9	—	2	—	—	32	1·1
Above mean	18	10	1	—	1	1	—	31	0·7
No answer	—	1	—	—	—	—	—	1	
Total	31	19	10	—	3	1	—	64	
City:									
Below mean	12	9	1	1	—	—	—	23	0·6
Above mean	18	7	5	2	—	—	—	32	0·8
Total	30	16	6	3	—	—	—	55	

Summary

Interdependence with the police scores were found to be associated with career satisfaction (city) and also with type of post, the real association with the latter occasioning the apparent link with the former. They were also associated with 'awareness and appreciation' score (city) and place of posting (both forces).

City men were observed to be highly dependent on one another as a result of legal and other infringements, the risk of physical injury, easing behaviour and the need for co-operation in the achievement of organizationally set goals. As a result there was a considerable degree of colleague solidarity and mutual support and backing. However, discretion and secrecy were highly valued, both as a defence against the relatively high visibility to colleagues of the various illicit activities, and so as not to place too great a responsibility on the colleague and thereby too great a strain on the colleague relationship itself. But information about other men was valued— as an insurance perhaps against ever being 'shopped' by them. The qualities admired in colleagues stemmed directly from the structure of these relationships.

The group of experienced policemen had considerable power over recruits, having many sanctions, both positive and negative, at their disposal. Recruits therefore tended to be socialized into the ways of beat men rather than senior officers where these were opposed. Recruits who resisted socialization were negatively sanctioned. Social controls were also observed to be put into operation against older policemen who proved deviant, either by talking too much, backing out of a fight, or in some way threatening the solidarity of of the work group.

In the county there were fewer identifiable reasons for solidarity between the men. In the small town the structure of the power hierarchy operated to prevent colleague solidarity. On the rural one-man beats there was a feeling of comradeship which developed from an intimate understanding of each other's work coupled with the feeling that other men and particularly senior officers lacked this understanding. There was some evidence of solidarity but it was inhibited by the close promotion contest. 'Covering' of mistakes in the county was usually an individual affair though there were exceptional situations. But despite this the beat men gave priority to their relationship with the local community rather than to senior officers in the matter of the reporting of all offences. There thus arose a difference in approach between beat men and other patrol men.

Relationships between uniform men and members of specialist departments tended to be better in the city where lines of responsibility were clearly demarcated and the uniform men did not have strongly possessive feelings, involving their status, about their beats. Specialists tended to be resented in the county because they were thought to be favoured for promotion, in the city because they reinforced the beat man's feeling of belonging to an undervalued residual category. Communications between departments were bad in both forces.

City men claimed to have more friends in the police than county men, but their social contacts with them, like their work contacts, tended to be informal. In the county a higher proportion of both work and social contacts were formalized. In both forces these social contacts provided a means of communication between some sub-systems, but reinforced the boundaries between others.

Like their husbands, city wives claimed to have more friendships within the police force than county wives. They also saw other police families more often and more people on each occasion than the county wives. Again, their contacts with each other were less formal than in the county, and there were more opportunities in the city for wives and husbands from police families to meet together informally. It was relatively difficult for the wife of a one-man beat man to make new friends within the police force. But even so two-thirds of the county wives had had at least one social contact with another police family during the fortnight before the interview, which suggests that contact was low only in relation to the city wives, and not in relation to any external standard concerning contact between wives of workmates.

City men more frequently than county men were found to act in accordance with the role definitions projected by their colleagues. This was as expected on the basis of the hypotheses as outlined, since interdependence with colleagues was higher in the city. Men with low scores on the police interdependence index in both forces perceived a greater number of disagreements on the part of colleagues than men with high police interdependence scores. Low scorers also perceived lack of consensus among their colleagues more frequently than high scorers on the police interdependence index.

8 Summary, conclusions and a forward look

City Sergeant: The thing about this job today, and our
superintendent, is that he expects you to do everything right
to the book. That's how he wants it. And you know as well as
I do that you can't in an area like this; you just can't. So
you see, you're against everyone, and you've got to pit your
wits with him as well as the public . . . But I like my job.
You see, I have the advantage over the men because I see them
all, whereas they only know their own turn, and naturally
they think their turn is the best. That's only natural . . .

Introduction

This final chapter has three discrete aims. The first is to summarize
the body of the foregoing analysis; the second is to present some
further data which draw together the necessarily segmented picture
which has been presented, and go some way towards testing the
propositions outlined in chapter 1; the third is to raise 'so what'
questions—so what in terms of sociological theory and so what in
terms of practical policing.

Who defines the policeman's role? A recapitulation

This section uses results from interviews, observations and administrative records. It presents a total picture of each police force and
of the web of relationships which constrain and support the police
officer in the rural and urban areas. Interdependence with the four
role-defining groups remains the focus of attention, though the
differential effects of the pressures from these sources are examined
more systematically in the next section of this chapter. Here, in so
far as is possible, the relationship with the four 'groups' as they

focus upon and are linked through a single police officer is *qualitatively* examined. The questions posed and answered in this section concern how the world looks to a policeman. The sergeant quoted explains how three of the four sets of relationships felt to him. How far was he typical?

This question is answered first for men in the county force, and then for city men. Five concepts have been introduced and defined in the preceding pages which facilitate this. These are easing behaviour (pp. 37, 72–5, 190–2), perks (p. 36), gimmicks (p. 73), infringements (pp. 161–3) and dependent uncertainty (pp. 150–2, 157). Of these, *easing behaviour* and *dependent uncertainty* add a new *dimension* to the traditional view of the structure of the relationship between higher and lower participants in an organization. *Infringements* as here defined are probably unique to the police situation. Within the police force their effect on structure is similar to that of easing, though probably it is more important in determining that structure (cf. Westley, 1956). *Perks* and *gimmicks* have less important effects on structure. The former help to consolidate the police group because they represent an experience not shared with those in other occupations. The latter emphasize the divisions within the colleague groups, and conversely reinforce the bonds between sub-groups of colleagues. In the city, by reducing the available manpower, gimmicks also limit the definitions of police work which it would be possible for the men to adhere to.

Policing in a county force

Considerable differences were found between city and county men in their relationships with members of the community which they served. Biographical characteristics which were examined (place of birth and number and type of previous jobs held) showed that county men had more in common with those they policed than city men. Amount of social contact with the community was also greater for county men. It was argued that previous exposure to similar definitions together with opportunity to learn local norms would make it at least possible for county men to police by consensus (chapters 2 and 4).

Moreover, the county policeman, in particular the man working a one-man rural beat, was highly motivated to accept the community's definition of reality and of his role. In the first place, he was dependent on the co-operation of local people in order to do his work. Rural crimes tended to be approached in the traditional 'detective story' manner, beginning with looking for evidence or 'clues' at the scene of the crime (pp. 44–5; also p. 106). A policeman trying to solve a crime in a rural area is heavily dependent on what local people know or have seen and are prepared to tell him; professional informers figure less prominently. Although crime constituted a small amount of the rural policeman's work, the clearing up of crimes on his beat mattered disproportionately to the beat man because the community defined certain aspects of this work as important, because of the prestige attached to this form of work by the police value system, and because it was one way of attracting the favourable attention of senior officers (chapter 2, pp. 30–2; chapter 3, p. 71; chapter 4, pp. 105–6; chapter 6, pp. 148–51; chapter 7, pp. 210–12).

The rural policeman also needed the co-operation of the local people in maintaining order, a 'quiet patch' being his main objective. He needed their help in coming forward as witnesses of accidents and non-indictable offences; sometimes he needed immediate practical help such as holding traffic warning lights while he himself dealt with witnesses. In addition, he was dependent on their hospitality and friendliness to make his work congenial (chapter 2, pp. 35–8; chapter 4, 105–11).

In the county, policemen spoke of being 'friendly' with the people on their beats, but emphasized that these people were not 'friends'. They felt it necessary to maintain social distance in order to carry out their work (chapter 4, pp. 85, 88).

County wives were in a similar position. But in their case the social distance was felt to result from pressures from the community rather than being their own choice. Yet country wives paid and received more social visits than city wives. Again, the pattern of being 'friendly but not friends' is apparent. County police families were thus heavily dependent on their relatives for affective relationships and, despite the distances involved, saw them as frequently as city men (chapter 4, pp. 92–8). The social dependence of the wives on the local people reinforced the community's power over their policeman, and enhanced the probability that he would come to accept their definitions of the world in general and his place within it.

For county men, the relationships which they formed in the course of their work were often sufficient compensation for their status isolation; for the wives, however, the isolation, which was often both social and geographical, could be a cause of considerable distress. This, coupled with the constant intrusions upon domestic life which resulted from living in the police station, the anxiety caused by the state of dependent uncertainty about transfer and the relatively frequent uprooting for the whole family which a posting entailed, meant that wives who were not themselves committed to and interested in police work were under a considerable strain. There was a feedback effect of this on the men, who were more interdependent with the police force if their families too accepted it.

These are the facts which underlie the positive correlations between both career satisfaction and interdependence with the police (IDP) and marital integration in the county (pp. 127–31, 152–58).

While the county beat man is heavily dependent on the community for the carrying out of his work, he is not very much dependent upon his colleagues. The county policeman met his colleagues socially more often than did the city man, but he did not see them every day at work. Usually, the only contact with other policemen for a rural beat man was the daily phone call to the section sergeant. Interdependence with colleagues as observed and as shown by IDP scores was less in the county than in the city. Yet there was a great deal of understanding of each other's problems between men on one-man beats, and a respect for each other's work and territory. PC 'A', for example, would notify PC 'B' if he had any work to do on B's beat. One-man beat men shared a definition of police work—projected, I would argue, by members of the community policed. Town policemen, even within the county force, had a different definition of their role (chapter 2, pp. 40–2), arguably because in their case community power was less and the source of the role definition different. These differences were reflected in the behaviour of the men both at work (chapter 7, pp. 204–5) and socially; one-man beat men always sat together at section meetings at DHQ; one-man beat men and others tended to join different police sports teams (chapter 7, p. 216).

Senior and intermediate officers did not have much direct impact on the work of men on one-man beats. The PC's area of discretion was very wide, and even the sergeant did not issue many instructions about the day-to-day work on the beat. Sergeants, however, could directly influence the work of the men by requiring them to do a duty in the section station, and more senior officers would allocate men to carry out other special duties away from beat stations (chapter 6, pp. 160, 164–5). Section sergeants in the country played a particularly important buffer role, and the importance of their individual orientations was shown, for example, by marked differences between sections in the men's perceptions of senior officers (chapter 6, pp. 172–7).

The dependence of the men on senior officers stemmed mostly from the state of *dependent uncertainty* concerning transfers and promotions. Qualified PCs were in direct competition with each other for the few vacancies within the higher ranks. Since approximately half the men with the requisite amount of service for promotion were equally well qualified on paper, selection had to be made on the basis of more particularistic criteria. One 'lucky break', it was thought, was enough to bring a man to the favourable attention of senior officers; similarly it was thought that one mistake could ruin a man's promotion chances indefinitely. But because much of the work was invisible from other constables this did not give rise to a code of secrecy between the men. It was not necessary. What did result from this was a manner of evaluating sergeants in terms of the amount of 'backing' the individual constable could expect from them in the event of a possible disagreement with higher authority (chapter 6, pp. 148–58, 176).

Senior officers were not in a position directly to supervise the work of the beat men. They were, therefore, presumed to attach considerable importance to the number of reports which the men submitted of non-indictable offences, this being the only visible evidence of on-going work. This was resented by the rural beat men who felt that it conflicted with their peace-keeping role; they felt that by cautioning rather than reporting offences they could create or consolidate the essential good relationship with the community. The men were thus highly motivated to keep certain of their actions secret from intermediate and senior officers. On the other hand, county men had more regular contact with senior officers than city men, with the exception of those city men who were posted to the divisional headquarters (pp. 106–10, 176–7, 204–5).

Small towns Men in the towns within the county were in a different position in respect of each of these variables. The extreme case of this was Hillbridge, the largest of these towns, which is considered here. An above-average number of less experienced men were posted to the towns where supervision could be closer. Five of the seven men posted to Hillbridge had less than five years' service. Town men could, therefore, anticipate a transfer away from the area relatively soon, since it was customary to give younger men as wide a range of experience as possible. Members of the community policed therefore had little power over them. Conversely, intermediate and immediate superiors had considerable powers. Most important, they could control the hours the men worked. The staff of the station was two men below establishment, and it was, therefore, necessary for the available men to work a high proportion of late evening and night shifts. This had detrimental effects on their domestic lives. But resentment of this was directed not so much against the late duties themselves as against the inequitable distribution of them. This shows the arbitrary nature of senior officers' power in a situation where bureaucratization was incomplete but the policeman was no longer embedded in the local community (pp. 40–2; 164–5). Relationships between colleagues in Hillbridge were characterized by mutual distrust and competition for the favours of superiors. This situation was not found anywhere else in either police force (chapter 7, pp. 203–7).

City force

The nature of the relationship between city policemen and the community they served differed again from that of county men. Few city men had been born locally, and a high proportion of them had joined direct from the police cadets. There were, therefore, fewer bases for the development of common understanding, or a value consensus with members of the local community (chapter 4, pp. 98–104). Because of the separation of home and work and specialization within the police force, as well as the generally less integrated pattern of urban life, the non-police community was perceived as fragmented. Broadly, it was divided into the two categories of the 'rough' and the 'respectable'. A degree of understanding, possibly leading to more lenient treatment, was possible with the 'respectable'; there was less consensus with 'rough' groups, such as criminals and coloured people, although encounters with them could be re-defined so as to make understanding possible. The main constraints on the handling of 'rough' citizens were how much superiors and the law would stand, and something akin to Bittner's demonstrated need for economy in encounters, which would also include the avoidance of 'unnecessary' visits. There was thus considerable variation between individual policemen in their handling of people who fell within these categories (chapter 3, pp. 64–72; chapter 4, pp. 89, 112–19).

Understanding was extended to rough categories on occasions which could be accepted by the policemen as 'special', such as a wedding or Christmas. There were also positive relationships with members of 'rough' categories on a contractual basis. For such relationships value consensus was not required. It was possible, for example, for a policeman to bargain with a criminal or an informer, but this involved an exchange of services rather than empathetic understanding (chapter 4, pp. 113–16).

Not only did city men have fewer bases for the development of a shared meaning system and value consensus with their public than county men, but they were also less motivated to develop one. The power over them of the local community was low.

City wives were not dependent on the people their husbands policed. They had fewer purely social contacts than rural wives, but they saw members of as many non-police families because a higher proportion of city wives worked. So they were not isolated and dependent on their neighbours in the same way. Both the men and their wives in the city spoke of selected 'friends' among the 'respectable'; the element of social distance apparent in the 'friendly with but not friends' relationship of county men was not apparent (chapter 4, pp. 84–98).

Furthermore, city men were not dependent on the community as a whole in order to do their work. Uniform men did not deal with criminal investigations; CID personnel were not dependent on receiving information from people living in the area of a crime, but rather on known informers who could help them select likely culprits from among those who were permanently in the area of suspicion. Similarly, uniform men were not dependent on the whole community for the provision of job easing facilities but rather on a limited segment of it. Again, for support in the event of physical danger and other immediate practical assistance, city men turned to their colleagues rather than to local people (chapter 7, pp. 189–94).

In the city there were insufficient men for a peace-keeping role to be adopted, yet many of the functions of an emergency service and the more interesting aspects of the work were hived off by mobile patrols and various specialist departments. The result of this was that the average beat patrol could have been both unpleasant and monotonous (chapter 3, pp. 54–64). Several means of compensating for this were developed. In the first place, uniform men could 'make the job interesting' by 'booking' members of 'rough' categories, for such offences as being drunk and disorderly. 'Respectable' people were not similarly at risk, though as much for independent structural reasons as because of police selections. The availability in the central area of large numbers of these vulnerable members of the population meant that the policemen, by very frequently arresting them for drunkenness and other 'public order' offences could achieve two things. First they could avoid potential monotony in their work. For this alone they were envied by some of their colleagues on quieter sub-divisions. Second, they enhanced their status because the activity which they were engaging in—frequent arrests—was closely analogous to the 'thief-taking' activity which is believed to be consensually backed, and therefore provides a blanket legitimation for other police tasks. There was some ambivalence, because some men acknowledged that the 'drunks' were not 'real criminals', but none the less it was generally understood that a 'good' night meant a busy night for prisoners (chapter 3, pp. 64–72).

The second way, and the officially encouraged way, of preventing boredom was for a man to develop contacts with individual people living on his beat. But his ability to do this was limited by the size of the area and population he was responsible for, and by the fact that at the time of the research there were no permanent beats (chapter 3, p. 65). *Because the definition of good police work in the city was more closely linked with thief-taking, 'working up' a beat in this way did not necessarily give a man status* (as it did in the country where the community defined the policeman's role, and defined it in peace-keeping rather than thief-taking terms (pp. 70–2)).

Third, a man could have recourse to official or unofficial methods of job easing. Official job easing, while alleviating the problem of monotony for individual officers, exacerbated the total situation. Considerable advantage was taken of officially provided facilities for sports and other activities, with the result that manpower on the ground was further reduced and a satisfying 'peace-keeping' role made even less possible (chapter 3, pp. 72–5).

Unofficial easing behaviour had equally far-reaching consequences. The form of these activities varied according to the characteristics of the beat and time of day. In high density areas the men could make use of the many cafés, pubs and clubs; in the more surburban areas the men had to take their unofficial breaks in the police station. Cutting across this broad distinction was a second: it was easier for men working in small section stations unofficially to call back to their base than it was for men in sub-divisional stations, who might be seen by intermediate superiors if they did so. Easing behaviour also varied from shift to shift according to the amount of work and the times when pubs and clubs could be used. In the central areas there was a peak period of work in the late evenings, which meant that easing behaviour was both less necessary and less possible. *The men prided themselves on always doing the work that was there to be done. It was in their much narrower definition of 'work' that they differed from county men.* A thief-taking definition meant that for much of their tour of duty there was 'no work'. Easing behaviour was legitimate because it was engaged in only at times when there was 'nothing to do'. On the 10.00 p.m.–6.00 a.m. shift it was easy to make an after hours call to a public house, and also on occasion to find a congenial put-up for a short nap (chapter 3, pp. 54–72).

Easing behaviours were often engaged in collectively, since the number of convenient places to visit late at night was restricted. As a result men were dependent on each other's silence to ensure that they were not 'shopped' to intermediate senior officers. They were similarly dependent on each other's tact to ensure that legal infringements against members of the 'rough' out-group were not drawn to their superiors' attention. Thus strong bonds of trust were developed between men on the same 'turn' or shift cycle. These were further strengthened by the fact that the men ran considerable risks of physical injury in the course of their work, and felt dependent on their colleagues to come to their assistance in the event of a fracas with members of the public (chapter 7, pp. 189–97). The other side of this penny was that men who could not be trusted were excluded from the supportive fellowship of the group. They could not be sure of backing if they got into difficulties *vis-à-vis* senior officers, though any policeman would be supported in a dispute with members of the public. Men whose work or social activities brought them into frequent informal contact with senior officers were not trusted, since there was a danger that they might inadvertently 'drop' information. Recruits were not fully trusted until they had had an opportunity to prove themselves in the three areas of legal infringements, easing behaviour and support in a fight. Recruits were particularly motivated to conform to the unofficial norms since they were dependent on the older policemen to teach them the job and show them ways of making it more pleasant, and because a sergeant would mention in his report on a recruit how well that recruit got on with other officers. The stress for recruits was considerable, for they were also more highly dependent than other men on the approval of senior officers during the probationary period, and the pressures from senior officers often ran counter to those from the men. Senior officers, for example, expected probationary constables to put in frequent offence reports for traffic offences, while treating the 'respectable' in this way was generally disapproved by experienced men as not being 'real police work' (chapter 7, pp. 197–201).

Senior officers had a considerable battery of sanctions which could be used against experienced constables, too, if necessary. It was thus essential that information about specific instances of illicit activities of all kinds should be kept from them. Both rewards and punishments were administered more formally in the city than in the county force, though in the city intermediate officers had greater informal control over the working conditions of the men (Hillbridge excepted). Rewards took the form of compliments, commendations and merit stripes, while punishments took the form of formal disciplinary proceedings leading to a reprimand, fine or dismissal. Informal control over a man's career prospects was less than in the county, since the relative shortage of qualified men meant that most of those who *did* qualify were automatically promoted. This also served to reduce one possible source of competition between the men, and was therefore an enabling factor for the development of strong colleague ties (chapter 6, pp. 147–60). Thus, the power of senior officers in the city was less than the more arbitrary, unrecorded power of senior officers in the county.

Moreover, in the city the men's superiors were in turn dependent upon them. Senior officers depended on the men to feed information about the work into the formal communication system, and all superiors were dependent on the men to carry out the work adequately, since tasks were initiated at ground level, and the men could not be directly supervised (chapter 6, pp. 144–6, 166–8). Except where relatively inexperienced men had been rapidly promoted through a series of specialist departments, city men did not feel the same gap in understanding between themselves and their senior officers as a one-man beat men did.

Interdependence with intermediate officers was even higher, for the inspector was accountable for the work of the shift. If the beat man made a mistake, he had to 'carry the can'. He was dependent on them not to take their illicit activities too far. This was particularly so in the case of legal infringements. Often it was the inspector's responsibility to accept the charge. Although in theory he could refuse to do so, in practice this would antagonize the men, which he could not afford to do as he was largely dependent for his own advancement on the results of their work. So in practice the inspector often had to accept responsibility for the decisions made by the men, and rely on them to be discreet. They in turn relied on him for legal advice about the formulation of charges and the recording of events, and for 'practical' advice as to how best to avoid trouble from senior officers, the public and the courts. The men also relied on the inspector to back them if such trouble did arise (pp. 160–6).

Partly because of this close interlinking of dependency, sets of informal rules developed about the appropriate behaviour for an inspector in a variety of situations. Thus it was expected that an inspector would 'send it down town' (institute formal disciplinary proceedings) if a man were found drinking on duty. On the other hand, it was also expected that the 'stick' would not go around seeking out such offences against the Discipline Code. He was expected to turn a blind eye to illicit activities unless the man concerned were caught red-handed (chapter 6, pp. 174–6).

Sergeants in the city indulged in the same legal infringements, prisoner-getting and easing behaviours as the men, and were to the same extent at risk of becoming embroiled in a fight. Their interdependence with the men was based on the same variables as interdependence between colleagues, and they were subjected to the same testing out procedures.

The picture which emerges from the analysis of the city police force is therefore one of a body of men with strong ties of mutual dependence which are both horizontal and vertical. The police force is a tight, integrated whole facing a community, which is seen as segmented[1] and in part undesirable. Family life is separate and has no effect upon this almost confrontation style relationship. The community has no power over the beat officer, and so cannot define his role. There is thus no mechanism by which shared definitions of the world between policeman and policed could be brought about.

Consequently, the police role definitions in the city were virtually autonomous. The family was irrelevant to the work situation, the community policed powerless. The power of senior officers was limited, so that they could project neither their own autonomously evolved definitions, nor those presented to them and accepted by them from other sources such as the Home Office or localized power groups. Agreement between ranks resulted from senior officers accepting beat men's definitions. The colleague group evolved its own definitions of role and of relevant others from legal categories, an estimate of the amount of police work likely to be generated by each type, and an assessment of consensual support, 'evidence' of which was available only for 'thief-taking'.

Quantitative evidence

The analysis so far has shown the usefulness of taking the differential power of role-definers as the core of an examination of police work. Although some doubt was expressed (chapter 1, pp. 9–10) about the value of attempting to quantify the effects of this power on police action, none the less responses to the 'hypothetical situation' questions have by and large been in anticipated directions. Thus one-man beat men said that members of the community would disagree with their action less often than policemen in any other type of post (although the scale which estimated wish for integration with the community had no predictive value); in the city men with high marital integration said that their wives would disagree with their action less often than men with low marital integration; in the county, marital integration was related to police interdependence and career satisfaction, and perhaps for this reason was not related to the number of situations in which the wife would disagree, or think a different action should be taken; in the city force, where interdependence with the police as observed and as measured was higher, fewer men than in the county said that either senior officers or colleagues would think they ought to take a different action from the one which they chose. Within forces here the differences were slight, though there was a tendency for county men scoring high on police interdependence to say that their senior officers would disagree with them less often than men scoring low on police interdependence (pp. 179–80).

What then can be said about role conflict? If two role-defining groups projected different definitions, which would win? The marital integration index provided one useful measure of inter-dependence, and the interdependence with the police index, although open to attack on many grounds, has been shown in these pages to work. These provided the basis for the first set of tests.

One would expect that in situations which are by definition police work relevant in the role definition of colleagues and superiors would be more relevant, and powerful, than that of the wife. The proposition on p. 7, however, would lead us to predict that where

233

marital integration is low and police interdependence is high action would be in the direction of police (colleagues') expectations more frequently than in the reverse situation where marital integration is high and police interdependence is low. This applies only in situations where the man sees wife and colleagues as thinking he ought to do different things, i.e., situations of disagreement.

This prediction was borne out in the city force, but not in the county. In the county, owing to the relationship between MI and IDP already discussed, there were only five men in the first category (high IDP, low MI) and three in the second (high MI, low IDP). Figures for city men are given in Table 96.

TABLE 96 *Probability of action being in accordance with police role definitions (city force)—situations in which wife and colleagues or wife and superiors disagree about action to be taken*

IDP	MI	% actions in direction of colleagues	% actions in direction of superiors
Above mean	Below mean	100·0	73·9
Below mean	Above mean	75·0	61·6

When high and low scorers on the wish for integration with the community scale are related to high and low scorers on the police interdependence index the results are as expected in the county; in the city, wish for integration with the community is seen to have no effect on action when in competition with the colleague group (this can be readily understood now, although it was not predicted) but the results are as anticipated when actions in the direction of superiors' expectations are considered (Table 97). Again, only situations of discrepant role definition are considered.

For county men, to want to be integrated with the community could mean adopting a whole policing style. Thus if you wanted to be integrated you would have to be prepared, in police relevant situations, to go against senior officers and colleagues if that was what the community demanded. The role segregation of city men and the variety of structural factors reducing the power of those actually policed meant that for city men this was less of a problem. Integration to them meant being accepted by neighbours, if they lived away from the beat and in private housing, by a loose built network of friends of their own choosing, and having people generally not regard their occupation as relevant when they were off

TABLE 97   *Probability of action being in accordance with police role definitions—situations in which community and colleagues or community and superiors disagree.*

IDP	Wish for integration with community	% actions in direction of colleagues	% actions in direction of superiors
County:			
Above mean	Below mean	93·1	73·7
Below mean	Above mean	69·3	33·3
City:			
Above mean	Below mean	100·0	83·3
Below mean	Above mean	100·0	78·3

duty. Thus their friends were not expected to have an opinion about how they handled matters which could be defined as police work. On the other hand, the magnitude of interdependence with colleagues has been emphasized again and again. Thus it is no surprise that those wishing for integration with the community, in the sense outlined above, were also able to act consistently in the direction of colleagues' expectations in potentially police work relevant situations.

The relative power of the four role-definers can also be assessed by a comparison of the mean number of situations in which there would be disagreement from each of these groups. This is a risky enterprise; the situations were selected and did not in any sense represent a range of normal life experience, or even a sample of potentially conflictful, police work salient situations. The data must therefore be handled with extreme caution.

Another problem is that the influence of the different groups varied in an uncontrolled way from situation to situation. In the situation in the public house, for example, where the wife was stated to be present, her influence was seen to be relatively more important.

With these major reservations in mind it is possible only to make remarks about, rather than draw conclusions from, the evidence. Table 98 sets out the mean number of disagreements perceived from each group.[2]

This shows that despite the divergencies between the two forces in the relative influence of each of the four groups taken separately, nevertheless the hierarchy of potency, the rank ordering of the groups, was similar. County men may have paid less attention to colleagues' expectations than city men, but they still acted in accordance with the expectations of colleagues more frequently

TABLE 98 *Mean number of situations in which each role-defining group would 'disagree', i.e., think the respondent ought to take a different action*

Role-definer	Mean County	City
Colleagues	0·5	0·2
Senior officers	1·4	0·9
Wife	1·4	1·2
'Community' or 'public'	2·1	1·8

than they conformed to the expectations of any other role-defining group or person. *In both forces colleagues' expectations carried more weight than did opinions of senior officers.*

The only difference between the forces in respect of the effectiveness ranking was in the relative importance of the wife. Her expectations in the county area carried as much weight as did those of senior officers. In chapter 5 it was shown that the county wife had a considerable part to play in her husband's work, and that her attitude to and involvement in this work both affected the man's own satisfaction with his work and also had a feedback effect on the integration of the marriage itself. It is, therefore, understandable that her opinion should carry more weight in a work relevant situation—however broadly interpreted—than the opinion of the city wife in a similar situation.

Another deduction which can be made from these data is that county men on the whole acted more independently. They were in a situation of great structural conflict, in that they tended to perceive more disagreements from all role-definers than city men; they were independent in their judgments in that there was no group with whose role expectations they conformed as routinely as city men conformed to the expectations of colleagues.

Consensus within role-defining groups Respondents were not specifically asked about lack of consensus, but were free to answer if they chose that members of the role-defining groups would be at variance with each other. Where the perception was that the group would be equally divided within itself this was separately coded; otherwise the majority view was coded as either 'agreement' or 'disagreement'. Some results of this analysis are given in Table 99.

Senior officers were seen as having a more internally consistent set of values than members of other role-defining groups, as shown by the proportions of men in each force who perceived lack of consensus in at least one of the presented situations. Thus half the

TABLE 99 *Consensus within role-defining groups*

Role-defining group	% of men perceiving lack of consensus in at least one situation				% of all situations in which reference group perceived as internally divided			
	County		City		County		City	
	no.	%	no.	%	no.	%	no.	%
Colleagues	32	51·6	25	45·4	56	14·6	37	11·2
Senior officers	9	15·6	12	27·3	10	2·6	15	4·5
Public	19	43·7	19	54·5	28	7·2	30	9·1

men, approximately, conceived the possibility of disagreement between colleagues. City men, who were more highly interdependent with colleagues, were less likely to perceive lack of consensus within the colleague group. As already shown (p. 220), within both forces below average scorers on the police interdependence index were more likely to see colleagues as having divided opinions.

City men were, however, more likely to perceive lack of consensus on the part of senior officers. This could be the result of two structural features. First, there were more senior officers in the city, so mathematically the chance of some disagreement among them was greater: the perception could have been a realistic one. (The same, of course, is true of colleagues, though the effect is reversed. In other words the 'real' difference between forces discussed in the previous paragraph may be even greater than the figures suggest.) Second, city men were more closely in contact with intermediate superiors especially, and were, therefore, in a position to be aware of real disagreements. Senior officers in the county were remote and their informal contacts with the large majority of the men were limited; their opinions were therefore made known through official channels or formal meetings when actual discrepancies, if they existed, would not become apparent.

City men perceived disagreement within the general public more frequently than did county men. This is understandable since it has here been argued (chapter 4) that county men perceived themselves as part of a relatively unified community, whereas city men perceived the community as essentially segmented, with many sub-divisions within the two broad groups of the rough and the respectable. But

237

again, although approximately half the men were overtly aware of the possibility of lack of consensus, and chose to express their answers in these terms, yet this was not seen as applying in the overwhelming majority of presented situations.

This is as far as the questionnaire based statistical data can take us. The data in the main support the propositions outlined in the first chapter, and are in line with the more substantial argument developed in the intervening chapters. It should be remembered that the argument was completely written up *before* the solutions to the hypothetical situations—the core analysis of the research as originally conceived—were analysed. This prevented bending the interpretation of the 'softer' data to create a fit.

Conclusions

In this section I want to draw some more general conclusions from the analysis as presented. I want to raise the questions, what power will the citizenry have over their policemen in the future and what are the likely effects of the massive changes in police organization which have taken place in the decade since this research was begun? Answers to large questions must be tentative, but they can also be rewarding.

This whole monograph has been produced without any attention to one fundamental conceptual question, namely, how do we define a police force? I would suggest the following: an institutionalized group expected by those who support it to be predominantly oriented to the maintenance of their rules in a specific way, i.e., by preventing specific offences or types of offence or by dealing with specific rule-breakers. Thus the symbolic representational role discussed by Silver would not be a defining characteristic of police forces in so far as they represented in a *generalized* way the behavioural norms of the society. A definition such as that suggested would enable one to examine the accretion to the role of other tasks and other effects. It would also leave open to question the *source* of the norms governing the policeman's work. Again, it is unhelpful to define policemen by what they do (a functional definition) or what they think they should do (a definition in terms of *their own* orientations) because these are precisely the areas which one most wishes to investigate. The definition also makes possible the application of theories of policing to private police forces, both legitimate and illegitimate in terms of the wider society. It is based on the meaning of this group to relevant actors, but since the actors are those who support the group in existence rather than its members, the choice between metaphysical organizational goals and the empirically disparate orientations and actions of those in the organization is avoided. The definition implies that the group must legitimate itself to those who support it in terms of its success in maintaining the rules in the specified ways. The members must convince those who support them that the ways in which they operate achieve the desired result. This would apply whether or not the shared premise of action was that (1) apprehension and punishment was necessary to show that a rule is a rule, or that (2) everyone (including the rule-breaker) 'knew' that the rule was a rule, so a quiet word of admonition from the policeman to make the rule-breaker realize that he had erred would be enough.

The use of a definition of policing of this kind also enables us to see the question of who defines the policeman's role in a new light. Policing and police work are no longer givens, but mutable. It becomes necessary to distinguish between different levels of the enforcement process. The definitions of police work projected by those who support the police service—the Home Office and local authorities—may be different from those projected by other individuals and groups with different kinds of power. I would argue that the 'formal' definitions are probably more relevant for senior officers, whose status and career advancement in part depend upon their complying with these definitions, than for the man on the beat who is subject to a whole host of different pressures.

Take the rural area described as an example. So long as 'formal' and community dictates remained the same there was no difficulty. But at the time of the research a discrepancy between these two sets of role definitions was beginning to become apparent. This was shown up by the superintendent's emphasis (imposed on him from above) on central recording, which the beat men rejected. For men on one-man beats, I have argued, *the members of the community policed defined their role.* Complying with this definition precluded complying with the instruction to report all offences, however trivial, and to leave the decision as to action with the superintendent.[3]

Interesting questions as to the exact nature of the formal definition and how it was arrived at remain open. One can only guess that officials working in the Home Office require evidence of output to legitimate their decisions about expenditure. The chief constables need money to police better in their existing way, but in some cases the negotiation for the money is self-defeating in their terms, since in order to get it it may be necessary to redefine their task and start policing in a *different* way. This would certainly apply where 'peace-keeping' involving a low level of enforcement was the predominant mode.

In the city neither community nor senior officers predominantly defined the policeman's role. Most important in this was the group of constables itself. They had considerable autonomy from senior officers and an almost total independence of the community policed. In fact, however, the police task was defined in very similar ways by senior officers and patrol men. Both used categories of thought about the work which derived from legal categories. It seems plausible that this is also in line with the definitions used by central government. About the relationship of the local police authorities with the chief constable in the city I know and can guess nothing. Thus, given a measure of agreement about the police task, beat officers needed to use their relative autonomy only to devise ways which were more efficient, in their terms, of carrying it out, and means of making the job more pleasant. The first is the central point of Skolnick's work, yet he does not very clearly tell us the *source* of the 'societal' demand for output.

Despite discrepancies in the definition of the police role from 'community' and 'formal' sources, the policemen maintained a firm belief in a single consensual society. The formal definition may have been derived from that of a particular class or other grouping, which would indicate the absence of consensus. Policemen, however, in so far as they were aware of the discrepancy, blamed it on 'the Home Office'. In other words, the world in which they lived, their model of society, contained a populace with agreement at least about standards of legal and moral behaviour and a quasi-autonomous bureaucracy which sometimes got out of step. This blaming of discrepancies in definition on to the Home Office enabled them to continue to legitimate their role as enforcer's of 'the people's' standards.

In raising the question about whose norms the police enforce, and according to whose procedural norms, we have to return briefly to the point made in chapter 1, and reiterated in chapters 2–4. Policing according to local norms is possible only where the community to be policed is relatively homogeneous—the presence of a single unified definition of the police role of itself increases community power to some extent—or where the local community, although differentiated, has a stable power structure, so that police consistently enforce the law 'informally' in accordance with a particular set of interests. Both modes have been described as 'peace-keeping', though the intent and meaning of the under-enforcement and the source of the policeman's role definition differ markedly. The term 'peace-keeping' is perhaps best reserved for policing according to consensual community standards as in Goldman's middle-class suburb, or Wilson's very similar 'service style' area, or in Esselstyn's (1953) rural county, or the rural division discussed in this study.

I want to suggest that policing in this country is moving away from both these types towards a more autonomous mode, involving a new kind of consensual acceptance.[4]

Effects of changes in police organization

Since this research was carried out a number of changes in police organization have taken place. The Police College at Bramshill has strengthened its grip on professional training. This means that autonomous professional standards are being developed which will be another source of role definition for senior officers orientated to career advancement. We do not know what these role definitions are. Their effect on 'practical policing', should they be different from those of the men, cannot be assessed until one has examined the changes in the power structure resulting from the introduction of Unit Beat Policing.

The outline of this scheme is given in a report of the Home Office (1967). In the rural area, beats have been amalgamated so that there are fewer one-man beat men, and those who remain are equipped with motor vehicles. The effects of the changes are easier to assess in the rural areas, where they continue a trend which was already under way. At the time of the research, policemen were already being 'released' from their dependence on the local community, being put into a position where it was easier for them to make a decision contrary to the local expectations. And the community itself was changing to include an increasing proportion of town workers with different attitudes. The pay rise of 1961 played a not inconsiderable part in freeing men from the area they policed. Thereafter it was more common for the men to own cars and to have a more active social life outside their area. Changes in the structure of the community to be served, bureaucratic processes and technological developments, had between them made both necessary and possible a different disposition of manpower. So already a PC posted to a one-man rural beat could spend a considerable amount of time on centrally organized duties (cf. chapter 2). In this way the constable's contact with his beat and the people on it was reduced. This made the traditional role of rule by consensus more difficult; it also reduced the power of the local community and made it easier for the man to conform to police standards—these being the only other unified set of expectations available in his environment.

At the time of the research these processes were resented. The men felt that their status was involved with their traditional independence, and they felt they were not being offered an alternative role which seemed equally attractive. The amalgamations of beats and the increasing use of motorized patrols which have happened since carry the process a good way further. But by giving the men vehicles and putting them into radio contact with headquarers, and by drafting others to work a unit beat system of policing in the towns within the county area, it is hoped that some of the resentments will be overcome. There will at least be less ambiguity concerning the formal order of priority in a man's work, for the men will be given clearly specified tasks, and it will be clear to them where their primary loyalty lies. Reductions in the competition for promotion resulting from force amalgamations will serve to strengthen the horizontal groupings between colleagues at the same time as the power of the local community is broken down. The informal structure of county police forces will henceforth approximate more closely to that of the cities. For the rural policeman life may be made easier, but the changes will signify the end of peace-keeping as we have defined it. Members of the local communities will be less happy with the new system.

In the cities unit beats have been established on the model of rural one-man beats, with the beat man living in his area where possible. To supplement this there is the now well-known system of panda cars. Car crews, beat men and detectives (who have been transferred to the divisional strength) work together in area teams. A central information bank is kept. In addition, and perhaps most important, each man has been put into radio contact with headquarters.

It has been shown that under the old scheme strong resistances to formal authority developed. These resulted largely from infringements of the law and to a lesser extent from easing behaviour, and were reinforced by the fact that actual support was necessary in the face of a high risk of physical attack and injury. The dependence resulted from the need to keep specific acts secret from senior officers despite high visibility as between colleagues, and from the need to preserve the easing facilities for the benefit of the whole group. At the same time as ties with the colleague group and, to a lesser extent, with more senior officers were strong, ties with the local community were relatively weak. Qualities most admired in colleagues were, therefore, discretion, reliability in a fight, a knowledge of easing facilities, and 'know how' concerning the handling of extra-legal situations. Men who lacked these qualities, or who were at risk of being indiscreet because they had frequent informal contacts with senior officers, were not fully trusted. Nor were recruits until they had been tried and tested, and exclusion from the colleague group meant, as well as a less friendly atmosphere to work in, being unable to rely on colleagues when one needed to be 'covered' oneself, and exclusion from or non-introduction to many communal easing facilities.

In this way opinions and methods of working were perpetuated in spite of instructions from senior officers. Senior officers could not supervise directly. They were dependent for information on a highly formalized system of upwards communication and one or two individuals who were known and suspect to the men. It was, therefore, possible for the lower ranks to stop at source any information which they preferred that senior officers should not have.

The new system will make possible more control from above. It will improve efficiency in the direction of patrol men to incidents. For most men any residual notion of 'peace-keeping' is now removed. For unit beat men, on the other hand, this is now an officially defined part of their role. What has not been understood, perhaps, is that peace-keeping in the country areas worked only so long as senior police officers approved, if they did not share, the definition of the police role projected by the community. The urban working-class communities will be projecting different definitions of the good policeman. Conceivably, senior officers will not approve them all. The urban community will still lack the power over its beat officer which the rural community had; the officer will still have fewer biographical characteristics in common with them. Thus in the event of a discrepancy of role definitions, senior officers or colleagues will still 'win'.

Some of the motivation for harassment of drunks—but only in so far as this was a device to prevent boredom—will be removed. But the culture pattern may persist for a time and status attached to bringing in *any* prisoner will almost certainly remain. The effects of Unit Beat Policing on this kind of work are shown in Table 100. The figures relate to the first full year after the introduction of the new scheme. They do not show a very marked change from the figures under the old system, given on p. 68. At the beginning of October, Walker Street and Central station records were amalgamated, hence the adjustment in the table.

The adjustment for the whole year may not reflect the actual total, but there is no reason to suppose that the proportionate distribution

TABLE 100   *Central station arrests, 1968*

	Against the person	Property with violence	Breaks	Lar-ceny	Other pro-perty	Drunken driving	Drunk and public order	Solicit-ing, etc.	Other	Total
First nine months:										
Uniform	17	—	49	96	24	3	281	4	30	504
CID	7	1	22	47	1	—	2	—	13	93
Other	—	—	—	—	—	—	—	—	1	1
Total	24	1	71	143	25	3	283	4	44	598
Figures, multiplied up for whole year: Uniform	23	—	65	128	32	4	375	5	40	672
CID	9	1	29	63	1	—	3	—	17	124
Other	—	—	—	—	—	—	—	—	1	1

243

would be altered. This shows that 47·3 per cent of the arrests in the first nine months were for public order offences, as compared with 67·2 per cent of the arrests under the old system. So infringements in connection with these arrests have still to be concealed, but they play a less significant part in the policeman's work.

There is no reason to suppose that arrest for any other offence would be affected by the change. The uniform men, however, had an increasing share in handling those proceded against for indictable offences. This change began as soon as Unit Beat Policing did, midway through 1967. The absolute numbers also increased (Table 101).

TABLE 101 *Persons proceeded against for indictable offences by uniform and CID officers**

	Uniform	CID
Jan.–June 1967	254	285
July–Dec. 1967	282	233
1968	632	527

*Policewomen are excluded.

So uniform men should be doing more interesting, varied and prestigeful work, in their terms. The need for easing behaviour may consequently have been reduced. Thus another reason for the vertical communication gap has been weakened.

The third reason identified for colleague solidarity, protection in the face of physical violence, remains, and seems to be increasing. This, however, does not involve secrecy from senior officers.

Thus, in both types of area, the power of senior officers to define the policeman's role will be increased: in the country because community power is rapidly being broken down; in the city because the range of situations is being reduced in which the patrol man's actions must be kept secret from senior officers. Colleague support, however, will still be necessary both because physical risks appear to increase rather than decrease, and because colleague support against *public* question—in court or in complaints investigations—will continue to be necessary. At the same time the increasingly similar definitions of tasks and proper behaviour between ranks will mean that secrecy *vis-à-vis* intermediate officers in these situations may be less necessary. Senior officers,* of course, would not wish to support their men against members of the public where an allegation is

*This paragraph is speculative, and not in any way based on discussions or observations in the two research forces.

proven, yet in part their authority is legitimated only to the extent to which they give 'backing'. To avoid impalement on the horns of this dilemma it is better, from senior officers' standpoint, for complaints to be dealt with privately and internally, so unofficial understandings about what constitutes 'going too far' can be taken into account. This is not to say that senior officers would 'cover' all infringements. They may be very severe on those who by carelessness or by 'going too far' expose the force to public censure, and place its methods of operation at risk of public scrutiny. It is the day-to-day routine infringements which are 'necessary' for effective police work (as defined by senior officers, by constables, and by the press and police authorities), that is, for effective thief-taking and analogous work, which 'must' continue. Indeed, the new Commissioner of the Metropolitan Police, Mr Robert Mark, has argued strongly that police powers should be increased to make thief-taking more effective and 'minor' infringements unnecessary.[5]

What is not treated as problematic in these discussions is that question which is treated as central here, that is, the definition of the policeman's role itself. Arguments like those of the commissioner follow with a seeming logic from one kind of definition (given that we don't raise questions about how offences and offenders come to be so defined). It would seem that this kind of definition of policing is gaining ground in the rural areas, while in the city the existence of the unit beat officer is not undermining it. What policemen in fact do will progressively limit the range of ways in which the police role is conceived. When thief-taker and policeman become synonymous in the minds of the people one will have a new consensus, but of a qualitatively different kind from that which I have described as existing in the rural areas in 1962. This new consensus will result not from the community defining the policeman's role for him at a local level. It will result from (1) an increasing sameness between police forces in different areas, so that a single model of what policing is about is available, (2) increasing differentiation and mobility of local populations so that no other agreed definition of the police role is available, (3) the decline in structural power over the local police of local communities so that if an agreed definition were arrived at it could not be projected (here there is a feedback loop to points 1 and 2), and (4) the increasing acceptance by people, as memories fade, of the only definition of policing available to them. Thus, I would predict increasing agreement about what policing *is*, to the extent that questions about what it *should be* appear irrelevant, indeed nonsensical. This new style consensus is not indigenous but imposed. Thus, paradoxically, although there will be greater agreement about the policeman's role, the separation between policemen and those who accept (rather than project) this definition may be very wide; nor does a consensus of this kind in any way ensure that policemen will be 'liked' or approved of. In this new world policemen *are*, which is a fact that must be accepted. For the first time questions about whether people approve or disapprove of 'the police' become possible. In the earlier type of consensus they were not possible; people approved of policemen who worked one way and not of policemen who worked another, and they made efforts to ensure that they got what they wanted. In the new style consensus everybody knows what is meant by the police, and people can take a stand for or against this unitary 'thing'.

The question which remains to be explored is that of the source of the high level norms which filter down from government to police forces. Do they derive from an autonomous bureaucracy, as policemen argue, or do they result from pressures on government from a ruling class, or from an élite? These questions become more important as the power of senior officers to influence the actions of their men increases. We can make even fewer enlightened guesses about the source of locally based norms. We do know, however, that the Police College plays an increasing part in the role definition at the top. Research is necessary here, too, to identify the content of this new set of autonomous professional norms. Whatever the content of these role definitions—and they may be diverse rather than unitary—the pattern is clear. Community power is decreasing; both central power and autonomous police power to define the role are increasing. There is less and less chance of our mythical Welsh policeman (p. 26) supporting the Celts.

Appendix I The policemen's interview schedule*

Following on the recent enquiries of the Royal Commission on the Police, we are carrying out an investigation into what policeman themselves feel about their work, and the difficulties which they have to encounter in the course of it. Your Chief Constable has agreed to let us carry out [the first stages of] this enquiry in your force.

All the answers you give will be completely confidential, and no names will be mentioned in the final report.

We shall be very grateful for your help in this enquiry, and hope that the results will be of benefit to policemen in general.

M. E. CAIN

(1) To be filled in by the interviewer.

Date of appointment ....
Date of birth ....
Date of posting ....
Date of promotion ....
(if applicable)

Name ....
Whether married ....

Could you please give me a brief account of all the jobs you held before joining the force?

....
....
....
....

How old were you when you left school? .... years.
Where were you born?   City, town or village..
County ....

* Items are not spaced as in the original schedules.

I

247

(Items (1) to (12) on detachable sheets to be filled in by respondent.)

Here are two sets of questions about your satisfaction with your work. In answering the following twelve questions, please consider the police force as a career, rather than your particular job at the moment.

(1) How much does the work of a policeman give you a chance to do the things at which you are best?

  A very good chance ....
  A fairly good chance...
  Some chance ....
  Very little chance ....
  No chance at all ....

(2) How does the work of a policeman compare with other types of work?

  It is the most satisfying career a man could follow ....
  It is one of the most satisfying careers ....
  It is as satisfying as some other careers ....
  It is not a satisfying career at all ....

(3) Considering the work of a policeman as a whole, how well do you like it?

  I like it very much ....
  I like it fairly well ....
  I'm more or less indifferent ....
  I don't like it any too well ....
  I don't like it at all ....

(4) Are there any features of the work of a policeman which you dislike?

  Very many ....
  Quite a few ....
  A moderate number ....
  Only one or two...
  None ....

(5) If you had your time over again, would you still become a policeman?

  Definitely yes ....
  Probably yes ....
  I don't really know ....
  Probably not ....
  Definitely not ....

(6) Are you making progress towards the aims which you had for yourself when you chose your career?

  I have achieved my aims ....
  I am making very good progress towards my aims ....
  I am making fairly good progress towards my aims ....
  I seem to be making rather slow progress ....
  I don't seem to be getting anywhere ....

(7) Has the career of a policeman lived up to the expectations you had before you entered it?

     Yes, in all respects ....

     Yes, in most ways ....

     Yes, in some ways ....

     In only a few ways ....

     Not at all ....

(8) If a young friend of yours who appeared to be suitable was thinking of becoming a policeman, would you advise him to do it?

     Definitely yes ....

     Probably yes ....

     I wouldn't advise him either way ....

     Probably no ....

     Definitely no ....

(9) Do you feel that the work which you do as a policeman is satisfying?

     Very satisfying ....

     Fairly satisfying ....

     Neither satisfying nor dissatisfying ....

     Fairly dissatisfying ....

     Very dissatisfying ....

(10) How many features of the work of a policeman do you especially like?

     Very many ....

     Quite a few ....

     Some ....

     Only one or two ....

     None ....

(11) In general, do you feel that policeman are given adequate recognition, compared with that received by other occupational groups?

     Yes, definitely ....

     In most respects ....

     In some respects ....

     In only one or two respects ....

     Not at all ....

(12) How much opportunity does the job of a policeman give you to follow your leisure time interests?

     Very adequate opportunity ....

     Adequate opportunity ....

     More or less adequate opportunity ....

     Inadequate opportunity ....

     Very inadequate opportunity ....

The next twelve questions are rather similar, but would you consider now your present job at this station. Please put a tick in the column on the right which best indicates your satisfaction or dissatisfaction with respect to the particular question.

	Very well satisfied	Fairly well satisfied	Neither satisfied nor dis-satisfied	Fairly dis-satisfied	Very dis-satisfied
(1) Are you satisfied that you have been given enough authority by your superiors to do your job well?					
(2) How satisfied are you with your present job when you compare it with that of men of your rank in other forces?					
(3) Are you satisfied with the progress you are making towards the aims which you had for yourself when you came to you present position?					
(4) Are you satisfied that the people of your community give proper recognition to your work as a policeman?					
(5) How satisfied are you with your present salary?					
(6) How satisfied are you with your immediate superiors?					
(7) How satisfied are you with the amount of time which you must devote to your job?					

	Very well satisfied	Fairly well satisfied	Neither satisfied nor dis- satisfied	Fairly dis- satisfied	Very dis- satisfied
(8) How satisfied are you with the amount of interest shown by your sup- eriors in the work you do?					
(9) How satisfied are you that your judg- ment is accepted as that of a profes- sional expert to the extent to which you are entitled by reason of your position, training and experience?					
(10) How satisfied are you with your pre- sent job when you consider the expectations you had when you took the job?					
(11) How satisfied are you with your present job with regard to your expectations of promotion?					
(12) How satisfied are you with the effect that your present job has on your private life?					

Here are several situations in which different people might want you to do different things: for example, your superiors in the police force might think that you ought to do one thing in a certain situation, whereas you as the man on the spot might in fact decide to do something else. Alternatively, in some cases your wife, colleagues, or non-policemen might disagree with the action which you decided to take. I want to find out how often this sort of things happens, and how much it worries you when it does occur.

(1) You have arranged to take your family out for the day if possible, on your rest day. Everything is ready, and you have packed up a picnic, etc. You are outside your home ready to leave when you hear the phone ringing. If you go back and answer it, it could mean that you would be delayed so that the whole day's outing would be ruined, perhaps for some quite trivial reason.

    (a) What do you think you should do?

    (b) What would your colleagues think you ought to do?

    (c) What would your superiors in the police force think you ought to do?

    (d) What would your wife think you ought to do?

    (e) What would the non-policemen who live in the area think you ought to do?

    (f) Would it cause you any anxiety that what you were doing differed from what .... thought you ought to do?
(Interviewer to repeat for each of four reference groups)

	Superiors	Colleagues	Wife	Non-policemen
Yes, a great deal				
Yes, a fair amount				
Yes, a little				
Only a passing thought				
None at all				

252

(g) How often have you been in this sort of situation?
Very often............... Fairly often............... Occasionally...............
Once or twice at most............... Never...............

(2) You are at a gathering in a friend's house, and someone whom you do not know unjustifiably criticises the police force. By revealing that you are a policeman yourself and arguing with him you might upset your host, but yet you feel that other people there might expect you to speak in defence of your colleagues.

(a) What do you think you would do?

....
....
....

(b) What would your colleagues think you ought to do?

....
....
....

(c) What would your wife think you ought to do?

....
....
....

(d) What would your superiors in the police force think you ought to do?

....
....
....
....

(e) What would non-policemen who live in the area think you ought to do?

....
....
....

(f) Would it cause you any anxiety that what you were doing differed from what...............thought you ought to do?

	Superiors	Colleagues	Wife	Non-policemen
Yes, a great deal				
Yes, a fair amount				
Yes, a little				
Only a passing thought				
None at all				

253

(g)   How often have you been in this sort of situation?
Very often...............   Fairly often..............   Occasionally...............
Once or twice at most..............   Never...............

(3) Your wife has been asked to join a local women's organization, and is very pleased at the idea. You, however, know that the husbands of a few of the other members are not the sort of people that you, as a policeman, feel you ought to mix with socially.

(a)   What do you think you ought to do?

....
....
....
....

(b)   What would your wife think you ought to do?

....
....
....

(c)   What would your superiors in the police force think you ought to do?

....
....
....

(d)   What would non-policemen who live in the area think you ought to do?

....
....
....

(e)   What would your colleagues think you ought to do?

....
....
....

(f)   Would it cause you any anxiety that what you were doing differed from what..............thought you ought to do?

	Superiors	Colleagues	Wife	Non-policemen
Yes, a great deal				
Yes, a fair amount				
Yes, a little				
Only a passing thought				
None at all				

254

(g) How often have you been in this sort of situation?

Very often.............. Fairly often.............. Occasionally..............
Once or twice at most.............. Never..............

(4) You are out one day in your car, but not on duty, and driving along a street which has a 30 m.p.h. speed limit. A young man goes past you on a motor bike, obviously exceeding the limit. You take his number, and then realize that he is the son of a friend you have known for many years.

(a) What would you do?

....
....
....

(b) What would your superiors in the police force think you ought to do?

....
....
....

(c) What would the non-policemen who live in the area think you ought to do?

....
....
....

(d) What would your colleagues think you ought to do?

....
....
....

(e) What would your wife think you ought to do?

....
....
....

(f) Would it cause you any anxiety that what you were doing differed from what..............thought you ought to do?

	Superiors	Colleagues	Wife	Non-policemen
Yes, a great deal				
Yes, a fair amount				
Yes, a little				
Only a passing thought				
None at all				

I*

    (g) How often have you been in this sort of situation?

        Very often............ Fairly often............ Occasionally............
        Once or twice at most............ Never............

(5) You are staying away from home in an area which is in a different division of your police force. In the evening you go to a local pub with your wife and the relatives with whom you are staying, but nobody else there realizes that you are a policeman. Towards the end of the evening one of the other customers starts shouting and causing rather a disturbance, but doesn't actually hurt anyone, although he threatens to. Several other men join in the argument, which shows signs of getting even more rowdy.

    (a) What do you think you would do?

    (b) What would non-policemen who live in the area think you ought to do?

    (c) What would your wife think you ought to do?

    (d) What would your colleagues think you ought to do?

    (e) What would your superiors in the police force think you ought to do?

    (f) Would it cause you any anxiety that what you were doing differed from what............thought you ought to do?

	Superiors	Colleagues	Wife	Non-policemen
Yes, a great deal				
Yes, a fair amount				
Yes, a little				
Only a passing thought				
None at all				

(g) How often have you been in this sort of situation?

Very often.............   Fairly often.............   Occasionally.............
Once or twice at most.............   Never.............

(6) You have made arrangements for some family friends to come and spend an evening with you. It is not possible for them to come any other night. On the day before you are asked if you will take over duties of a fellow policeman who is ill, but you are not officially required to do this. It is impossible for you to contact the friends and explain the situation.

(a) What do you think you would do?

(b) What would non-policemen in the area think you ought to do?

(c) What would your colleagues think you ought to do?

(d) What would your wife think you ought to do?

(e) What would your superiors think you ought to do?

(f) Would it cause you any anxiety that what you were doing differed from what.............thought you ought to do?

	Superiors	Colleagues	Wife	Non-policemen
Yes, a great deal				
Yes, a fair amount				
Yes, a little				
Only a passing thought				
None at all				

(g)   How often have you been is this sort of situation?

Very often............   Fairly often.............   Occasionally.............
Once or twice at most............   Never.............

Can you state whether or not you agree with the following statements. Please put a single tick in the column on the right which seems most nearly to express your own opinion.

	Strongly Agree	Agree	Uncertain	Disagree	Strongly disagree
In this work it's important to know that your colleagues will be behind you if you have to make an on the spot decision.					
If I had to give up being a policeman I should feel that I had lost an important part of my life.					
A policeman is helped by the knowledge that his authority is dependent on the public respect for the force as a whole.					
When you are a policeman you are aware that you are part of a body much larger and more powerful than yourself, and this helps you to carry on under difficult circumstances.					
It is important to be certain that your superiors will support you if you have to make a difficult decision.					
Being a policeman is so important to me now that I can't imagine myself otherwise.					
When you appear in court it is always a help to know that the rest of the force will support you, even if the defending counsel should attack you.					

Can you answer the next three questions in the same way, by putting a tick in the column on the right which seems to be the most appropriate expression of your own views.

	Yes, both aware of and appreciate it.	Not really aware of it, but would appreciate it if they knew.	Aware of it but do not appreciate it.	Neither aware of it nor likely to appreciate it.
Do you think your colleagues are aware of and appreciate all the work you do or not?				
Do you think your section sergeant is aware of and appreciates all the work you do or not?				
Do you think your superiors at Division and Headquarters are aware of and appreciate all the work you do or not?				

Now could you please tell me what are your main activities and hobbies in your leisure hours?

....

....

....

What would you say is the attitude of your children towards your job?

....

....

....

What work did your own father do?

....

The following three sets of items, on detachable sheets, to be filled in by respondent.

Could you rank the following ten items in what you consider to be their order of importance to a family. There are no right or wrong answers to the question; all we want is your personal opinion on the matter. Mark them 1, 3, 8, 5, etc., or whatever order you think is most important, in the column on the right.

		Order of importance
A place in the community	The ability of a family to give its members a respected place in the community and make them good citizens (not criminals or undesirable people)	....
Healthy and happy children	....	....
Companionship	The family members feeling relaxed with each other and being able to get on well together	....
Personality development	Continued increase in the ability of members of the family to get along with and understand people, and to accept responsibility............	....
Satisfaction with affection shown	Satisfaction of the members of the family and of the husband and wife with the amount of affection and love shown............................	....
Economic security	Being sure that the family will be able to keep up or improve its standard of living	....
Moral and religious unity	Trying to live a family life according to religious and moral principles and teachings	....
Everyday interest	Having interesting day-to-day activities to do with the house and family which keep family life from being dull or boring	....
A home	Having a place where the members of the family feel they belong, where they feel at ease, and where other people do not interfere in their lives	....
Emotional security	Feeling that the members of the family need each other emotionally, and trust each other fully	....

In our last experimental questionnaire we tried asking people what sort of person they thought a policeman had to be, but people found this difficult to answer. This time, therefore, we are asking you to rate yourself on each of the following characteristics. Could you please say whether you think you have the characteristics very much, considerably, somewhat, a little, or not at all. Remember again that there are no right or wrong answers; nobody knows what characteristics policemen usually have. If you tell us what you consider to be your own characteristics it will be a great help. Please tick the appropriate column on the right, saying how much you think you have the characteristic in question.

	Very much	Con-siderably	Somewhat	A little	Not at all
Sense of humour					
Sense of duty					
Stubborn					
Get angry easily					
Easy-going					
Nervous or irritable					
Get on with people					
Feelings easily hurt					
Friendly					
Tolerant					
Moody					
Jealous					
Like to take responsibility					
Shy					
Easily excited					
Dominating or bossy					
Critical of others					
Like belonging to organizations					
Easily depressed					
Self-centred					
Cheerful					
Self-sufficient					

Several people have told me how important a policeman's wife can be to his work, and this does indeed seem to be the case, so perhaps you would rate your wife on the same set of characteristics, ticking the right hand column in the same way as before.

	Very much	Con-siderably	Somewhat	A little	Not at all
Sense of humour					
Sense of duty					
Stubborn					
Gets angry easily					
Easy-going					
Nervous or irritable					
Gets on with people					
Feelings easily hurt					
Friendly					
Tolerant					
Moody					
Jealous					
Likes to take responsibility					
Shy					
Easily excited					
Dominating or bossy					
Critical of others					
Likes belonging to organizations					
Easily depressed					
Self-centred					
Cheerful					
Self-sufficient					

Have you ever thought seriously about what you will do when you retire or not?

....

....

      Take another full time job ....

      Take another part time job ....

      Type of work preferred ....

      After how many years' service retirement

      preferred ....

Have you considered or made any arrangements for housing when you retire?

....

....

....

Can you please say whether or not the following have ever caused any inconvenience to yourself or your family. Give special examples if you can think of them.

	Very often	Fairly often	Occasionally	Once or twice at most	Never
(a) The particular place to which you were posted					
(b) The time at which you were transferred from one post to another					
(c) The requirement to work a particular shift					
(d) An accident, or other unforeseen occurrence or special duty					
(e) Training courses away from the county (home)					
(f) Others. Please give examples					

EXAMPLES particularly mentioned:

....

....

....

263

Here are some questions about how much opportunity you get for meeting other people socially out of working hours, whether they be other policemen, relations or non-police friends.

(1) How many times in the last two weeks have you visited socially the home of a friend who is not a policeman or a member of a policeman's family? (Do not include relatives here.)

....No. different people........................

(2) How many times in the last two weeks have you visited the home of a friend who is also a policeman or a member of a policeman's family?

....No. different people........................

(3) How many times in the last two weeks have you visited one of your relatives?

....

Which?..

(4) How many times in the last two weeks has a friend who is not a policeman or a member of a policeman's family been to visit you?

....No. different people........................

(5) How many times in the last two weeks has a friend who is also a policeman or a member of a policeman's family been to visit you?

....No. different people........................

(6) How many times in the last two weeks has one of your relatives been to visit you?

....Which?..

(7) How many times in the last two weeks have you been out—e.g., for a drink, with your family, to a sporting event, etc.—in the company of one or more other people who were not policemen or members of policemen's families?

....No. of people........................

(8) How many times in the last two weeks have you been out (examples if necessary) with other policemen or members of policemen's families?

....No. of people........................

(9) How many times in the last two weeks have you been out (e.g.,................) with one or more of your relatives?

....Which?..

(10) How many times in the last two weeks have you been out (e.g.,................) with only members of your immediate family—your wife or children?

....Which?..

How many close friends would you say you have among your colleagues in the force?

....

264

How many of these policemen friends are stationed sufficiently near for you to see them fairly regularly should you want to (e.g., once a week)?

....

How many close friends who are not policemen or members of policemen's families would you say that you have in this area?

....

How many close friends who are not policemen or members of policemen's families would you say that you have living further away?

....

Would you say that you have more, less, or about the same number of non-policemen friends in this area as people in other jobs have?

More............ Same............ Less............ Don't know............

Would you say that you have less, more, or about the same number of non-policemen friends living further away as people in other jobs have?

More............ Same............ Less............ Don't know............

What sort of people would you say these non-policemen friends were? (I think if you could give me a rough idea of the work they do, I should get a better picture of the sort of people who are willing to be friends with policemen.)

....
....
....

Now some more questions of the kind that you have already been answering. Once again would you put a tick in the column on the right which seems to be the closest to your own opinion.

	Strongly disagree	Disagree	Neither agree nor disagree	Agree	Strongly agree
Policemen are very much a race apart, and should try and stay that way by not having any close friends outside the force.					
Policemen must be self-sufficient and have no need of social ties with the general public.					
Life would be much easier if other people could forget that one was a policeman when one was off duty.					
It is always a good idea to try and make friends with non-policemen and their families in the area in which one lives.					
It's a pity that so many non-policemen are unwilling to make friends, as it makes life very difficult for a policeman and his family.					
A policeman should try and avoid getting too friendly with the civilian population in the area in which he lives.					
It would be a good thing to be accepted by the general public as just one of the community like themselves.					

These are the last few questions. They are of the same type again, so just put a tick in the column which seems most nearly to express your own opinion.

	Strongly disagree	Disagree	Neither agree nor disagree	Agree	Strongly agree
A policeman must be aware all the time that the reputation of the force is in his hands.					
If I were to make a serious mistake, all the rest of the force would have to suffer for it as a result of the report in the press.					
Everyone in the force knows that it is what we do as individuals that determines what the general public think of policemen as a whole.					
Every policeman is aware that what he does at a particular time will have an effect on members of the force.					
People will always judge the force as a whole from the actions of a particular policeman whom they happen to know.					
All policemen are constantly aware that what they do now will influence the attitude of the public to those who come after them.					
Every policeman feels that the most important thing is not to let the force down in the eyes of an outsider.					

Thank you very much. There are just two very factual questions before we finish. Could you please give me a brief account of the various jobs you have done since you joined the force, i.e., where you have been stationed and for how long, whether you have been in a special section or on beat duty, etc.

....
....
....
....

Which of these jobs did you prefer, and why?

....
....
....

Have you any further comments about your work, or the questionnaire, that you would like to make before we finish?

....
....
....

Respondent's comments;

Interviewer's comments;

Thank you very much for your help in this enquiry. I hope it hasn't taken too much of your time.

We are very grateful that you have co-operated so willingly, and will ensure that a copy of the final report is sent to your force so that it will be available for you to read.

If possible I should like now to see your wife, and ask her opinion about one or two matters. I don't think I shall need to be quite as long with her as I have been with you.

Appendix II The wives' interview schedule

We are carrying out an experimental enquiry into what policemen themselves feel about their work, and the various difficulties that they have to encounter in the course of it. One of the main problems seems to be the effect that this has on their private lives. Several men have said that their wives are very important to their work, so we are interviewing policemen's wives as well, to get their opinions from another angle.

The Chief Constable of this force has agreed to let us carry out this study, and we should, therefore, be very grateful for your co-operation. If our results are to be beneficial at all, we need everybody's help so that we can have a complete picture.

All the answers will be entirely anonymous, so you need have no anxiety on that score. There are no right or wrong answers to any of the questions; all we want is your opinion on the matter.

Thank you very much.

MAUREEN E. CAIN

Date of birth .... Place of birth ....
Date married .... City, town or village ....
No. of children .... County ....
                   Distance from present home ....

Age and sex of children   *Age*   *Sex*
              ....
              ....
              ....
              ....

Free answer question on distance from home, etc. To be phrased by interviewer according to the circumstances. Find out where parents and other family members live, how respondent feels about this distance, and also how she feels about living where she does at present. General introductory chat.

269

(*Items* (1) *to* (12) *on a detachable sheet to be filled in by the respondent.*)
Here are two sets of questions about how satisfied you are with your husband's job. In answering the first twelve questions, please consider the police force in general as a career, rather than the particular work your husband is doing at the moment. Put one tick beside whichever answer you agree with most.

(1) How much does your husband's work as a policeman give you the opportunity of doing the things in which you are most interested?

A very good chance ....
A fairly good chance ....
Some chance ....
Very little chance ....
No chance at all ....

(2) How do you think the job of a policeman compares with other types of work?

It is the best career a man could follow ....
It is one of the best careers ....
It is about as good as most other careers ....
It is as good as some other careers ....
It does not compare well at all ....

(3) Considering your husband's job as a whole, how well do you like it?

I like it very much ....
I like it fairly well ....
I'm more or less indifferent ....
I don't like it any too well ....
I don't like it at all ....

(4) Are there any features of the work of a policeman which you dislike?

Very many ....
Quite a few ....
A moderate number ....
Only one or two ....
None ....

(5) If you could choose now—and assuming that you could still be married to your husband—would you still be willing to become a policeman's wife?

Definitely yes ....
Probably yes ....
I don't really know ....
Probably not ....
Definitely not ....

(6) Do you think that your husband is making progress in his career towards the goals which you had when you were married?

He has already achieved these goals ....
He is making very good progress towards these goals ....
He is making fairly good progress towards these goals ....
He is making rather slow progress towards these goals ....
He doesn't seem to be getting anywhere ....

(7) Has your husband's career as a policeman lived up to the expectations you had about it when you were married?

    Yes, in all respects ....

    Yes, in most ways ....

    Yes, in some ways ....

    In only a very few ways ....

    Not at all ....

(8) If the husband of a friend of yours were thinking of becoming a policeman would you tell your friend to advise him to do it?

    Definitely yes ....

    Probably yes ....

    I wouldn't say anything either way ....

    Probably no ....

    Definitely no ....

(9) Do you feel that your husband's career as a policeman makes life satisfying to you?

    Very satisfying ....

    Fairly satisfying ....

    Neither satisfying nor dissatisfying ....

    Fairly dissatisfying ....

    Very dissatisfying ....

(10) How many features of your husband's work do you especially like?

    Very many ....

    Quite a few ....

    Some ....

    Only one or two ....

    None ....

(11) In general, do you feel that policemen are given adequate recognition, compared with that received by other occupational groups?

    Yes, definitely ....

    In most respects ....

    In some respects ....

    In only one or two respects ....

    Not at all ....

(12) How much opportunity does your husband's job as a policeman give you to follow your leisure time interests?

    Very adequate opportunity ....

    Adequate opportunity ....

    More or less adequate opportunity ....

    Inadequate opportunity ....

    Very inadequate opportunity ....

In this second set of questions I want you to tick the answer which best indicates your satisfaction or dissatisfaction with respect to the particular question. Please consider now your husband's particular job at this station, and put your tick in one of the columns on the right-hand side.

	Very well satisfied	Fairly well satisfied	Neither satisfied nor dis-satisfied	Fairly dissatisfied	Very dissatisfied
(1) How satisfied are you with your husband's present job when you compare it with that of men of his rank in other forces?					
(2) How satisfied are you that your husband's superiors consider sufficiently the claims of his home life?					
(3) Are you satisfied with the progress your husband is making towards the aims which you had when he came to his present position?					
(4) How satisfied are you with the effect your husband's present job has—or would have—on the lives of your children?					
(5) Are you satisfied that the people of your community give proper recognition to your husband's work as a policeman?					
(6) How satisfied are you with your husband's present salary?					

	Very well satisfied	Fairly well satisfied	Neither satisfied nor dis-satisfied	Fairly dissatisfied	Very dissatisfied
(7) How satisfied are you with the amount of time your husband must devote to his job?					
(8) How satisfied are you with the amount of interest in your husband as a person shown by his superiors?					
(9) How satisfied are you that your husband's judgment is accepted as that of a professional expert to the degree to which you feel he is entitled by reason of his position, training and experience?					
(10) How satisfied are you with your husband's present job when you consider the expectations you had when you got married?					
(11) How satisfied are you with the effect that your husband's present job has on your family life?					

	Very well satisfied	Fairly well saisfied	Neither satisfied nor dis- satisfied	Fairly dissatisfied	Very dissatisfied
(12) How satisfied are you with your husband's present job with regard to his expectations of promotion?					
(13) How satisfied are you that your husband has been given enough authority by his superiors to do his job well?					

Now one or two questions about how your husband's work affects your children. Have your children had to change schools at all on account of your husband's being transferred?

Ist child ....   2nd child............................   3rd child............................
            ....
            ....

4th child............................   5th child............................   6th child............................
            ....
            ....

Are any of your children policemen, or do they want to be?
            ....
            ....

So, in general, what would you say is your children's attitude to their father's job? [NB Ask for comments on whether they make friends easily or not.]

Can you please say whether or not the following have ever caused any inconvenience to yourself or your family. Give special examples if you can think of them. The answers you can give are:

	Very often	Fairly often	Occasion- ally	Once or twice at most	Never
(a) The particular place to which your husband was posted					
(b) The time at which you were transferred from one post to another					
(c) The requirement that your husband should work a particular shift					
(d) An accident, or other unforeseen occurrence or special duty					
(e) Training courses for your husband, away from the county (home)					
(f) Other. Please give examples					

EXAMPLES particularly mentioned..

....

Could you rank the following ten items in what you consider to be their order of importance to a family. There are no right or wrong answers to the questions; all we want is your personal opinion on the matter. Mark the items 1, 3, 8, 5, etc., or in whatever order you think most important, in the column on the right. These numbers I have given are not suggestions; they are only examples of the way you should set about it.

[Items as in p. 260 (male questionnaire).]

In our last experimental questionnaire we tried asking people what sort of person they thought a policeman had to be, but found that people found this difficult to answer. This time, therefore, we are asking you to rate both yourself and your husband on each of the following characteristics. Several people told me how important a policeman's wife can be to his work, and this indeed seems to be the case, so perhaps you can rate your own characteristics first. Remember again that there are no right or wrong answers; nobody knows what characteristics policemen's wives usually have. If you tell us what you consider to be your own characteristics it will be a great help. Please put a tick in the

275

appropriate column on the right, saying how much you think you have the characteristic in question.

Now, on the assumption that wives know their husbands better than anyone else, perhaps you could rate your husband's characteristics in the same way. Please tick the right-hand column in the same way as before.

[Items as in pp. 261–2 (male questionnaire).]

Have you ever thought seriously about what you will do when your husband retires?

....

....

Have you considered or made any arrangements for housing when your husband retires?

....

....

What is your general opinion of the house you are living in at the moment?

....

....

Here are some questions about how much opportunity you get for meeting other people socially, whether they be other policemen or members of their families, relations or non-policemen.

(1) How many times in the last two weeks have you visited socially the home of a friend who is not a policeman or a member of a policeman's family? (Do not include relatives here.)

      No. times ....   No. different people ....

      ....

(2) How many times in the last two weeks have you visited socially the home of a friend who is not a policeman or member of a policeman's family?

      No. times ....   No. different people ....

      ....

(3) How many times in the last two weeks have you visited one of your relatives?

      ....   Which? ....

(4) How many times in the last two weeks has a friend or friends who are not policemen or members of policemen's families been to visit you?

      No. times ....   No. different people ....

      ....

(5) How many times in the last two weeks has a friend or friends who are also members of policemen's families been to visit you?

      No. times ....   No. different people ....

      ....

(6) How many times in the last two weeks has one of your relatives been to visit you?

No. times .... Which? ....

....

(7) How many times in the last two weeks have you been out for a drink, with your family, shopping, etc., in the company of one or more other people who are not policemen or members of policemen's families?

No. times .... No. different people ....

....

(8) How many times in the last two weeks have you been out (e.g., ...) with other policemen or members of their families?

No. times .... No. people ....

....

(9) How many times in the last two weeks have you been out with one or more of your relatives?

No. times .... Which? ....

....

(10) How many times in the last two weeks have you been out with only members of your immediate family, i.e., your husband or children?

No. times .... Which? ....

....

How many close friends would you say you have who are either policemen or members of policemen's families?

....

How many of these live sufficiently near for you to see them as often as you want to (e.g., once a week should you wish)?

....

How many close friends who are not policemen or members of policemen's families would you say that you have in this area?

....

How many close friends who are not policemen or members of policemen's families would you say that you have living further away?

....

Would you say that you have more, less, or about the same number of non-policemen friends in this area as people whose husbands are in other jobs have?

More............ Less............ Same............ Don't know............

What sort of people would you say these non-policemen were? (I think if you could give me some rough idea of the work their husbands do, it might throw a bit of light on the problem of whether or not policemen and their families find some other people unwilling to be friendly.)

....

....

Would you say that, for yourself, most of the people who live round about are friendly or unfriendly? Do you think that your husband's job makes any difference to this? [Free answer. Probe re. reaction of other people when meeting them informally, e.g., in shops, etc.]

These are more questions of the kind that you have already been answering. Once again would you please tick the column on the right which seems to be closest to your own opinion. For each statement say whether you strongly disagree, disagree, neither agree nor disagree, agree or strongly agree.

	Strongly disagree	Disagree	Neither agree nor disagree	Agree	Strongly agree
Policemen are very much a race apart, and their families should help them stay that way by not having any close friends outside the force.					
Policemen must be self-sufficient and neither they nor their families have any need of social ties with the general public.					
Life would be much easier if other people could forget sometimes that one was a policeman's wife.					
It is always a good idea to try and make friends with non-policemen and their families in the area in which one lives.					
It's a pity that so many non-policemen are unwilling to make friends, as it makes life very difficult for a policeman and his family.					
A policeman and his family should try and avoid getting too friendly with the civilian population in the area in which they live.					

	Strongly disagree	Disagree	Neither agree nor disagree	Agree	Strongly agree
It would be a good thing to be accepted by the general public as just one of the community like themselves.					

What would you say are your main activities and hobbies in your leisure time?

....

....

Do you belong to any clubs or organizations in which you take an active part?

Club .... Alone or with .... How often do you go....................

,, ... husband .... ,, ...

,, ... ,, ... ,, ...

Is your husband a member of any clubs or organizations in which he takes an active part—e.g., police sports clubs, non-police clubs, etc.?

Club .... Alone or with .... How often does he go....................

,, ... wife .... ,, ...

,, ... ,, ... ,, ...

Finally, a few factual questions about yourself. Would you mind telling me what work you did between leaving school and getting married?

[Probes—'You left school at 15 then, did you?' 'At this time you were still living in.................(place of birth), and your job was in................' etc.]

....

....

....

....

What work did your own father do then?..

What work would you like your children to do, if you could choose?

Son .... Daughter ....

....

Now I dare say that you've got a lot of comments of your own that you'd like to make, both about your husband's work, and about the questions I've been asking, so perhaps you could tell me in general what you feel about it all, and what is the point that sticks most in your mind.

Appendix III Supplementary information about research techniques

Pilot study

Permission to carry out the research was gained in the first instance from a single county force, and a pilot project was carried out there during three weeks in the early part of 1962. In the course of this pilot study a questionnaire was distributed to a 1 : 3 sample of the men, excluding those in the division chosen for the final research and those working in a largish seaside borough within the county area. The stations were ranged in alphabetical order to create a sampling list, and the sergeants and constables working from each were internally ordered likewise. A sample was then drawn from the chance selected starting point of one; the total sample numbered fifty-three cases. Since it was impossible to distribute all the questionnaires personally it was arranged that where several men in one section were involved all the questionnaires would be handed to the section sergeant who was able to report back to the men in his section what had transpired during his meeting with the researcher. In addition, a number of men were met at 'monthly assemblies' or section meetings, three of which were attended. Two of these were in areas in which the pilot was being carried out and one was in the research division. This gave further opportunities for the project to be discussed. Forty of the fifty-three schedules issued were returned, and in addition to answering the formal questions many of the men had useful criticisms as to the appropriateness and value of a number of items on the pilot questionnaire.

At the same time an effort was made to 'get a picture' of the force and some preliminary insight into the work. Shifts were worked in the information and control room and on various motor patrols; a number of training sessions and special functions were attended; discussions were held with officers of all ranks including the chairman of the Police Federation. A detailed field diary of the period was kept.

It was not possible to carry out a pilot study in the city force and this led to an important omission in the final questionnaire. In the county area the term 'the community' was readily understood; in the city the question was immediately raised as to which community was implied by the term, that in which the man lived or that in which he worked—the respectable or the undesirable. As Banton's work (1964a) has shown, consensus between police and community is at its highest in a rural area. In the city the community was perceived as fragmented, and the questions concerning it would have been more meaningful had they been further refined.

The questionnaire

Interdependence with the family

Farber's marital integration index (1957) was used as the indicator of marital interdependence. According to the assumptions on which this is based marital integration is a function of the degree of consensus of the husband and wife as to the rank ordering of ends and commitment to roles. Farber's own checks on the validity of this scale suggest that it is at least highly correlated with interdependence and, given the impossibility of devising and testing a new scale or even of carrying out a pilot study with the wives, it was decided to adopt this ready-made alternative which seemed so close an approximation to what was required. The only practical disadvantage of the scale was that if the wife refused to be interviewed then her husband's responses to the marital integration questions were of no use and he was lost as a case to this area of the research (pp. 260–2).

Interdependence with police

Interdependence with police was measured by means of two series of items subjectively thought to indicate perceived dependence of ego on the force and perceived dependence of the force on ego. The aim in both cases was to detect a psychological *sense* of dependence. Items were included which *a priori* would be relevant in both a rural and an urban setting. Matters of structural dependence which could be estimated by statistical fact gathering —such as type of housing—were not included among the items but separate questions were asked about these and the responses were used as an independent aid in interpreting the other findings.

The two series of items were treated as Guttman scales (Guttman, 1944; 1947; 1954). In this way unidimensionality was achieved. Farber's technique for producing a single index from the two scaled scores was then adopted. This involved the dividing of the scales into quartiles, scoring them 0–3, and adding the scores thus obtained from the two scales to give an overall index of perceived interdependence with scores ranging 0–6.

A number of problems inherent in this procedure are recognized. Equal weight is given to each scale, but without further extensive tests any alternative weighting would be equally arbitrary. Also, the chances of getting a high score on the index are greater than the chances of getting a low score. Only one possible combination of quartile scores produces an index score of 0; there are seven possible ways in which a score of 6 might be produced. But the index, albeit a somewhat blunt instrument at its upper limits, none the less serves as a useful indicator of *relative* interdependence as between respondents, particularly when comparing groups of respondents in different structural settings. It could not be relied upon as an accurate assessment in a single particular case. In those cases where a more refined analysis was necessary the scores for the two separate scales were used.

Interdependence with the community

As already pointed out, dependence of ego on the community is partly a function of whether ego wishes to be a member of the community or not. This is true whether or not ego has actual contact with the community. But contact or the lack of it itself produces structural factors which influence interdependence. Both variables were therefore estimated.

A scale of 'desired integration with the community' was devised, and items scored and reduced to a Guttman scale. Some problems arose in the scaling of these items owing to the fact that there was no pilot testing of them in the city area, for example concerning item 5 (cf. Appendix 1, p. 266).

As in the previous case, these items measured the psychological sense of dependence on the community. No attempt was made to estimate the perceived dependence of the community on the respondent, so in effect a dependence rather than an interdependence measure is used here.

Actual contact with members of the community was also estimated. (Contact with police and relatives was also estimated in the same way.) Respondents were asked to recall the number of people they had 'seen' in the fortnight prior to the interview, the number of occasions on which these contacts took place, and the venue of the contacts. This enabled a distinction to be made between twenty people 'seen' at one party and one neighbour calling at the house on twenty occasions. These data were collected from both the men and their wives. The facts were scored by dividing the cases into quartile groupings on the basis of numbers of non-police (excluding relatives) 'seen' anywhere during the previous fortnight. A general mention of a club or party attended was arbitrarily scored as ten contacts, and for the wives work was counted as five contacts each weekday. The quartiles were then scored 3, 2, 1, 0. Similarly the sample was divided into quartiles on the basis of the number of occasions on which non-police were seen, and scored in the same way. The scores for the two indicators were added, giving a 'contact with the community' index for both husbands and wives, with scores ranging 0–6. This method is subject to the weaknesses already pointed out as inherent in these indices, plus the additional one that in this case an index score of 1 is impossible; if one person was seen there must also have been at least one occasion, scoring two.

Conflict

The measurement of conflict took the form of hypothetical situations which were presented to the respondents who were asked what they would do in such a position. They were then asked what colleagues, wife, non-policemen and subordinates would 'think they ought to do'. The order of the counterpositions for the questions concerning their expectations was different for each situation presented, but there were not enough situations for a full permutation of the alternative placings to be possible. If the order in which the questions were asked produced any bias this would be apparent here, but it was felt that this would show itself most strongly in the responses to the first situation, where the respondent was not quite sure what to expect. The ordering of the counterpositions for the first question was colleagues, wife, non-policemen, superiors. Bias could be expected to show itself as more men indicating that colleagues would agree with them than in other subsequent sets of responses. This was tested, and results showed that although a far higher proportion of county men said that colleagues would agree with them in this situation than in others, in the city the reverse was true although the differences were less great. This dispersal of the answers suggests that the differences found were 'real' rather than the results of bias. The differences found were in both cases statistically significant.

This method of 'measuring' conflict does not in fact constitute a measure; it does not yield a quantitative assessment of conflict in either absolute or relative terms. To do this one would have to be certain that all possible conflict situations had been presented to the respondents.

Moreover, the situations included had different relevance for rural and urban men. It was not possible, therefore, to compare *amounts* of conflict as between the two forces. What was possible was to test the hypotheses by comparing the numbers of conflicts arising from each source. Any conflict score produced had to be in terms of numbers of conflicts *from each source*. *Amounts* of conflict cannot be compared, even in a situation specific way (cf. Banton 1964a for an example of this).

Comparison with other techniques for measuring conflict It is worth considering other points raised by Banton (1964a, pp. 243–60), directly or by inference, in discussing his methodology since the seminal idea for this study was partially derived from his work, and some of the conflict situations presented in the questionnaire are free adaptations of his own— particularly situations 2, 3, and 5.

The approach of this study does not allow the identification of situations as posing conflicts *between roles*. Until we know the expectations of the various counterpositions we do not know what these roles are; we only know the positions in the structure which the focal person (ego) occupies. It was not intended to present the respondents with *conflicts* but with situations in which, *a priori*, conflict might be expected to arise.

The problem posed by Banton concerning the uniqueness of situations and the policeman's pragmatic approach and reluctance to generalize was encountered during the course of the interviewing. The pilot study proved that this problem was greater still with a postal questionnaire. But where the emphasis is on *who would agree* with the decision rather than on the course of action proposed this is of less importance. Qualifications made by the men were none the less noted, together with spontaneously offered examples of similar experiences. These were either allowed for in the coding or included in the field data as appropriate. It was not found that the men refused *in interview* to take the questions seriously, and they were free to leave unanswered any particular question which seemed to them too 'far-fetched'. In the case of situation 1, for example, four city men left this item unanswered but responded to the other five situations.

One further point, arising from the publication of Banton's work (ibid.)

283

on consensus, is that room was left for the respondent to indicate that he was aware of lack of consensus within the counterposition, and such responses were separately analysed.

The work of Ehrlich (1962) and his collaborators (Ehrlich *et al.*, 1962; Preiss and Ehrlich, 1966) has already been mentioned. His unpublished PhD dissertation (1959) cited by Banton was not available at the time the research was designed, nor had his published work then appeared. None the less, the methods of questioning chosen were similar to his, differences being:

(1) that he concerned himself with the expectations of a large number of 'audiences';
(2) that the present research emphasizes more strongly the normative quality of expectations;
(3) that the order of questioning in this research is reversed.

The first point needs little explication; this research concerns itself with only four of a possible myriad of counterpositions, and by doing so does not deny the possibility of other highly potent counterpositions. Second, the focus of concern of normative expectations—on what counterpositions think ego *ought* to do—was made because it was assumed that a normative expectation would constitute a stronger pressure and would therefore highlight better the area of differential potency under consideration. Results showed that in fact conflict could arise on a normative level where on an expectational level there was no discrepancy, e.g.: 'My wife would think I ought to stay in I suppose, but she knows me well enough by now . . .'.

Third, respondents were first asked what they would do and *then* what the several sets of expectations would be. (This was decided upon after the schedules had been printed, so it is not reflected in the copy in appendix 1.) This order was decided upon because it was felt that at the outset there might be mistrust of the researcher and a resultant attempt to make answers correspond with the expectations of superiors of whatever group the researcher was perceived as favouring, if the expectations of this group were first announced. The advantage of Ehrlich's alternative procedure is that the respondent has mapped out the structural setting for his hypothetical action in advance of his decision as to how he will 'act', and is therefore more fully aware of what conflicts he is hypothetically precipitating. The method used here records the spontaneous response, and it is contended that this approximates more closely to the process of real life.

Other items on the questionnaire

Other items on the questionnaire included adaptations of the job and career satisfaction scales used by Gross *et al.* (1958), and factual questions which helped to provide a structural framework for the analysis. These items require no additional explanation.

Wives' questionnaire

It was necessary to interview policemen's wives in order to gain a full set of responses to the marital integration scale. In addition it was possible to illuminate other areas of interdependence from these interviews. Wives were asked, for example, about their contacts and relationships with the community, and also with other police families. Again, factual questions to provide a structural framework for the responses of both the men and their wives were included in the questionnaire.

Appendix IV   Additional tables referred to in the text

TABLE A   *Men: wish for integration with the community*

							Scaled scores							
	9	*10*	*11*	*12*	*13*	*14*	*15*	*16*	*17*	*18*	*19*	*20*	*21*	*22*	*Total*
County	—	3	6	3	7	4	10	5	6	6	4	5	3	2	64
City	1	1	—	—	—	4	4	9	4	10	10	6	3	3	55

TABLE B   *Men: number of occasions in previous two weeks on which a non-policeman was 'seen' socially*

	0	*1*	*2*	*3*	*4*	*5*	*6*	*7–10*	*11–15*	*16+*	*Unknown*	*Total*
County	12	11	8	5	6	5	2	8	3	3	1	64
City	16	10	7	3	5	—	4	5	2	2	1	55

TABLE C   *Men: number of non-policemen 'seen' socially in previous two weeks*

	0	*1*	*2*	*3*	*4*	*5*	*6*	*7–10*	*11–15*	*16+*	*Unknown*	*Total*
County	12	12	6	5	4	3	6	8	3	4	1	64
City	16	16	5	3	—	1	3	8	2	—	1	55

286

TABLE D   *Number of non-police friends in the area in which you live*

	Number							Over 6	No. of respondents	No answer
	0	1	2	3	4	5	6			
County	30	7	7	5	4	0	2	9	64	—
City	19	4	5	4	2	1	6	13	54	1

TABLE E   *Number of non-police friends 'further away'*

	Number							Over 6	'Numerous', 'several', etc.	No. of respondents	No answer
	0	1	2	3	4	5	6				
County	9	3	6	6	2	0	3	27	8	64	—
City	12	0	4	1	2	1	7	13	14	54	1

TABLE F   *Wish for integration with the community—wives*

	DIC							Total
	14	15	16	17	18	19	20	
County	6	8	15	10	6	9	3	57
City	4	5	12	3	2	—	4	30

TABLE G   *Wives: number of non-police friends in the 'area in which you live'*

	Number							Over 6	'Several', etc.	No. of respondents	No answer
	0	1	2	3	4	5	6				
County	24	12	6	2	6	—	2	3	1	56	1
City	15	4	1	3	—	—	2	—	4	29	1

TABLE H   *Wives: number of non-police friends 'further away'*

	Number						Over	'Several',	No. of	No
	0	1	2	3	4	5	6	6	etc.	respondents	answer
County	10	4	7	3	5	3	8	15	1	56	1
City	4	—	4	3	1	—	3	8	6	29	1

TABLE I   *Wives: index of contact with non-police*

	Score											No. of respon-	No
	0	%	2	%	3	%	4	%	5	%	6	%	dents	answer
County	14	25·0	12	21·4	6	10·7	11	19·7	5	8·9	8	14·3	56	1
City	7	23·3	4	13·3	3	10·0	5	16·7	3	10·0	8	26·7	30	—

TABLE J   *Wives: number of occasions in previous two weeks on on which a relative was 'seen' socially**

	Occasions									No. of	No
	0	1	2	3	4	5	6	7–10	11+	respondents	answer
County	17	20	7	4	1	2	2	2	1	56	1
City	11	6	—	4	5	1	1	2	—	30	—

*The comparable table for men is presented in chapter 4, Table 20, p. 86.

TABLE K   *Social class of wife's father**

	1	2	3	4	5	No information	Total
County	1	15	26	11	1	3	57
City	—	7	17	4	1	1	30

*Data from interviews with wives.

TABLE L   *Age of male sample*

	Under 20	Years				No. of respondents
		20–9	30–9	40–9	50+	
County	2	24	13	21	4	64
City	1	20	23	9	2	55

TABLE M   *Number of situations in which community perceived as divided, i.e. some thinking the policeman ought to take the same action as he did, others thinking he ought to take a different action*

	Situations							Total
	0	1	2	3	4	5	6	
County	45	10	9	—	—	—	—	64
City	36	11	6	1	1	—	—	55

TABLE N   *Career satisfaction: summary of scaled scores**

Score	Men		Women	
	County	City	County	City
Up to 15	—	1	2	1
16–20	2	4	15	7
21–5	8	5	15	7
26–30	21	15	15	11
31–5	27	16	9	4
36–40	6	14	—	—
Unknown	—	—	1	—
n	64	55	57	30

*Men and women cannot be compared as the items are scaled differently for the two groups.

TABLE O   *Interdependence with police by marital states (city)*

	\multicolumn{8}{c}{IDP score}	
	0	1	2	3	4	5	6	Total
Married	1	3	7	8	7	12	7	45
Single	—	3	1	—	2	2	—	8
Divorced/separated	—	—	—	—	1	—	1	2
	1	6	8	8	10	14	8	55

TABLE P   *Interdependence with police by marital integration indices (city)*

IDP	0	1	2	MI 3	4	5	6	Single men	No answer	No. of respondents	n
—	—	—	—	—	—	—	—	—	1	0	1
1	—	—	—	—	—	—	—	3	3	0	6
2	1	1	1	1	1	—	1	1	1	6	8
3	—	2	—	1	1	3	—	—	1	7	8
4	—	1	1	1	1	—	—	2	4	4	10
5	—	—	3	3	—	1	1	2	4	8	14
6	1	—	—	1	2	—	—	—	4	4	8
	2	4	5	7	5	4	2	8	18	29	55

TABLE Q   *Career satisfaction by marital integration (city)*

CS score	0	1	2	MI score 3	4	5	6	No answer/ not applicable	Total
13	—	—	—	—	—	—	—	1	1
19	1	—	—	—	—	1	1	1	4
20	—	—	—	—	—	—	—	—	—
21	—	—	1	1	—	—	—	—	2
22	—	—	1	—	—	—	—	—	1
23	—	1	—	—	—	—	—	1	2
24	—	—	—	—	—	—	—	—	—
25	—	—	—	—	—	—	—	—	—
26	—	—	—	—	1	—	—	3	4
27	—	—	1	1	—	—	—	—	2

290

TABLE Q—*continued*

CS score	MI score 0	1	2	3	4	5	6	No answer/ not applicable	Total
28	—	—	—	1	1	1	1	—	4
29	—	—	—	—	—	—	—	1	1
30	—	—	—	—	—	—	—	4	4
31	—	1	1	—	—	—	—	3	5
32	—	—	—	—	—	—	—	3	3
33	—	—	—	—	—	1	—	1	2
34	—	—	—	2	—	—	—	1	3
35	—	1	—	—	1	—	—	1	3
36	—	—	1	1	—	—	—	1	3
37	—	1	—	—	—	—	—	—	1
38	—	—	—	1	1	—	—	1	3
39	—	—	—	—	2	—	—	2	4
40	—	—	—	—	—	—	1	2	3
	1	4	5	7	6	3	3	26	55

TABLE R *Women: numbers of responses about each cause of inconvenience**

	County	City
Concerned with transfers	42	2
Place posted	11	2
Night duties/training courses/ being left alone	12	5
Home is police station/disruption domestic life	28	4
Disruption social life	20	7
Hours	7	33
Leave days/holidays at different times from children and other people	3	10
DHQ duties (away from home/ wife had to do police work)	7	—
Accommodation when retire	3	—
Other	11	5
None	3	2
	n57	n30

*A woman might mention more than one inconvenience connected with one item, e.g., the expense of moves as well as the uncertainty generated by transfers.

TABLE S *Men: children's attitude to father's job and/or perceived effect of job on them*

Attitude/effect	County	City
Too young/ not applicable/no answer	40	38
Neutral/accept it	1	3
Pleased that father a policeman	8	8
Negatively affected by hours	8	5
Too high a standard expected	2	—
Meet with antagonism from others	3	1
Poor education because of transfers and village schools	1	—
Children are embarrassed by it	1	—
Number of respondents	64	55

TABLE T *Children's attitude to father's job and/or perceived effect of the job on the child—wives' answers*

Attitude/effect	County	City
Too young/not applicable/no answer	19	13
Neutral/accept it	3	5
Good for them/something to live up to	3	1
Pleased that father is a policeman	5	5
Embarrassed by it, don't like it	2	—
Negatively affected by hours	8	1
Father more strict than non-police	1	1
Too high a standard expected	5	1
Meet with antagonism from others	5	1
Poor education because of transfers and village schools	16	2
See more of father than other children	3	4
Emotionally upset by frequent moves/transfers	10	—
Number of respondents	57	30

292

TABLE U *Interdependence with police score by qualification, length of service and rank (county force: research division only)*

Length of service	*Qualification*	IDP *score* 0	*1*	*2*	*3*	*4*	*5*	*6*	*Unknown*	*Total*
Under 4 years	Not qualified	2	1	1	1	2	2	—	—	9
4 under	Qualified	—	1	1	1	—	—	—	—	3
9 years	Not qualified	1	3	3	5	1	4	—	1	18
9 under	Qualified	—	3	2	1	—	2	—	—	8
15 years	Not qualified	1	—	1	1	1	—	—	—	4
15 years	Qualified	—	4	2	1	—	—	1	—	8
and over	Not qualified	—	1	1	1	—	—	—	—	3
15+	Unknown	—	—	—	—	1	—	—	—	1
Sergeants and higher ranks	—	2	1	1	1	2	2	1	—	10
Total		6	14	12	12	7	10	2	1	64

TABLE V *Number of children**

	Number 0	*1*	*2*	*3*	*4*	*5*	*Over 5*	*Total respondents*
County	3	14	29	7	2	1	1	57
City	5	11	9	4	—	1	—	30

*Information got from wives.

Appendix V The Police (Discipline) Regulations, 1952

Regulation 1

FIRST SCHEDULE

Discipline Code

1. Discreditable conduct, that is to say, if a member of a police force acts in a disorderly manner or any manner prejudicial to discipline or reasonably likely to bring discredit on the reputation of the force or of the police service.

2. Insubordinate or oppressive conduct, that is to say, if a member of a police force—

    (a) is unsubordinate by word, act or demeanour, or

    (b) is guilty of oppressive or tyrannical conduct towards an inferior in rank, or

    (c) uses obscene, abusive or insulting language to any other member of the force, or

    (d) wilfully or negligently makes any false complaint or statement against any member of the force, or

    (e) assaults any other member of the force, or

    (f) improperly withholds any report or allegation against any member of the force.

3. Disobedience to orders, that is to say, if a member of a police force disobeys or without good and sufficient cause omits or neglects to carry out any lawful order, written or otherwise, or contravenes any requirements of the Third Schedule to the Police Regulations, 1952.

4. Neglect of duty, that is to say, if a member of a police force—

    (a) neglects, or without good and sufficient cause omits, promptly and diligently to attend to or carry out anything which is his duty as a constable, or

    (b) idles or gossips while on duty, or

(c) fails to work his beat in accordance with orders, or leaves his beat, point, or other place of duty to which he has been ordered, without due permission or sufficient cause, or

(d) by carelessness or neglect permits a prisoner to escape, or

(e) fails, when knowing where any offender is to be found, to report the same, or to make due exertions for making him amenable to justice, or

(f) fails to report any matter which it is his duty to report, or

(g) fails to report anything which he knows concerning a criminal charge, or fails to disclose any evidence which he, or any person within his knowledge, can give for or against any prisoner or defendant to a criminal charge, or

(h) omits to make any necessary entry in any official document or book, or

(i) neglects, or without good and sufficient cause omits, to carry out any instructions of a medical officer appointed by the police authority or, while absent from duty on account of sickness, is guilty of any act or conduct calculated to retard his return to duty.

5. Falsehood or prevarication, that is to say, if a member of a police force—

(a) knowingly makes or signs any false statement in any official document or book, or

(b) wilfully or negligently makes any false, misleading or inaccurate statement, or

(c) without good and sufficient cause destroys or mutilates any official document or record, or alters or erases any entry therein.

6. Breach of confidence, that is to say, if a member of a police force—

(a) divulges any matter which it is his duty to keep secret, or

(b) gives notice, directly or indirectly, to any person against whom any warrant or summons has been or is about to be issued, except in the lawful execution of such warrant or service of such summons, or

(c) without proper authority communicates to the public press, or to any unauthorised person, any matter connected with the force, or

(d) without proper authority shows to any person outside the force any book or written or printed document the property of the police authority, or

(e) makes any anonymous communication to the police authority or the chief constable or any superior officer, or

(f) canvasses any member of the police authority or of any county, city or borough council with regard to any matter concerning the force, or

(g) signs or circulates any petition or statement with regard to any matter concerning the force, except through the proper channel of correspondence to the chief constable or the police authority, or in accordance with the constitution of the Police Federation, or

(h) calls or attends any unauthorised meeting to discuss any matter concerning the force

7. Corrupt practice, that is to say, if a member of a police force—

(a) receives any bribe, or
(b) fails to account for or to make a prompt and true return of any money or property received by him in his official capacity, or
(c) directly or indirectly solicits or receives any gratuity, present, subscription or testimonial, without the consent of the chief constable or the police authority, or
(d) places himself under pecuniary obligation to any publican, beer-retailer, spirit-grocer, or any person who holds a licence concerning the granting or renewal of which the police may have to report or give evidence, or
(e) improperly uses his character and position as a member of the force for his private advantage, or
(f) in his capacity as a member of the force, writes, signs or gives, without the sanction of the chief constable, any testimonial of character or other recommendation with the object of obtaining employment for any person or of supporting an application for the grant of a licence of any kind, or
(g) without the sanction of the chief constable, supports an application for the grant of a licence of any kind.

8. Unlawful or unnecessary exercise of authority, that is to say, if a member of a police force—

(a) without good and sufficient cause makes any unlawful or unnecessary arrest, or
(b) uses any unnecessary violence to any prisoner or other person with whom he may be brought into contact in the execution of his duty, or
(c) is uncivil to any member of the public.

9. Malingering, that is to say if a member of a police force feigns or exaggerates any sickness or injury with a view to evading duty.

10. Absence without leave or being late for duty, that is to say, if a member of a police force without reasonable excuse is absent without leave from, or is late for, parade, court or any other duty.

11. Uncleanliness, that is to say, if a member of a police force while on duty or while off duty in uniform in a public place is improperly dressed or is dirty or untidy in his person, clothing or accoutrements.

12. Damage to clothing or other articles supplied, that is to say, if a member of a police force—

(a) wilfully or by carelessness causes any waste, loss or damage to any article of clothing or accoutrement, or to any book, document or other property of the police authority, served out to him or used by him or entrusted to his care, or
(b) fails to report any loss or damage as above however caused.

13. Drunkenness, that is to say, if a member of a police force, while on or off duty, is unfit for duty through drink.

14. Drinking on duty or soliciting drink, that is to say, if a member of a police force—

   (a) without the consent of his superior officer, drinks, or receives from any other person, any intoxicating liquor while he is on duty, or

   (b) demands, or endeavours to persuade any other person to give him, or to purchase or obtain for him, any intoxicating liquor while he is on duty.

15. Entering licensed premises, that is to say, if without permission a member of a police force enters:—

   (a) while on duty any premises licensed under the liquor licensing laws or any other premises where liquors are stored or distributed when his presence there is not required in the execution of his duty, or

   (b) any such premises in uniform while off duty.

16. Lending, borrowing or accepting presents, that is to say, if a member of a police force lends money to any superior in rank or borrows money or accepts any present from any inferior in rank.

17. Conviction for a criminal offence, that is to say, if a member of a police force has been found guilty by a court of law of a criminal offence.

18. Being an accessory to a disciplinary offence, that is to say, if a member of a police force connives at or is knowingly an accessory to an offence against discipline.

Notes

1 The background of the study

1 Westley's work (1951; 1953; 1956) was an exception. I was also able to discuss his as yet unpublished research with Professor M. Banton.
2 Wilson's study also differentiates between types of offences for which enforcement is likely to be high or low in each area. Under a 'watchman' style, for example, there is likely to be a very high arrest rate for public order offences such as drunkenness.
3 Her health category includes investigation of accidents, and there may be an enforcement possibility here.
4 See Tobias (1970) for a discussion of the changing loyalties of the RIC and RUC.

2 Rural police work

1 These nightly patrols had not been operating long enough for a meaningful average to be calculated when the research period ended.
2 Because night cars had beat men as observers this is an overestimate of the number of reports, etc., dealt with by each driver.

3 City police work

1 Subsequent re-organization has modified this pattern somewhat, and the system of patrolling has also been changed. These modifications and their probable effects are discussed in the final chapter.
2 Some postings such as one carpenter were only semi-official and therefore impermanent.
3 There was, of course, also a main stables for the force where training was carried out.
4 The 'traditional' procedure was followed in cases of murder and child rape if the offender were not readily apparent. In these cases the bringing to justice of the offender was deemed imperative regardless of expenditure of time, money and effort. Other crimes were mere

statistics, and the non-solution of crime A could be compensated for by the probably simpler 'clearing up' of B.

5 Money spent on the purchase of information was recorded by the men and claimed back from the police force as legitimate expenses. These were paid monthly in arrears. Small amounts—a few shillings or so—were not usually claimed for, but expected to be covered by the CID allowance. These smaller amounts would be spent on keeping informers (or potential informers) 'sweet' rather than on a direct purchase of information.

6 The emphasis on these types of premises confirms to CID men the value of such sources; the information available at such places limits their search for criminals to a particular section of the population.

7 Attempts to minimize this waste were made by the pooling of information at CID conferences, and by encouraging CID men to attend 'lock-up parade'—a line-up of overnight prisoners at the central cells—before attending court. Here relevant details of each man were read out, and the officers were encouraged to remember the faces. The recent introduction of the practice of attaching CID officers to a unit team, and of centralized collation of information (cf. last chapter) is intended to increase the efficiency of this process.

8 'Watched' means kept track of rather than literally kept in view. This, of course, increases the chance of a known offender getting picked up for a further offence with the effects on future behaviour described by Wilkins (1964) as 'deviance amplification'.

9 Hall (1953) claims that there are 'several million' illegal arrests each year in the USA. There is no evidence that the figure is as high, proportionately, in this country. But a strict interpretation of the legal position would make it very difficult for police officers to carry out the 'thief-catching' function which society presently requires of them. Either the task or the formal authority given to police officers would have to be changed if the two elements—task and authority—were to be brought into line. From the point of view of a senior police officer in this country C. V. Hearn (1965) has also stated that 'any system which ties policemen hands and feet must accept full responsibility when things go wrong'. His critical discussion of the revised Judges' Rules (Home Office, 1964) is of value to the sociologist again because it puts the policeman's point of view. He points out, for example, that they are *embarrassing* to administer, for example, when motorists who are only suspected of an offence must formally be cautioned.

10 In 1956 magistrates' courts were not allowed to deal with 'breaking' offences.

11 At the time of the study this term was used for foot patrol men. Today it is used to distinguish the unit beat officer from the panda-car men.

12 The concept 'turn' included both the hours being worked (early turn, late turn, nights) and also the group of constables who regularly worked each shift together ('it's a good turn this').

13 Since the research all men have been issued with pocket radio equipment.

14 Inspector, so called because of the cane carried.

15 Lieberman (1950) has shown that newly-appointed foremen rapidly adopt management attitudes. His work also suggests that when there is a change in position that is known to be temporary—as Sid's was—the attitude change still occurs but is less marked.

16 Cf. chapter 8 for discussion of the system of Unit Beat Policing in relation to this.

17 Martin and Wilson (1969) have now shown beyond all doubt how widespread this problem is, and how intractable of short-term solution.

18 This was the term used by the policemen for those arrested. The book in which the charge was recorded was officially known as the 'prisoners book'. The term tells us a lot about the fiction of the 'presumption of innocence'.

19 It was pointed out to the researcher that people arrested by divisional personnel would in some cases be taken to stations in the town centre or on other divisions, and recorded in their figures rather than in those of the 'R' Division. Although these would in part be cancelled out by men from other divisions bringing their prisoners into 'R' Division stations, it was felt that the balance would be in favour of the other divisions and that 'R' Division, and Central sub-division in particular, would be under-represented.

20 Both these proportions are slightly lower than those cited in my paper (Cain, 1971) owing to coding changes.

21 This is what one would expect on the basis of Stinchcombe's (1963) argument that lower-class persons, having restricted access to private places, are more at risk in relation to these offences. The law itself is directed against them.

22 'Drunks' was a category of others regularly used by the policemen. When I use it in this and other sections of the work I am operating with their thought categories and not my own.

23 For the official view see a quotation from the Select Committee on Estimates in Martin and Wilson (1969), p. 160; for a judge's view see Cecil (1971); for policemen's views, other than those expressed to sociological researchers (which all bear this out), see 'Two Scotland Yard Officers', *The Times*, 24 August 1971, and Hearn (1965). The policy of the Police Federation is to rid the force of 'extraneous duties'. For the views of the general public see Royal Commission on the Police (1962b).

24 Like all the averages per man suggested in this chapter, these figures result from a rather rough and ready calculation. Since the official figures include plain clothes and attached CID men with the uniform strength, I have here included them with the uniform constables for purposes of averaging. I have subtracted sixteen from the total of 193 constables on the division: four station office constables; ten permanent administration, etc., constables, and two others representing detachments to regional and force-wide specialist squads, the courts, and so on. The mean is an overestimate because it includes attached CID figures. On the other hand, sergeants are not included in the calculation, which may partly compensate for this.

25 Senior officers object to the use of this term, but it is common parlance among the men. Its connotation was, however, different in the county from the city. County men regarded 'gimmick' activities, such as perhaps playing bowls, as improving the promotion prospects of those participating; city men regarded gimmicks simply as time off work.

26 See Hollowell (1968) for an example of these priorities in another occupation where the men worked long and irregular hours.

4 Interdependence with the community

1 See appendices I and III for a description of the scale formation and a list of items, and appendix V, Table A for results.

2 Appendix III describes the construction of the index. Lists of items are given on p. 264.

3 The data from which these means are derived are presented in appendix IV, Tables B and C.

4 These data are presented in appendix IV, Tables D and E.

5 The survey conducted for the Royal Commission on the Police (1962b) found 66·8 per cent of sergeants and constables said that the job affected their friendships with non-police.

6 This issue is discussed at length for both the men and their wives because in the county many of the respondents thought it was important. Tables showing the amount of contact with relatives are given in appendix IV, Table J and Table 20.

7 This no doubt prevented simple deviancy labelling and the onset of the deviance amplification cycle, noted by Becker (1963; 1964) and Wilkins (1964) as a mainly urban phenomenon.

8 The police can be embarrassed when the 'respectable' behave in a 'rough' way, as at a political demonstration. It is necessary for them to perceive the 'respectable' participants as having been led astray by a calculating minority of the 'rough'. For a discussion of the police and demonstrators see Bowes (1966).

9 For a description of similar indifference to offenders see American Civil Liberties Union (1962).

10 The following description of a CID inspector, given in a novel written by a serving policeman, aptly describes the speaker: 'He loves his work. Especially the end product of that work. The putting away of fellow creatures. . . .' Both in the novel and in the research division such attitudes were rarely expressed in this extreme form (Wainwright, 1965).

11 For discussions of the contractual relationship with criminals and informers, see Newman, 1962 and 1966; Skolnick, 1966; Blumberg, 1967.

12 This will be referred to in future as 'disagreement' on the part of the role-defining group concerned. The negative situation of 'disagreement' is used as the basis of the analysis since this was a 'harder' answer than those coded into the agreement category. The letter included a number of responses such as, for example, 'They'd accept it whatever I did'.

5 Interdependence with family

1 This is 'required' in so far as high career satisfaction is considered desirable as an end in itself. It also seemed highly probable that a man whose wife's satisfaction with his career was high might perform his work tasks more wholeheartedly; certainly increased efficiency would be an expected concomitant of high career satisfaction on his own part. But there is no concrete evidence from this study that men scoring low or having low scoring wives were in fact less efficient.

2 See Parsons and Bales (1956) for a discussion of the distribution of instrumental and expressive tasks within a marriage in American culture.

3 The table showing the number of wives who ever mentioned each of these items is given in appendix IV, Table R.

4 The table showing the number of occasions in the previous fortnight in which a relative was seen is given in appendix IV, Table J.

6 Interdependence with senior officers

1 It will be apparent from this that I regard power as existing in its own right and not as something socially created. There is as yet no resolution of the difference between these two standpoints at a sociological or a philosophical level.

2 This difference in the powers between county and city chief constables was abolished by the 1964 Police Act. A new *ex post facto* accountability to the Home Secretary was introduced by the same Act for all chief constables.

3 Men could take the general education examination for inspector at any stage. They were not allowed to sit the police duties paper until after promotion to sergeant.

4 'Averaging' of income over the three years prior to retirement as the basis for pension meant that for three years following the 1962 pay increase retirement figures were 'artificially' kept down.

5 Subsequent amalgamation temporarily improved these promotion prospects. At the time of the study there was no definite proposal about this, but the men generally expressed themselves in favour of such a move because of its predicted effects on promotion opportunities (cf. Cain, 1964).

6 Crozier (1964) emphasizes this point (p. 192): 'Individuals or groups who control a source of uncertainty . . . have at their disposal a significant amount of power over those whose situations are affected by this uncertainty. . . .'

7 Kephart (1957) reports similar anxieties about promotion on the part of negro policemen in Pennsylvania Police Department.

8 There are difficulties in making these calculations. Number of transfers is taken from data collected on number of posts, the number of in service transfers being one less in each case. But for men with more than six posts data were grouped, so that to find the number of transfers I have shifted men a whole category lower. The estimates given here are therefore low. The problem is the same when, for example, trying

to subtract four 'promotion moves' from the superintendent's total. I have consistently underestimated, because it seemed that if the argument could stand even so, any error could only strengthen it.

9 See Skolnick (1966) for the most telling discussion of this argument emphasizing the contradictory demands which society places on its police officers.

10 Korn and McCorkle (1959) have pointed out that police actions are initiated by the public or by a junior police officer rather than by the 'management'.

11 This closely parallels Gouldner's (1954) finding: 'formal rules gave superiors something with which they could bargain in order to gain informal co-operation from workers'.

12 The first 'special course' for constables at the Police College was started in 1962. It was designed to provide an avenue of rapid promotion for men likely to rise to the most senior ranks. Selection was based on results of the promotion examinations to sergeant coupled with an extended interview. A constable successfully completing the course was promoted substantive sergeant immediately on returning to his force. Promotion regulations have also been amended so that at the time of writing it is possible to become an inspector in a minimum of five years and a sergeant in three.

13 There are links here with Crozier's (1964) analysis of inter-level segregation. But the need for *co-operation* between level, in particular the interdependence between constables and sergeants/inspectors, needs at least as much emphasis. It would seem that the same factors in the work situation, giving rise to infringements for example, are part causes of both the segregation and the interdependence. There are elements of Crozier's ideal type—the intensified importance of the peer or stratum group is another—but the articulating factors between strata include not only formal authority and rules but also a mass of variables which hinge round bargaining and exchange patterns.

7 Interdependence with colleagues

1 See appendix III, p. 281 for a discussion of statistical problems.

2 This is also briefly discussed in chapter 6, p. 146. The police force was conceived in the research design from an outsider's standpoint, that is, it was thought of as an undifferentiated group. The pilot study in the rural area did not reveal the fallacy of this. However, as soon as the intensive observations were started it became apparent that (among others) a distinction was drawn between senior officers and colleagues. It was by then too late to incorporate this new knowledge about the force from the policeman's standpoint into the interview schedule.

3 Cardarelli (1968) exposes the considerably greater extent of this risk in the American situation.

4 'No intelligent policeman can conceive it to be a duty of his to tag cars for parking overtime. It is child's work and consumes time that should be employed profitably otherwise.' Vollmer (1936)—himself a police chief.

5 Cf. Du Cann (1963) and Donnelly (1962) for discussions of the difficulties of 'working to rule', as well as Skolnick (1966).

8 Summary, conclusions and a forward look

1 This is an urban phenomenon rather than a phenomenon peculiar to the police. See, among others, Davis (1949), Wirth (1957) and Wilkins (1964).
2 The distributions can be found in the final sections of chapters 4, 5, 6, 7, pp. 120–3, 138–9, 179–80, 218–20.
3 The similarity in empirical application between this approach and that advocated by Wenninger and Clark must be noted. Their general model directs attention to important empirical problems (which is the main indicator of a useful and therefore good theory). It does not, however, indicate where solutions should be sought.
4 A more detailed discussion of the points made here and in the next section can be found in Cain (1972).
5 Discussed in *The Times*, 4 November 1971, pp. 1–2. It is suggested that an increase in police powers be coupled with a liberalization of the penal regime.

References

ALLEN, R. F. *et. al.* (1969) 'Conflict resolution: team building for police and ghetto residents', *Journal of Criminal Law, Criminology and Police Science*, vol. 60, no. 2, 251–5.

AMERICAN CIVIL LIBERTIES UNION (1962) 'Illegal detention by police' in Johnston, N., Savitz, L., and Wolfgang, M. (eds), *The Sociology of Punishment and Correction*, New York: Wiley, 12–17.

ASSOCIATION OF CHIEF POLICE OFFICERS (1960), *see* Royal Commission on the Police (1960a).

BAIN, R. (1939) 'The policeman on the beat', *Scientific Monthly*, vol. 48 (May), 450–8.

BANTON, M. (1963) 'Social integration and police authority', *The Police Chief* (April), 8–20, International Association of Chiefs of Police.

BANTON, M. (1964a) *The Policeman in the Community*, London: Tavistock.

BANTON, M. (1964b) 'Concepts 4—role', *New Society*, 7 May (no. 84), 23–4.

BANTON, M. (1965) *Roles—An Introduction to the Study of Social Relations*, London: Tavistock.

BAYLEY, D. H. and MENDELSOHN, H. A. (1969) *Minorities and the Police: Confrontation in America*, New York: Free Press.

BECKER, H. S. (1963) *Outsiders*, New York and London.

BECKER, H. S. (ed.) (1964) *The Other Side*, New York: Free Press.

BELL, R. L. *et al.* (1969) 'Small group dialogue and discussion: an approach to police–community relations', *Journal of Criminal Law, Criminology and Police Science*, vol. 60, no. 2, 242–6.

BEN-DAVID, J. (1958) 'The professional role of the physician in bureaucratised medicine: a study in role conflict', *Human Relations*, vol. 11, no. 3, 255–73.

BERKOWITZ, L. (1957) 'Effects of perceived dependency relations upon conformity to group expectations', *Journal of Abnormal and Social Psychology*, vol. 55, no. 3, 350–4.

BERKOWITZ, L. and LEVY, B. I. (1956) 'Pride in group performance and group task motivation', *Journal of Abnormal and Social Psychology*, vol. 53, 300–6.

REFERENCES

BIDDLE, B. J. (1961) 'The Present Status of Role Theory' (monograph), Columbia, Missouri: Social Psychology Laboratory, University of Missouri (mimeo).

BIDDLE, B. J. and THOMAS, E. J. (eds) (1966) *Role Theory, Concepts, and Research*, New York: Wiley.

BIRCH, A. H. (1959) *Small Town Politics*, Oxford University Press.

BITTNER, E. (1967a) 'The police on skid row', *American Sociological Review*, vol. 32, no. 5, 699–715.

BITTNER, E. (1967b) 'Police discretion in emergency apprehension of mentally ill persons', *Social Problems*, vol. 14, no. 3, 278–92.

BLACK, M. (ed.) (1962) *The Social Theories of Talcott Parsons*, London: Routledge & Kegan Paul.

BLUMBERG, A. S. (1967) *Criminal Justice*, Chicago: Quadrangle.

BOTT, E. (1957) *Family and Social Network*, London: Tavistock.

BOWES, S. (1966) *The Police and Civil Liberties*, London: Lawrence & Wishart.

BREDEMEIER, M. C. (1962) 'Law as an integrative mechanism' in Evan, W. M. (ed.), *Law and Sociology*, New York and London.

CAIN, M. E. (1964) 'Recruitment, wastage, and career' and 'The life of a policeman and his family' in Whitaker, B., *The Police*, London: Eyre & Spottiswoode and Penguin, Chapters 5 and 6.

CAIN, M. E. (1968a) 'Role conflict among police juvenile liaison officers', *British Journal of Criminology*, vol. 8, no. 4, 366–82.

CAIN, M. E. (1968b) 'Some links between role and reference group analysis', *British Journal of Sociology*, vol. 19, no. 2, 191–205.

CAIN, M. E. (1969) 'Conflict and its Solution', PhD dissertation, University of London.

CAIN, M. E. (1971) 'On the beat; interactions and relations in urban and rural police forces' in Cohen, S. (ed.), *Images of Deviance*, Penguin.

CAIN, M. E. (1972) 'Police professionalism: its meaning and consequences', *Anglo-American Law Review*, vol. 1, no. 2, 217–31.

CAIN, M. E. and DEARDEN, M. (1966) 'Initial reactions to a new juvenile liason scheme', *British Journal of Criminology*, vol. 6 (October), 421–30.

CAIN, M. E. and HALL WILLIAMS, J. E. (1963) 'Higher Court Sentencing Policy', unpublished MS. Typescript available from author.

CARDARELLI, A. P. (1968) 'An analysis of police killed by criminal action: 1961–1963', *Journal of Criminal Law, Criminology and Police Science*, vol. 59, no. 3, 447–53.

CECIL, H. (1971) *The English Judge*, London: Stevens.

CHAMBLISS, W. J. (1964) 'A sociological analysis of the law of vagrancy', *Social Problems*, vol. 12 (summer), 67–77.

CHAPMAN, B. (1970) *Police State*, London: Pall Mall.

CHAPMAN, D. (1968) *Sociology and the Stereotype of the Criminal*, London: Tavistock.

CICOUREL, A. V. (1968) *The Social Organisation of Juvenile Justice*, New York and London.

CLARK, J. P. (1965) 'Isolation of the police: a comparison of the British and American situations', *Journal of Criminal Law, Criminology and Police Science*, vol. 56, no. 3, 307–19.

306

COOLEY, C. (1902) *Human Nature and the Social Order*, New York: Scribner.

CRESSEY, D. and ELGESEM, E. (1968) 'The police and the administration of justice' in Christie, N. (ed.), *Scandinavian Studies in Sociology*, vol. 2, London: Tavistock, 53–72.

CRITCHLEY, T. A. (1967) *A History of Police in England and Wales 1900–1966*, London: Constable.

CROZIER, M. (1964) *The Bureaucratic Phenomenon*, London: Tavistock.

CUMMING, E. *et al* (1965) 'Policeman as philosopher, guide and friend', *Social Problems*, vol. 12, no. 3, 276–86.

DAVIS, K. (1949) *Human Society*, London: Collier-Macmillan.

DICKIE-CLARK, H. F. (1966) *The Marginal Situation*, London: Routledge & Kegan Paul.

DITTES, J. E. and KELLY, H. H. (1956) 'Effects of different conditions of acceptance upon conformity to group norms', *Journal of Abnormal and Social Psychology*, vol. 53, no. 1, 100–7.

DONNELLY, R. C. (1962) 'Police authority and practises', *Annals of the American Academy of Political and Social Science* (January), 90–110.

DU CANN, R. (1963) 'Police evidence, I', *Lawyer*, vol. 6, no. 2.

EHRLICH, H. J. (1962) 'Role Theory and the Study of Role Conflict', paper presented to the Society for Social Research, University of Chicago (mimeo).

EHRLICH, H. J., RINEHART, J. W. and HOWELL, J. C. (1962) 'The study of role conflict: explorations in methodology', *Sociometry*, vol. 25, no. 1, 85–97.

ESSELSTYN, T. C. (1953) 'The social role of the county sheriff', *Journal of Criminal Law, Criminology and Police Science*, vol. 4, 177–84.

FARBER, B. (1957) 'An index of marital integration', *Sociometry*, vol. 20, no. 2, 117–34.

GARDINER, J. A. (1968) 'Police enforcement of traffic laws: a comparative analysis' in Wilson, J. Q. (ed.), *Controlling Delinquents*, New York: Wiley.

GARFINKEL, H. (1967) *Studies in Ethnomethodology*, Englewood Cliffs: Prentice-Hall.

GETZELS, J. W. and GUBA, E. G. (1954) 'Role, role conflict and effectiveness', *American Sociological Review*, vol. 19, no. 2, 164–75.

GOFFMAN, I. (1956) *The Presentation of Self in Everyday Life*, University of Edinburgh Social Sciences Research Centre, Monograph 2.

GOLDMAN, N. (1963) 'The Differential Selection of Juvenile Offenders for Court Appearance', National Research and Information Centre: National Council on Crime and Delinquency.

GOLDSTEIN, H. (1960) 'Police discretion not to invoke the legal process', *Yale Law Journal*, vol. 68, 543–94.

GOLDSTEIN, H. (1963) 'Police discretion: the ideal versus the real', *Public Administration Review*, vol. 23, 140–8.

GOODE, W. J. (1960) 'Norm commitment and conformity to role-status obligations', *American Journal of Sociology*, vol. 66, no. 3, 246–58.

GOULDNER, A. W. (1954) *Patterns of Industrial Bureaucracy* (reissued 1964), New York: Free Press.

GOULDNER, A. W. (1959) 'Organisational analysis' in Merton, R. K. et al., Sociology Today: Problems and Prospects, New York: Basic Books, 400–28.

GROSS, N. et al. (1958) Explorations in Role Analysis, London: Chapman & Hall.

GULLAHORN, J. T. (1956) 'Measuring role conflict', American Journal of Sociology, vol. 61, no. 4, 299–303.

GUTTMAN, L. (1944) 'A basis for scaling qualitative data', American Sociological Review, vol. 9, no. 2, 139–50.

GUTTMAN, L. (1947) 'The Cornell technique for scale and intensity analysis' in Churchman C. W. et al. (eds), Measurement of Consumer Interest, Philadelphia: University of Pennsylvania Press, 60–84.

GUTTMAN, L. (1954) 'The principal components of scaleable attitudes' in Lazarsfeld, P., Mathematical Thinking in the Social Sciences, Chicago: Free Press, 216–49.

HALL, J. (1952) Theft, Law and Society (2nd ed.), Indianapolis: Bobbs-Merrill.

HALL, J. (1953) 'Police and law in a democratic society', Indiana Law Journal, vol. 28, 133–42.

HAMMOND, W. H. and CHAYEN, E. (1963) Studies in the Causes of Delinquency and the Treatment of Offenders, 5. Persistent criminals: a study of all offenders liable to preventive detention in 1956, Home Office Research Unit Report, London: HMSO.

HARTLEY, E. (1951) 'Psychological problems of multiple group membership' in Rohrer, J. H., and Sherif, M. (eds), Social Psychology at the Crossroads, 371–87, New York: Harper & Row.

HEARN, C. V. (1965) A Duty to the Public, London: Muller.

HERMANN, S. N. and SCHILD, E. (1960) 'Ethnic role conflict in a cross-cultural setting', Human Relations, vol. 13, no. 3, 215–28.

HOLLOWELL, P. G. (1968) The Lorry Driver, Routledge & Kegan Paul.

HOME OFFICE (1964) Judges' Rules and Administrative Directions to the Police, London: HMSO.

HOME OFFICE (1967) Police Manpower, Equipment and Efficiency: Reports of Three Working Parties, London: HMSO.

HUGHES, E. C. (1944) 'Dilemmas and contradictions of status', American Journal of Sociology, vol. 50, quoted in Coser, L. A. and Rosenberg, B., Sociological Theory, London: Collier-Macmillan, 1964, 353–9.

HUGHES, E. C. (1949) 'Social change and status protest: an essay on the marginal man', Phylon, vol. 10, 58–65.

HYMAN, H. H. (1942) 'The psychology of status', Archives of Psychology, no. 269.

JEFFERY, L. R. (1957) 'The development of crime in early England', Journal of Criminal Law, Criminology and Police Science, vol. 47, 647–66.

KADISH, S. M. (1962) 'Legal norms and discretion in police and sentencing process', Harvard Law Review, vol 75, 904–31.

KAHN, R. L. et al. (1964) Organisational Stress—Studies in Role Conflict and Ambiguity, New York and London.

KEPHART, W. (1957) Racial Factors and Urban Law Enforcement, Philadelphia and Oxford.

KILLIAN, L. M. (1952) 'The significance of multiple group membership in disaster', *American Journal of Sociology*, vol. 58, no. 4, 309–14.

KORN, R. R. and MCCORKLE, L. W. (1959) 'The police' in *Criminology and Penology* by the same authors, New York: Holt.

LA FAVE, W. R. (1965) *Arrest: the decision to take a suspect into custody*, Boston: Little, Brown.

LAMBERT, J. L. (1969) 'Race Relations: the Role of the Police', paper presented to British Sociological Association Annual Conference.

LAMBERT, J. L. (1970) *Crime, Police and Race Relations*, Oxford University Press.

LEVINSON, D. J. (1959) 'Role, personality and social structure in an organisational setting', *Journal of Abnormal amd Social Psychology*, vol. 58, 170–80.

LIEBERMAN, S. (1950) 'The effects of changes in roles on attitudes of role occupants', *Human Relations*, vol. 9, 385–403.

LINDESMITH, A. R. and STRAUSS, A. L. (1949) *Social Psychology*, New York: Dryden Press.

LINTON, R. (1936) *The Study of Man*, New York and London.

LINTON, R. (1945) *The Cultural Background of Personality* (republished 1947), London: Routledge & Kegan Paul.

LOCKWOOD, D. (1956) 'Some remarks on "The Social System"', *British Journal of Sociology*, vol. 7, 134–47.

LOCKWOOD, D. (1958) *The Blackcoated Worker*, London: Allen & Unwin.

MCGLASHAN, C. (1967) 'Growing up with pinky', *Observer*, 10 September, 17.

MCINTYRE, D. M. *et al.* (1967) *Detection of Crime*, Boston: Little, Brown.

MARSHALL, G. (1965) *Police and Government*, London: Methuen.

MARTIN, J. P. and WILSON, G. (1969) *The Police: a Study in Manpower*, London: Heinemann.

MATZA, D. (1964) *Delinquency and Drift*, New York: Wiley.

MEAD, G. H. (1934) 'Play the game, and the generalised other' in *Mind, Self and Society*, University of Chicago Press.

MERTON, R. K. (1957a) *Social Theory and Social Structure* (revised ed.), Chicago: Free Press.

MERTON, R. K. (1957b) 'The role-set: problems in social theory', *British Journal of Sociology*, vol. 8, 106–20.

MERTON, R. K. and KITT, A. S. (1951) 'Contributions to the theory of reference group behavior' in Merton, R. K. and Lazarsfeld, P. (eds), *Continuities in Social Research: Studies in the Scope and Method of the American Soldier*, Chicago: Free Press.

MEYERS, A. C. (1962) 'Statistical controls in a police department', *Crime and Delinquency*, vol. 8, no. 1, 58–63.

MINTO, G. A. (1965) *The Thin Blue Line*, London: Hodder & Stoughton.

MITCHELL, R. E. (1966) 'Organisation as a key to police effectiveness', *Crime and Delinquency*, vol. 12, 344–53.

MUSGROVE, F. (1967) 'Teachers' role conflicts in the English grammar and secondary modern school', *Current Journal of Educational Science*, vol. 2, 61–9.

NADEL, S. F. (1957) *The Theory of Social Structure*, London: Cohen & West.

REFERENCES

NELSON, H. A. (1967) 'The defenders: a case study of an informal police organisation', *Social Problems*, vol. 15, no. 2, 127–47.

NEWCOMB, T. and CHARTERS, W. W. (1950) *Social Psychology*, New York and London.

NEWMAN, D. J. (1962) 'Pleading guilty for considerations: a study of bargain justice', *Journal of Criminal Law, Criminology and Police Science*, vol. 46, 780–90.

NEWMAN, D. J. (1966) *Conviction: the determination of guilt or innocence without trial*, Boston: Little, Brown.

NIEDERHOFFER, A. (1967) *Behind the Shield*, New York: Doubleday.

OSBOROUGH, N. (1965) 'Police discretion not to prosecute juveniles', *Modern Law Review*, vol. 28, 421–31.

PARSONS, T. (1951) *The Social System*, Chicago and London.

PARSONS, T. and BALES, R. F. (1956) *Family: Socialization and Interaction Process*, London: Routledge & Kegan Paul.

PILIAVIN, I. and BRIAR, S. (1964) 'Police encounters with juveniles', *American Journal of Sociology*, vol. 70, 206–14.

POLICE FEDERATION (1963) *Police Federation Newsletter*, vol. 4, no. 5 (June).

PREISS, J. J. and EHRLICH, H. J. (1966) *An Examination of Role Theory: The Case of the State Police*, Lincoln: University of Nebraska Press.

QUINNEY, R. (1970) *The Social Reality of Crime*, Boston: Little, Brown.

REISS, A. J. and BORDUA, D. J. (1967) 'Environment and organisation: a perspective on the police' in Bordua, D. J. (ed.), *The Police: Six Sociological Essays*, New York: Wiley.

REMINGTON, F. J. (1962) 'The law relating to "on the street" detention, questioning, and frisking of suspected persons, and police arrest privileges in general' in Sowle, C. R. (ed.), *Police Power and Individual Freedom*, Chicago: Aldine.

REMINGTON, F. J. (1965) 'The role of police in a democratic society', *Journal of Criminal Law, Criminology and Police Science*, vol. 56, 361–5.

ROETHLISBERGER, F. J. (1945) 'The foreman: master and victim of double talk', *Harvard Business Review*, 23, no. 3, 283–98

ROMMETVEIT, R. (1957) *Social Norms and Roles*, Oslo: Academisk Forlag.

ROSENBERG, D. (1971) 'The sociology of the police and institutional liberalism', unpublished paper, privately circulated.

ROYAL COMMISSION ON THE POLICE (1960a) *Minutes of Evidence* (part 2), Association of Chief Police Officers of England and Wales, London: HMSO.

ROYAL COMMISSION ON THE POLICE (1960b) *Interim Report*, Cmnd. 1222, London: HMSO.

ROYAL COMMISSION ON THE POLICE (1962a) *Final Report*, Cmnd. 1728, London: HMSO.

ROYAL COMMISSION ON THE POLICE (1962b) *Appendix IV to the Minutes of Evidence*. 'Relations between the police and the public', London: HMSO.

SARBIN, T. R. (1954) 'The concept of role taking', *Sociometry*, vol. 6, no. 1, 273–85.

SARGENT, S. E. (1951) 'Conceptions of role and ego in contemporary psychology' in Rohrer, J. H., and Sherif, M., (eds), *Social Pyschology at the Crossroads*, New York and London.

SEEMAN, M. (1953) 'Role conflict and ambivalence in leadership', *American Sociological Review*, vol. 18, no. 4, 373–80.

SHERIF, M. (1951) 'A preliminary experimental study of intergroup relations' in Rohrer, J. H. and Sherif, M. (eds), *Social Psychology at the Crossroads*, New York and London, 388–424.

SHERIF, M. (1953) 'The concept of reference groups in human relations' in Sherif, M. and Wilson, M. (eds), *Group Relations at the Crossroads*, New York: Harper & Row, 203–31.

SHERIF, M. and CANTRIL, H. (1947) *The Psychology of Ego Involvements*, New York: Wiley.

SHERIF, M. and SHERIF, F. C. (1948) *An Outline of Social Psychology* (new ed. 1956), New York: Harper & Row.

SILVER, A. (1967) 'The demand for order in civil society' in Bordua, D. J. (ed.), *The Police: Six Sociological Essays*, New York: Wiley.

SKOLNICK, J. H. (1966) *Justice without Trial*, New York & London.

SKOLNICK, J. H. and WOODWORTH, J. R. (1967) 'Bureaucracy, information and social control: a study of a morals detail' in Bordua, D. J. (ed.), *The Police: Six Sociological Essays*, New York: Wiley.

SOWLE, C. R. (ed.) (1962) *Police Power and Individual Freedom*, Chicago: Aldine.

STEER, D. (1970) *Police Cautions: a Study in the Exercise of Police Discretion*, Oxford: Blackwell.

STERN, E. and KELLER, S. (1953) 'Spontaneous group relations in France', *Public Opinion Quarterly*, vol. 17, no. 2, 208–17.

STINCHCOMBE, A. (1963) 'Institutions of privacy in the determination of police administrative practice', *American Journal of Sociology*, vol. 69, 150–60.

STODDARD, E. R. (1968) 'The informal code of police deviancy: a group approach to "blue-coat crime"', *Journal of Criminal Law, Criminology and Police Science*, vol. 59, 201–13.

STONEQUIST, E. V. (1937) *The Marginal Man*, New York: Scribner.

STOUFFER, S. A. (1949a) *The American Soldier: Adjustment during Army Life*, Social Science Research Council, Studies in Social Psychology in World War II, Princeton University Press.

STOUFFER, S. A. (1949b) 'An analysis of conflicting social norms', *American Sociological Review*, vol. 14, monograph.

TAPPAN, P. W. (1959) *Crime, Justice and Correction*, New York: McGraw-Hill.

TOBIAS, J. J. (1970) 'The policing of Ireland', *Criminologist*, vol. 5, 99–104.

TURK, A. T. (1969) *Criminality and Legal Order*, New York: Rand McNally.

TURNER, R. H. (1956) 'Role taking, role standpoint and reference group behavior', *American Journal of Sociology*, vol. 61, 316–28.

VOLLMER, A. (1936) *The Police and Modern Society*, University of California Press.

WAINWRIGHT, J. (1965) *Death in a Sleeping City*, London: Collins.

WENNINGER, E. P. and CLARK, J. P. (1967) 'A theoretical orientation for police studies' in Klein, M. W. (ed.), *Juvenile Gangs in Context*, New Jersey: Prentice-Hall, 161–72.

REFERENCES

WERTHMAN, C. and PILIAVIN, I. (1967) 'Gang members and the police' in Bordua, D. J. (ed.), *The Police: Six Sociological Essays*, New York: Wiley.

WESTLEY, W. (1951) 'The police: a sociological study of law, custom and morality', PhD dissertation, University of Chicago (microfilm).

WESTLEY, W. (1953) 'Violence and the police', *American Journal of Sociology*, vol. 59, 34–41.

WESTLEY, W. (1956) 'Secrecy and the police', *Social Forces*, vol. 34, 254–7.

WESTLEY, W. (1970) *Violence and the Police*, Cambridge, Mass.: MIT Press.

WHEELER, S. *et al.* (1968) 'Agents of delinquency control' in Wheeler, S. (ed.), *Controlling Delinquents*, New York: Wiley, 31–60.

WHYTE, W. F. (1948) *Street Corner Society*, University of Chicago Press.

WHYTE, W. F. *et al.* (1945) 'Facing the foreman's problems', *Applied Anthropology*, vol. 4, no. 2, 1–17.

WILKINS, L. T. (1964) *Social Deviance*, London: Tavistock.

WILLETT, T. (1964) *Criminal on the Road*, London: Tavistock.

WILLMOTT, P. and YOUNG, M. (1960) *Family and Class in a London Suburb*, Institute of Community Studies Reports 4, London: Routledge & Kegan Paul.

WILSON, J. Q. (1963) 'The police and their problems: a theory', *Public Policy*, vol. 12, 189–216.

WILSON, J. Q. (1968a) *Varieties of Police Behavior*, Cambridge, Mass.: Harvard University Press.

WILSON, J. Q. (1968b) 'The police and delinquents in two cities' in Wheeler, S. (ed.), *Controlling Delinquents*, New York: Wiley.

WIRTH, L. (1957) 'Urbanism as a way of life' in Hatt, P. K. and Reiss, A. J., *Cities and Society*, Chicago: Free Press.

YOUNG, J. (1971) 'The role of the police as amplifiers of deviancy, negotiators of reality and translators of fantasy' in Cohen, S. (ed.), *Images of Deviance*, 27–61, Penguin.

YOUNG, M. and WILLMOTT, P. (1957) *Family and Kinship in East London*, Institute of Community Studies Reports 1, London: Routledge & Kegan Paul.

Index

accommodation, 84, 85–6, 156–7, 158–60
administration, 44, 79
armed forces, experience in, 103
arrests: county, 35; city, 66–8, 243
Association of Chief Police Officers, 7, 8
attachments, 50, 73

beat:
city, 53–4; first watch, 54–7; need for 'action', 65–70; night crime patrol, 60–4; nights, 59–60; second watch, 57–9
county, 33–7; beat patrols, 35–6; crime patrols, 38–9; work away from beat, 38–40
Unit Beat Policing, 1–2, 241–4
birthplace, 100
bureaucratization, 106, 168–71, 227–39, 241

career satisfaction: by type of post, 187; and interdependence with colleagues, 185; and marital integration, 127–9, 226, 290–1; measurement, 248–9, 270–1, 284, 289
chief inspectors' duties, 142–3
children: attitude to father's job, 291–3; effect of father's job, 137–8; effect of transfers, 154–6
CID: city, 50–3, 208–10; county, 44–5, 210–13, hours, 50–1; informers, 51, 106; and uniform men, 106, 208–13
city police: administration, 79; CID work, 50–3, 208–10; crime, 50; definition of role, 65–72, 114, 230, 240; divisions, 46–9; dog section, 78–9, 171; mobile patrols, 75–8;

city police (contd.)
patrols: first watch, 54–7, second watch, 57–9, nights, 59–60, night crime patrols, 60–4; plain clothes, 78; research division, 46–9, 54; station office, 78; workload, 50, 56, 58, 59, 65–8, 77, 243–4
colleagues: attitudes to, 196–7, 207, 237; dependence on, 61–4, 189, 195, 200–1, 226, 230–2, 242; evidence of dependence, 195–6, 197, 203–4; and role definition, 218–20, 234–6; social control of, 200–1; social relationships, 214–16; town versus country, 203–5, 205–7, 226, 227; wives' relationships, 218–20, 234–6
communication: 'down' the hierarchy, 144–5, 166–7; formal, 144–242; informal, 145–6; and transfers, 156–8
community: contact, 84–5, 88–9, 224, 241, 286–7; conceptions of, 81–2, 111–12, 114–19, 228, 237; measure of interdependence, 282; mobile patrol men, 110–11; power, 87, 90, 105–6, 113–14, 224–5, 228, 235, 239–40, 241, 242; relationship of wives with, 90–8, 154, 225, 227–8; and role definition, 71, 89–90, 98–104, 104–5, 106, 108–10, 111–23, 224, 228, 240, 289; social relationships with, 84–90, 154, 224–5, 286–7
county police: administration, 44; CID, 44–5, 210–13; crime, 29–32, 71; crime patrols, 38–9; definition of role, 70–1, 105, 204–5, 224–5, 227, 241; diseases of animals, 32–4; divisions, 28–9; mobile patrols,

county police (*contd.*)
42–4, 170, 213–14; research division, 27–9, rural beats, 29–36; section duties, 39–40, 41; town work, 40–2, 177, 227; work away from beat, 37–40; work load, 30, 32–4, 70–1
crime, 29–32, 105–6, 225; and CID, 44–5, 50–3, 208–13; and police role definition, 50, 53, 65–70, 72, 105–6, 114, 225
criminals, 51, 81–2, 106, 114–17, 229

definition of role by policemen, 65–72, 105, 114, 230, 232, 239–40, 244–6
dependent uncertainty, 150–1, 157, 224, 226
discipline, 147–8, 169, 231; police regulations (1952), 294–7
dog section: city work, 78–9; chain of command, 171

easing: county, 36–7, 202; city, 56, 58–9, 61–2, 72, 190–1, 230–1, 242; definition, 37; interdependence with colleagues, 190–2; official, 37, 72–4, 80, 230; and role definition, 72, 224, 229
educational background, 101

family life, 7, 8; children, 137–8, 154, 156, 292–3
  marital integration, 125–30, 225–6; and career satisfaction, 127–30, 226, 290–1; and conflict solution, 138–9, 234–5; and interdependence with police, 130–1; measure, 260–2, 275, 281
  problems, 131–8, 291; intrusions, 34, 136; shifts, 136–7; transfers, 134; unpredicability, 40, 133, 136
  role definition, 138–9
  wife's contact with community, 91–3, 98, 225
  wife's isolation, 94–7
  wives' questionnaire, 269–79, 284–5

gimmicks, 73–4, 224

hours of duty, 7–8, 34, 40, 42, 132–3, 135–8, 165, 227
housing, *see* accommodation

immigrants, policemen's conception of, 117–19, 161
informers, 51, 106, 111–12, 115–16, 161–3
infringements, 52, 190, 192, 202, 224, 229, 242
inspectors: duties, 142–3; promotion, 152

legitimation of police role, 67, 69, 229–30, 240

manpower, 74–5, 229–30
marital integration, *see* family life
Mark, Robert, 245
methods of research, 7–13; access, 8; choice of force, 8; discussion and critique, 8–10, 281–4; interviews, 9–12; observation, 9, 11–13; pilot study, 8, 280–1; questionnaires, 9–11, 248–79 (items), 280–5; sample, 10–11
mobile patrols, 42–4, 75–8; and community, 110–11; hours, 12; relationships between departments, 213–14

occupation, previous, 102
offences TIC, 52–3
organization, police: effect of changes, 241–6; and relationship with public, 82–3; and relationship with senior officers, 168–71

perks, 36–7, 74, 224
physical danger, 190, 192–4, 202, 230
plain clothes work, 78
Police Act (1964), 2, 302n
Police Federation, 7–8, 171, 300n
police interdependence, index of, 146–7, 183–9, 281–2, 293; and conflict solution, 179–80, 218–20, 233–6; and marital integration, 130
prisoners: county, 35, 111; city, 65–70, 113, 243
professionalism, 241, 246
promotion, 106, 148–51, 169, 204, 226–7, 231, 241; and police interdependence, 150–1

reference groups, 5
rewards, formal, 148, 160, 163–4, 169, 231
Richardson, Superintendent, 69
role, 2–7; definition, 3–8, 26–7; conflict, 4–8; conflict solution, 233–6, 282–4; lack of consensus, 236–7; hypotheses, 7, 119–23, 138–9, 179–80, 218–20; power, 4–7; and reference groups, 5; source of definitions (theoretical), 5–6, 25–6,
Royal Commission on the Police, 7, 300n, 301n

senior officers: communication, 144–6, 166–7, 227, 242–3; dependence of men on highest ranks, 147–60, 226, 231, 244; dependence of men on intermediate ranks, 160–6, 226;

senior officers (*contd.*)
dependence of senior officers on constables, 166–8, 231–2, 244; duties of senior officers, 141–5; men's attitude to senior officers, 65, 106, 174–6, 177–9, 227, 232, 237, 242; paternalism, 165–6; sergeants' attitudes to men, 172–4, 176–7; senior officers and role definition, 179–80, 234–6, 240, 242–4, 246

sergeants: attitudes to men, 172; attitudes to senior officers, 176–7; constables' perception, 177–8, 226; duties, 143, 226; promotion, 151

social class: of men, 100–2; of wives, 101, 288

social control: between colleagues, 200–1

socialization, 197–200, 205–7, 231, 242

social relationships: between police wives, 217–18; of men with colleagues, 214–16; of men with community, 84–90; of wives with community, 90–6

sociology of police work: citizen rights, 14–15; differences in police practice, 15–18; effects of police actions, 18–21; remaining problems, 18–21, 238–46; research perspective, 25–6; social order, the macro framework, 21–5

superintendents: duties, 141–2; qualities admired in, 175

town police work: characteristics, 40–2, 177, 227; hours, 41–2, 136, 164–5; colleague relationships, 177, 202–3

transfers, 134, 152–8; effect on children, 155–6; effect on wives, 156–7; frequency, 153–4; punitiveness, 154–5; tables, 291–2

uniform branch: description of work, 33–40, 42–4, 53–64, 75–8, 243–4, role definition, 65–72, 105, 114, 230–2, 239–40, 244–6; relationship with CID, 208–13, 243–4

Unit Beat Policing, 1–2, 241–4

welfare, 165–6

wives: relationship in the community, 90–3, 94, 225, 287–8; career satisfaction, 128, 290–1, 226; and conflict solution, 138–9, 234–6; employment, 92; interdependence with police, 130–1, 226, 290; isolation, 94, 95–6, 97–8, 225, 228; practical difficulties, 131–7, 156–7, 158–9, 225–6; relationships between wives, 217–18; social class, 101, 288

work load: city, 50, 56, 58, 59, 65–8, 77, 243–4; county, 30, 32–4, 70–1

315